THE STORY OF
TOBACCO
IN AMERICA

JOSEPH C. ROBERT

✧

THE STORY OF
TOBACCO
IN AMERICA

✧

NEW YORK: ALFRED A. KNOPF

1949

To the Memory of

MY FATHER

PREFACE

WILLIAM BYRD of Westover named tobacco "that bewitching vegetable." His description was accurate and prophetic; the leaf has enthralled hosts of men, and it has shaped societies and events since the epochal experiments of John Rolfe at Jamestown in 1612. In these chapters I have attempted to tell something of farm, leaf-market, and factory operations, and also to trace the effect of tobacco on the political, economic, and social life of the nation. The staple guaranteed the permanence of the Virginia settlement; created the pattern of the Southern plantation; encouraged the introduction of Negro slavery, then softened the institution; begot an immortal group of colonial leaders; strained the bonds between mother country and Chesapeake colonies; burdened the diplomacy of the post-Revolutionary period; promoted the Louisiana Purchase; and, after the Civil War, helped create the New South. The story of tobacco illustrates many themes—states' rights in the Confederacy, the growth of big business, the agrarian aspects of the New Deal, among them. Decisive events in the careers of great Americans are integral parts of the his-

tory of tobacco: Patrick Henry achieved prominence and
first heard the cry of "Treason" in a county-court tobacco
case; Theodore Roosevelt began to question economic and
judicial systems after examining sweated labor in the cigar
industry. Dispute and violence are milestones along this tobacco road; Culpeper's Rebellion marked the seventeenth
century, the Black Patch War the twentieth. Colonial Virginians used tobacco as money; in the confusion following
the Second World War, the American cigarette was currency "from Paris to Peking."

Herein are described the fluctuating nicotine manners of
America: the descent from snuffing to dipping, the banishment of the quid from polite society (when the United
States District Court in Washington, D. C., in 1945 authorized elimination of the cuspidor from federal buildings over the nation, an era had ended), the persistent
revivals of the pipe, the rise of the cigar as the symbol of
wealth, the amazing growth of the cigarette. Our bad tobacco habits have incensed many observers, including
Charles Dickens, who, after watching the poor marksmanship of chewers, doubted reports of American proficiency
with the rifle. Consumption of tobacco increased, despite
antitobacco tracts running from the *Counterblaste to Tobacco*, a pamphlet by King James I, to "Nicotine Knockout,
or the Slow Count," an article by Gene Tunney. There was
a hundred-year struggle over the question of cigarette-
smoking by women. As early as 1854 a horrified reformer
discovered that a few urban ladies had adopted "a weaker
and more *feminine* article, which has been most delicately
denominated *cigarette*." The average consumer, heedless
of sermons and statistics, preferred to recite the doggerel,
"Tobacco is a dirty weed. I like it."

The industry has bred a host of colorful characters and
a calendar of good stories. There are profane wagoners,
riotous boatmen, chanting auctioneers, gaudy drummers,
and conniving "blockaders," as the illicit rural manufacturers were called. Famous anecdotes have become part of

the tobacco heritage: Commissary Blair's rebuff by Sir Edward Seymour; Gilbert Stuart's explanation of his tobacco habits; Van Buren's parliamentary maneuver with Clay's snuff box; the naming of the Lone Jack brand of smoking tobacco; George Washington Hill's own testimony, under oath, as to his creation of "Reach for a Lucky Instead of a Sweet."

For the preparation of this history of tobacco, various libraries have generously made available rare source materials. Of special importance are manuscripts, pamphlets, and books in the Arents Tobacco Collection of the New York Public Library; the Ellis & Allan papers in the Library of Congress; Confederate imprints, reform pamphlets, and the E. F. Small Manuscripts in the Duke University Library; manuscript census returns and county tax lists in the Virginia State Library; and the 1941 anti-trust trial records in the University of Kentucky Library.

This book owes a large debt to the labors of others. Elsewhere I have made specific acknowledgment of the major monographs from which I have drawn. Many individuals, by interviews or by permission to use private papers, have illuminated otherwise dark corners in the history of tobacco. Among these persons are the late Mr. A. W. Patterson of Richmond, son of the manufacturer, Dr. R. A. Patterson, who coined the brand name Lucky Strike; Mr. Richard Duckhardt of Richmond, once a tobacco head-label lithographer; Mr. J. L. Crumpton of Durham, a great nephew of John W. Carroll, creator of Lone Jack smoking tobacco; Mr. Mercer Young and Miss Elsie Young of Richmond, son and daughter of William J. Young, manager of the Cameron plants in Australia in the 1880's; Mr. James C. Stone of Louisville, leading figure in the Burley cooperative of the 1920's; and Mr. Maurice Moore of Lynchburg, grandson of the first Maurice Moore, maker of Killikinnick. Memoranda of early market days, prepared by Mrs. Moore, wife of the present Maurice Moore, included the music of the call to Friend's Warehouse, reproduced in the text. I shall not soon forget my visits to the Burley fields of Mr. J. Winston Coleman, Jr., at hospitable Winburn Farm in the Blue Grass, or a tour of the Perique country in St. James Parish under the cordial supervision of Mr. Joseph Lamendola.

I appreciate the wise counsel given me throughout my researches by Dr. Francis Pendleton Gaines, Professor W. T. Laprade, and Mr. George Arents, Jr. Parts of the manuscript have been read by Dr. F. R. Darkis, Mr. W. B. Pace, Mr. E. G. Moss, Dr. Lodwick Hartley, Mr. Donald E. Deichmann, Dr. Robert H. Woody, and Dr. Charles S. Sydnor. Dr. William B. Hamilton has given a critical review of all the chapters. To these and to those numerous friends, unnamed here, who have passed on to me bits of information collected in their own investigations, I am profoundly grateful. The errors that undoubtedly exist in this volume are fewer because of their generosity.

Although Duke University is in no sense responsible for the conclusions reached in these pages, I am indebted to the Duke University Press for permission to paraphrase portions of my earlier work, *The Tobacco Kingdom*, which it published in 1938; to the Duke University Research Council for financial support of various research problems; and to the University itself for sabbatical leave during which basic study was completed.

J. C. R.

Durham, North Carolina
January 17, 1949

CONTENTS

1492 ✳ 1776

1776 ✳ 1860

xi

CONTENTS

1860 ＊ 1911

1911 ＊ 1941

1941 ＊ 1948

ILLUSTRATIONS

*1492 * 1776*

[Chapter 1]

THE DISCOVERY OF "THAT BEWITCHING VEGETABLE"

On his first voyage to the New World, Christopher Columbus was offered strange dry leaves, tokens of friendship, by the natives of San Salvador. Two of the admiral's party, Luis de Torres, the official interpreter, and Rodrigo de Xeres, able seaman, while in the interior of Cuba looking for the Grand Khan, marveled as they saw men and women drawing smoke from the rolled and twisted herb. In this manner Europeans obtained their first knowledge of tobacco. Later explorers discovered that the Indians used the leaf for ceremonial, social, and, to a small degree, therapeutic purposes. They chewed and snuffed, and had developed all basic types of smoking: the pipe, cigar, and a husk-wrapped cigarette. Tobacco enriched Indian myths, enlivened festivals, and gave meaning to rituals, especially in the North American groups. Of particular importance in tribal etiquette was the sacred calumet, the long stemmed pipe used for sealing a peace.

No one knows when or by whom tobacco was first taken to Europe. The city fathers of Ayamonte celebrate Rodrigo de Xeres, their townsman, as the person first to smoke in

Europe. This was the Rodrigo who saw natives of Cuba smoking. If not Rodrigo probably some other common sailor dared copy the Indians and boastfully paraded his accomplishments on the wharves and in the streets of one of the Spanish port towns. It is certain that the leaf had traveled to the Iberian peninsula by the early sixteenth century, and soon was known in other western European areas. But there was little interest in the plant for fully half a century after it was observed by Europeans, though botanists in a perfunctory way cultivated a few specimen plants.

About the middle of the sixteenth century, tobacco received sensational attention as a divinely-sent remedy for virtually all ailments of the human body. Apparently Portugal, the tight little trading country, was the scene of the "great discovery." Tobacco was recommended in powders, unguents and otherwise, as cathartics, clysters, dentifrices. A disease-ridden world pathetically rushed to worship at the shrine of the leaf. One of the first to proclaim the virtues of tobacco as a poultice was a kinsman of a page employed by Jean Nicot, French ambassador at the Portuguese court. About 1560 Nicot sent to the Queen Mother of France, the notorious Florentine, Catherine de' Medici, seeds of the fabulous plant. The leaves grown from these seeds reportedly cured many ailing Frenchmen. It seemed only just to name the remedy Nicotiane. While the gospel of the nicotine therapy was echoing to the corners of the land, the social use of tobacco was more quietly diffused. As a recreative herb tobacco was carried by sailors and merchants along the trade routes of Europe, then to Africa and to the Orient.

In some uncharted fashion, specimens of the tobacco plant were soon brought from the continent across the channel to England. As to the direct importation of tobacco into England from America, the most reasonable theory is that Sir John Hawkins or some member of his famous second expedition obtained leaves in Florida and brought them home in September, 1565, to display with the gold, silver, and pearls which had been taken from the Spanish by way of trade or plunder. At any rate, the Hawkins fleet, headed by the Queen's 700-ton ship *Jesus*, visited Florida, saw the Indians of that region smoking, and knew that the ill-fated group of Huguenots under René de Laudonnière were using tobacco.

The habit was substantially encouraged in 1586 when Sir Francis Drake returned to England with quantities of tobacco captured in the West Indies and with the exhausted settlers rescued from Roanoke Island. These colonists had adopted the native custom of smoking, and presumably they carried with them on their return Indian clay pipes as well as leaf and seed. From this date the pipe was a well-established institution in England. Sir Walter Raleigh, who holds the center of tobacco tradition, was one of the earliest to adopt smoking. He helped make the custom acceptable in Elizabethan court circles, and he learned to plant and to cure the leaf. He did indeed give impetus to the fashion, but in no wise did he initiate the custom. As if to make up for tardy beginnings, the Englishmen took up the habit with a rush, and this despite such exceedingly high prices that in some markets the purchaser was forced to balance the weight of tobacco with silver shillings.

To the disgust of the sober element in the country, the fashionable young men of London entered on a period of exaggerated and affected display. Strutting in the middle aisle of St. Paul's, they would exhibit tricks with smoke called "the slights," properly named with such designations as the Gulpe, the Retention, and the Cuban Ebolition. Both the extravagancies of the dandies and the extreme medical claims made by herbalists invited satirical comments from leading literary figures.

The best-known diatribes were those coined by James I himself, who had come down from Scotland to assume the British throne and, he hoped, to cure the English of sundry bad habits, among them smoking. Most famous of all anti-tobacco tracts is his *Counterblaste to Tobacco*, published in 1604 anonymously though soon known as the king's work. In the *Counterblaste* James frankly surveyed his new dominion and discovered "a generall sluggishnesse, which makes us wallow in all sorts of idle delights," one of the corruptions being "the vile use (or rather abuse) of taking *Tobacco*." He tried to shame his people by reminding them that tobacco was first used as an antidote against the "Pockes" and mocked the absurdities of the light-headed people claiming the leaf as a cure for divers and contradictory diseases. But, in truth, as for the user of tobacco, said James, "all his members shall become feeble, his spirits dull, and in the end, as a drowsie lazie bellygod, he shall evanish in a Lethargie." The use of the "precious stink" was a folly, an extravagance, a sin. In summation and conclusion, James called it "A custome Lothsome to the eye, hatefull to the Nose, harmefull to the braine, daungerous to the Lungs, and in the blacke stinking fume thereof, neerest resembling the horrible Stigian smoke of the pit that is bottomelesse." Fewer suppositions in history are more certain than that James would never have issued the charter to the adventurers of London and Plymouth in 1606 could he have foreseen this same despised tobacco as the first fruit of the New World, as the staple of the plantations strung along the river ironically enough named for him.

The story of tobacco in the English colonies properly begins with John Rolfe. One day in May, 1609, when the Jamestown settlement was scarcely two years old, this personable young Englishman and his wife went aboard the *Sea Adventure*, then loading at the London docks. They were two of a bustling company of five hundred emigrants sailing in nine vessels for the new colony of Virginia, where, so the stories ran, there were grapevines the size of a man's leg, and perhaps gold. All went well until some eight days from Virginia when the little fleet was scattered by a storm of fabulous temper. Under a blackened sky the *Sea Adventure* ran before a roaring northeast wind until, in miraculous fashion, on July 25th the vessel became wedged between two rocks less than a mile from the uninhabited and treacherous Bermudas, or Devil's Islands, as the sailors called them. All lives and many goods were saved. This was the storm of which Shakespeare read, echoing in the *Tempest* the contemporary accounts by William Strachey and by Silvester Jourdain. On the Bermuda Islands, with their strange birds and wild hogs, the company lived for over nine months and built for themselves from the native cedars and the wrecked *Sea Adventure* two pinnaces. They were carried through the ordeal by the ingenuity of their chief men, Sir Thomas Gates and Sir George Somers. Rolfe's wife gave birth to a girl, christened Bermuda, but the infant died before the company left the islands.

The two pinnaces, named the *Deliverance* and the *Patience*, sailed from the Bermudas May 10, 1610, and arrived at Jamestown on May 24th to be greeted by a heart-rending spectacle, the wretched remnant of the terrible winter of 1609–1610, known since as the "Starving Time." The newly-arrived and the sixty survivors mournfully concluded that the Jamestown settlement, like the earlier venture at Roanoke, was a failure. But the arrival of Lord Delaware's three ships, well-provisioned, gave them spirit and they renewed their efforts to plant an English settlement in the New World. Sir Thomas Dale soon became deputy-governor, giving Virginia what it needed, order and stability. Most important of all, during his administration a suitable staple was discovered.

Like many other Englishmen Rolfe enjoyed his pipe, packed with the leaf grown in the Spanish colonies and imported only after paying tribute to the merchants and planters of the Catholic King, Philip III. Near the English settlements in Virginia he could see the Indians cultivating the indigenous *Nicotiana rustica*, a tough plant, which might do for the natives, but the colonists accustomed to the Spanish leaf found it "poore and weake, and of a byting tast . . ." In the memorable year 1612, when Rolfe had been in the Jamestown colony less than two years, hopeless of making a comforting smoke from the native leaf, he planted West Indian seed, *Nicotiana tabacum*, the larger variety used in the Spanish commerce, which chance or his own energy had brought his way. It is recorded that he had in mind both his own pipe and the possibility of an export commodity, sadly needed to bolster the fragile experiment in the New World. Never was a marriage of soil and seed more fruitful. In those great leaves was wealth beyond the gold of the Aztecs or the mines of Peru.

Thomas Dale, sensing the fever of interest in the commodity but fearing a new starving time, ordered that no man could raise tobacco unless he also each season manured and maintained two acres of corn. Experimentally some of the new tobacco was shipped in 1613, but in the period 1615–1616 the London receipts of the Virginia product amounted to only 2300 pounds as compared with the more than 50,000 pounds sent in by Spain. Rolfe confessed difficulty in curing the leaves, but the staple was undoubtedly an acceptable article. Ralph Hamor, Rolfe's friend and secretary of the colony, ventured a plot of tobacco and in his enthusiasm for the new staple declared after leaving Virginia, "no country under the Sunne, may, or doth affoord more pleasant, sweet, and strong Tobacco."

Rolfe's career blended stark tragedy, high romance, economic and political triumphs. His wife, after surviving the Bermudas, had died. His courtship and marriage of Pocahontas, daughter of Powhatan the mighty Werowance, is the best-known romance of the entire colonial period. Antiquarians delight in arguments over the maiden's countenance and her manners, but Rolfe found her agreeable enough, for in April, 1614, with the consent of Dale and of Powhatan, the marriage took place. This alliance insured peace with the Indians for eight years. Rolfe took his bride to England, where in 1616 he addressed to the King a propagandist brochure extolling in neat and enthusiastic style the virtues of the new land. His slightly apologetic tone with reference to tobacco, "the principall commoditie the colony for the present yieldeth," may have been accounted for by the fact that the *Counterblaste to Tobacco* in that same year was acknowledged as having come from the royal pen. Even Rolfe's Elizabethan imagination did not compass the future of the leaf.

When, after the death of Pocahontas, Rolfe returned to the colony he found the Virginians feverishly planting tobacco in every likely nook and cranny, even in the streets and market places of Jamestown. He had the satisfaction of seeing larger and better crops; the yield of 1618 was over 20,000 pounds and the following year England imported more Virginia than Spanish leaf. Thomas Lambert introduced a method of curing by hanging the leaves on lines rather than letting them ferment in piles in the sun as had been the custom. Rolfe again settled down in the community, married his third wife, received due honors including membership in the Council of State, and presumably lost his life in the famous Indian massacre at Bermuda Hundred in 1622. His son by Pocahontas, Thomas Rolfe, grew to manhood in England, but eventually came to Virginia, the Bollings, Randolphs, and others claiming descent from him.

The early English commercial and fiscal policy with respect to tobacco was determined, in large measure, by the belief that the use of tobacco was harmful, and that the colonies should be turned from the culture of a noxious article. After arguments between farmers of the customs and colonists, an agreement was made in 1620 whereby the government would force the agriculturists of England to cease growing tobacco, and the Virginia and Bermuda Companies would pay duties of one shilling a pound, twice that which could have been collected on the basis of the charters but only half the import being charged the Spanish. Then, following an exhausting series of internecine quarrels, the Virginia Company in 1623 agreed to restrict tobacco shipments to England; the government, in turn, gave the Virginia and Bermuda Companies a practical monopoly of the English market by narrowly limiting the importation of Spanish tobacco. Furthermore, the import duties on colonial tobacco were reduced from twelve pence to nine pence per pound. These agreements provided the framework of British tobacco policy down to the time of the American Revolution. The later Navigation Acts merely strengthened the structure erected under James.

The colonial industry was growing at a rate which grieved those English officials who looked on tobacco as a social evil, responsible administrators who feared that the colonials would neglect food crops, and planters who wanted to preserve the fantastically high prices received for the earliest shipments. Yearly exports from Virginia reached the half-million pound mark before 1630, and a decade later London, the principal port of entry, was receiving on an average almost 1,400,000 pounds annually. With the establishment of the colony of Maryland, new tobacco areas were opened, and the Marylanders listed the leaf as their major staple and medium of exchange.

To develop markets which would absorb their expanding staple the colonials wanted direct trade with the continent, but such freedom of commerce was, of course, directly contrary to the mercantilist theories dominating Europe at the time and to the specific bargains struck under James. For awhile Americans surreptitiously sampled the Dutch trade. During the 1640's while England was absorbed in the Civil Wars this traffic became a torrential stream. Whereupon the Navigation Acts formally restricted the shipment of certain "enumerated articles," including tobacco, to England and her dominions. The Act of 1660 in effect reaffirmed the Act of 1620, but it was understood that the rule was now to be enforced.

Although there were other factors, such as overly-large crops, the enforcement of the Navigation Acts contributed to the severe depression which existed in the tobacco areas for two decades after 1660. Failing to obtain relief from the statutes, the planters of the New World turned to crop control. The Virginians led in attempting to develop effective agreements, especially along the line of a stint-of-days plan which would limit transplanting to a certain date, but failed partly because of the objections advanced by Lord Baltimore, who saw a discrimination against Maryland in its more northerly location. Baltimore proclaimed that if planters were poor, "it is not from the low price of Tobacco, but from their owne sloth, ill husbandry, and profusely spending their cropps in Brandewine, and other liquors." In 1666 the three tobacco colonies, Virginia, Maryland, and Carolina, actually agreed among themselves to prohibit the cultivation of the staple during the season from February 1, 1667, to February 1, 1668, an astounding feat of diplomacy. But again Baltimore, the *bête noire* of control legislation, opposed, professing to take the part of the poorer planters and the King's customs.

The depression frame of mind, brought on by the low price of the Virginia staple in the 1670's, made possible Bacon's Rebellion. Even more directly did the meager returns from tobacco sales lead to an upheaval in the following decade, the first important plant-cutting riot, a type of illegal remedy with which the industry has been infected from time to time. In the spring of 1682 the Virginia Assembly adjourned without passing a local cessation act, desired by some, and several planters of Gloucester County destroyed their own plant beds and those of their neighbors. The idea spread rapidly and the "Cutters and Pluckers," as William Fitzhugh called them, began to operate in York, Middlesex, and New Kent Counties until some of the leaders were arrested. Prices gradually improved, in part because of the tobacco lost in the riots, the equivalent of about ten thousand hogsheads.[1]

While the earlier statutes prohibiting the shipment of tobacco to countries other than England had been flagrantly violated, especially during the upheaval in England of the 1640's, the Navigation Acts were, in general, well obeyed in the tobacco colonies. Such violations as did occur were principally the deeds of New York and New England traders, who freighted hogsheads to their own warehouses, then, by-passing English customs officials, marketed the leaf in the ports of Europe. In this manner they undersold the English merchants operating through ordinary channels. Sensitive to pressure from the merchant groups, Parliament in 1673 tried to check this illegal traffic by levying an export duty on "enumerated articles" sent from one colony to another. For tobacco the fee was specified as one penny per pound. Most of the violations at which the planters connived, either actively or passively, were in attempting to circumvent this special statute of 1673.

Through a tortuous maze of events, this levy of 1673 led to the disturbance known as Culpeper's Rebellion, one of the earliest popular outbreaks in American history. The rebellion, which reached its height in the years 1677–1679, was localized in the Albemarle section of the Carolina province, an area later designated as North Carolina. In migrating from Virginia the small planters of the Albemarle region had brought with them, in addition to the bad opinion of their creditors, a sound knowledge of tobacco culture, and by the 1670's their crop was properly

[1] The only other notable plant-cutting riots in the colonial period occurred in Maryland and in northern Virginia during the early summer of 1732, the disturbance centering in Prince George County, Maryland. The immediate provocation was the refusal of the Maryland Assembly to pass a satisfactory inspection act, which, it had been hoped, would raise the price of tobacco.

accounted the principal staple of the region. Because of the shifting sands along the coast, the major part of the traffic in the staple fell into the hands of ingenious New England traders, who pushed into the shallow bays with their light-draft coasters. The lesser fraction of the tobacco was hauled northward to the Virginia markets, where the local planters complained of its poor quality and the ruination of standards, all the while thinking of better prices which might come if the crops from "Rogues Harbour," as they termed Albemarle, were totally barred.[2] The statute of 1673, a sop thrown the London merchants, threatened to wreck the business of the New Englanders and troubled the planters, who saw no other avenue of trade open to them. Though the issues were partly obscured by the struggle of rival factions for power within the colony, in essence the outbreak occurred because of the enforcement of the trade law of 1673.

According to the affidavit of one of the frightened collectors, "y° Rable" demanded of the new Assembly "first absoelutely to insist upon a free traid to transport thier tobacco where they pleased and how they pleased without paying any duty to y° King; Upon wch some of them cryed out God dame y° Collecto^r and this Depon^t verily thought they would have murthered him." The rebellious group actually took over the government for awhile and made John Culpeper governor. The Lords Proprietors removed Culpeper but, fearing that their charter would be jeopardized by news of the violence and nullification of the statute of 1673, minimized the outbreak, and by 1680 proclaimed that all was quiet in the province and that the customs were being collected according to law.

The rebels were never punished, and, despite the declara-

---

[2] In April, 1679, the Virginians in their General Assembly resolved that the importation of Carolina tobacco "hath been found very prejudicial to this country and the inhabitants thereof" and forbade the continuance of the practice, wisely providing, however, that Virginia merchants to whom the Carolinians owed debts could fetch their debtors' tobacco without running afoul the law!

tions of the Lords Proprietors, Albemarle planters largely ignored the obnoxious statute of 1673. Some tobacco was run into Virginia contrary to Virginia statute—Colonel William Byrd of Westover in surveying the dividing line found in Nansemond River Virginia shipmasters who had come for North Carolina tobacco—but New England traders kept a large share of the Carolina tobacco trade until, in the next generation, the Virginians modified their restrictive policy. In some small measure the Culpeper rebellion trained the colonials in the circumvention of statutes running counter to accustomed routes of trade. It helps explain the flouting of the Molasses Act by a later generation.

By the last of the seventeenth century, British tobacco policy contained no hint of the moral opposition to the leaf which had partly determined those grudging regulations under the first James. Certainly there was now no thought of doing away with the tobacco industry; the revenue was precious and the Crown none too secure in its finances. The revenue idea, plus the insistence of a colonial and the temper of a crown official, provided the main ingredients in the well-known encounter between Commissary Blair and Attorney General Seymour.[3]

Commissary James Blair in 1691 was authorized by the Virginia Assembly to go to England and to obtain a charter for the proposed college at Williamsburg. The Queen was willing, the King consented, and they authorized a special grant of two thousand pounds. After his cordial reception by the reigning monarchs, Blair was

[3] This story, one of the most famous in all tobacco lore, was contributed by Benjamin Franklin in a letter to Mason Locke Weems, whom he was consoling because "a cross old Gentleman at Canterbury," the Archbishop, would not ordain him after the American Revolution. This Weems is, of course, the celebrated Parson Weems, creator of the cherry-tree story and other narratives of Washington that regale youths and exasperate scholars to this good day. As for Franklin, an examination of his testimony before the House of Commons in connection with the Stamp Act will show that, while not a user of tobacco himself, he was well informed as to the nature of the trade.

shocked at the objections of Sir Edward Seymour, whose task it was to draw the actual charter. England was at war and money was hard to get. But, said Blair, the new institution would prepare men for the ministry, and the Virginians had souls that needed saving. Then, according to Franklin's version of the story, the exasperated Seymour shouted, "Souls! damn your Souls. Make Tobacco!"

The reward of Blair's persistence was not only the charter and the two thousand pounds, to be taken out of Virginia quitrents, but also 20,000 acres of land, fees from the surveyor-general's office, and a tax of one penny per pound on all this self-same tobacco exported from either Virginia or Maryland to another colony. This last item obviously represented a turning over to the college the income from the controversial one-penny tax of 1673. The export tax on Maryland tobacco gave the youth of Maryland a special right to attend the College of William and Mary. In the year 1719 governor and assembly of Maryland ineffectively addressed the Lord Proprietor requesting that the one-penny tax be reserved for the cause of education in Maryland. The Lord Proprietor was forced to inform the governor and assembly that the grant to the College of William and Mary was perpetual. In such a manner was instituted the first connection between Rolfe's leaf and higher education in English-speaking America.

The discovery that tobacco could be successfully grown and profitably sold was the most momentous single fact in the first century of settlement on the Chesapeake Bay. Relentlessly the leaf shaped the economic, social, and political life of those who carried on its culture. It spread the people over the land. It created the plantation pattern. Its labor requirements soon meant hordes of African slaves. Present-day rural and racial problems below the Mason and Dixon Line are rooted in that first Southern staple, tobacco. But tobacco had guaranteed that the Jamestown experiment would not fail. And in the controversy over the acts of trade there lay ideas to germinate

[Chapter 2]

FIRST AMERICAN ARISTOCRATS

SWEET SCENTED AND ORONOKO

Two main types of *Nicotiana tabacum* were cultivated in
the Chesapeake region: the Sweet Scented and the Oronoko. The Oronoko, spelled quite as often Aronoko,
Oroonoko, or Orinoco, predominated in the Maryland district: the Sweet Scented, a more favored article, milder
in flavor and with shorter, broader leaves, along the James
and York rivers. At one time connoisseurs identified as the
particular plot from which the very best Sweet Scented
came, the Edward Digges property on the York known as
Digges Neck. Hogsheads from these plantations, with the
ED branded on the casks brought the fanciest prices in the
English markets, and to call a crop "E Dees" was the compliment of highest quality.

To start a crop, the seeds were sown in beds, much as
the English had been accustomed to treat their cabbage
plants. In May, after a shower of rain (called a *season*)
the slips were transplanted to hills set some four feet apart
in the cleared fields. The crop was carefully weeded and,
to insure growth and strength, the top of the plant includ-

ing the bud was removed.[1] Some nine to sixteen leaves remained, the number depending on the richness of the soil. Then the suckers, small growths appearing between the leaves and stem, were nipped off. Throughout the period of culture there was a constant fight against insect pests: the fly in the plant bed, the ground worm, and the green hornworm. In August when ripe the plants were cut and hung by pegs on sticks in a ventilated tobacco house. The curing by air was completed in about five or six weeks, then, when the leaves were in proper *case* (moist condition), the tobacco was *struck* (taken down), the stalks removed, the leaves bound in bundles and *prized* into hogsheads. During the eighteenth century the curing process was modified by the occasional use of open fires, and, instead of being pegged, the stalks were split and hung on the tobacco sticks. Hand cultivation dominated, the basic instruments of culture being hoes: grubbing, hilling, and weeding varieties.

Colonial cropmasters raised tobacco on a plot of land for three or four years, *wore out the soil*, as they phrased it, then moved on to another field.[2] Since the actual space devoted to tobacco on any one plantation was the merest fraction of the total—an able-bodied laborer could cultivate only two or three acres in addition to his other duties—this extravagant economy might continue for some time before its effects were felt in any community.

By the last of the seventeenth century the culture of tobacco dominated an area stretching in the tidewater zone from the southern boundary of Pennsylvania to Albemarle Sound. The 40,000,000 pounds being cured each

[1] Some of the yeomen who worked their own crops allowed their thumb nails to grow long and then hardened these talons in the flame of a candle. Suspicious travelers feared that the nails were cultivated for the purpose of gouging eyes in rough-and-tumble combat, but the true design was to pursue the innocent art of topping.

[2] Less prodigal in education than in agriculture, our ancestors used these so-called exhausted lots as building sites for neighborhood schools, known to a later generation as "little red schoolhouses," or more properly "old field schools."

season in this Chesapeake region now represented virtually all the leaf commercially produced in the British
dominions, domestic and colonial. Though some of the
larger plantations approached self-sufficiency, especially
in times when international crises made the leaf unsalable,
the typical planter concentrated on the staple, keeping in
mind all the while that he must produce his basic food
crops. To the satisfaction of English statesmen, trade statistics from the tobacco colonies fitted into the pattern of
imperial theory. The plantations produced a staple for
export, and, contrary to the tendencies perceivable in the
New England and middle colonies, the Marylanders and
Virginians relied on the British markets for manufactured
goods.

The details of crop husbandry, the planting, hilling,
transplanting, weeding, topping, suckering, cutting, hanging, stripping, and prizing, were carried out principally
by white labor in the seventeenth century. Indentured
servants arrived in considerable numbers, but on the ending of their terms most of them became landowners and
competed with their former masters in the production of
the staple to which they had become accustomed. With
an impermanent laboring group, large-scale operations
were exceptional in the seventeenth century. Most of the
huge initial grants were soon subdivided; the attempt to
institute a manorial system in Maryland failed.

Negro slavery, on which the pattern of large plantations eventually shaped itself, had been introduced in the
tobacco area in 1619, but slave traders did not import
Negroes in great numbers until the last decades of the
century. Soon thereafter there emerged a large-planter
class of wealth and influence which dominated the tobacco
regions.

GREAT PLANTERS OF THE TIDEWATER

"In every river there are from ten to thirty men who by trade and industry have gotten very competent estates," wrote Colonel Robert Quary in 1703 by way of reporting Virginia conditions to the Board of Trade. A fair sample of this great-planter class, which took root in the Chesapeake Bay in the late seventeenth century and flowered in the eighteenth, was William Fitzhugh, son of an English woolen draper, who arrived in the New World about the year 1670 and settled in Virginia near the Potomac River. There he acquired a fortune through tobacco production, trade, and the legal profession. Like many other tidewater planters he bought tobacco from those of his neighbors who operated on a smaller scale, and from his own wharf shipped this leaf together with that of his own plantations to merchants of London and Bristol. The ship captains, whom Fitzhugh sent off with wishes for "A prosperous voyage, a lucky market and a happy Return," brought him English goods, some of which Fitzhugh sold to his neighbors.

William Fitzhugh enjoyed the advantages of his wealth, purchasing handsome plate and a calash, accumulating a library, employing a French Huguenot minister to teach his son William, who was later sent to England for more schooling. Fitzhugh was judge of the county court, commanded the local militia, and sat in the House of Burgesses. Though to his mother he wrote, April 22, 1686, "Praised be God I neither live in poverty nor pomp, but in a very good indifference & to a full content," his modesty was hardly justified by a calendar of his possessions that year. His plantation, Bedford, was a thousand acres in extent, "at least 700 acres of it being rich thicket, the remainder good hearty plantable land," all equipped with proper houses, including dairy, dove-cote and hen-house, and with a sufficiency of labor, twenty-nine Negroes in all. His own house of thirteen rooms was "furnished with all accommodations for a comfortable & gentile living." In his orchard were 2500 apple trees, enclosed in a locust fence. The garden was one hundred feet square. From his water grist mill, a mile and a half distant from his house, came enough wheat and Indian corn by way of toll to satisfy his needs. Farther up the river he owned three more tracts, one containing 22,000 acres, another 500, and a third 1000. In addition, he had on hand crops and debts due him to the sum of 250,000 pounds of tobacco. His tobacco, corn, and meat, in terms of tobacco currency, were worth 60,000 pounds per year. And, added Fitzhugh, "the negroes increase being all young & a considerable parcel of breeders will keep that stock good for ever."

Later in that same year 1686, M. Durand, a French Huguenot, visited Bedford in the company of Fitzhugh's planter friend, Ralph Wormeley of Rosegill, and a party totaling twenty. Wormeley, it may be noted, was educated in Oriel College, Oxford, and possessed the largest library of seventeenth-century Virginia. The score of guests found good wine, a great fireplace, and such amusement as a fiddler, a jester, a tight-rope dancer, and an acrobat could afford. The next day Colonel Fitzhugh lent them his boat for the Potomac River crossing, and brought a punchbowl to the shore as a parting gesture of hospitality. At the time of his death in 1701, Fitzhugh possessed about 54,000 acres; named in his will were fifty-one slaves.

William Byrd II, otherwise termed William Byrd of Westover, is the best known and most brilliant representative of his class. His father, the first of the name, through inheritance, the Indian trade, and tobacco planting had accumulated a fortune and sent his children to English schools. Byrd visited Holland, then returned to England for business training under the general supervision of the merchants, Perry and Lane. He then entered the Middle Temple, was admitted to the bar and, at an early age, was

elected to the Royal Society. Byrd became not only agent
for the colony of Virginia and thus represented her in
England, but back in Virginia was elected a member of
the House of Burgesses and then chosen a member of the
Council, an office which he held from 1708 to the end of
his life. "The Merchants of England take care that none
of us grow very rich," he wryly commented, adding, however, that "the felicity of the Clymate hinders us from
being very poor." Yet he accumulated, with Westover as
the center, properties to add to his inheritance. In 1717 he
held 43,000 acres; by the time of his death in 1744, these
had been increased to 179,000.

This urbane and versatile gentleman read widely, accumulated a library of over 3600 volumes, rivaled in the
colonies only by Cotton Mather's collection, and corre-
sponded with the literary and scientific figures in England. His major writings, "History of the Dividing Line,"
"A Journey to the Land of Eden," and "A Progress to the
Mines," though unpublished until the nineteenth century,
prove his nimble wit and facile pen. And his "Secret
Diary" is a gem whose facets reflect with rare honesty the
life of the eighteenth-century gentleman on Virginia
plantation and in English society. His most extensive
work printed during his lifetime was *A Discourse Concerning the Plague, With some Preservatives Against it.
By a Lover of Mankind*, written in Virginia early in the
year 1721, when Byrd heard that the pestilence had reap-
peared in England. The principal theme of the one-shilling
pamphlet was that the generous use of tobacco constituted
an excellent preventive. Byrd reviewed and affirmed the
doctrine of nicotine therapy, calling attention to the fact
that "In *England* it [the plague] us'd formerly to make a
visit about once in twenty or thirty years: but since the
universal use of Tobacco, it has now been kept off above
fifty four years." The ordinary employment of the herb
was not enough. "We shou'd wear it about our clothes,
and about our coaches. We should hang bundles of it

round our beds, and in the apartments wherein we most converse." Though the "Lover of Mankind" fails to list the point, it is obvious that such a generous use of tobacco would benefit the planters of the New World.

The Carter family achieved its greatest fame in the person of Robert Carter, or King Carter as he was usually called, reputedly the most wealthy and certainly one of the most powerful of the ruling class. At the time of his death, in 1732, he was supposedly possessed of some 300,-000 acres of land and 700 or more slaves. He was consistently acquisitive, and often overbearing. During his lifetime he held a multitude of offices: justice of the peace, member of the House of Burgesses, Speaker of the House, member of the Council, President of the Council, colonial Treasurer, and, of course, commander of the local militia. He naturally assumed as his right and duty leadership in the local parish. In the vestry lists his name came ahead of the minister, and according to tradition no ordinary member had the temerity to enter Christ Church on a Sabbath before the arrival of King Carter!

His grandson was Robert Carter of Nomini Hall, whose life spanned the so-called "Golden Age" of the tidewater tobacco aristocracy. Dressed in new clothes and accompanied by a Negro attendant, at the age of nine he entered William and Mary. He inherited his property at the age of twenty-one, went to England for two years of undisciplined living, returned and in 1754 married Frances Ann Tasker, sixteen years of age and daughter of the wealthy Benjamin Tasker of Baltimore, who had been president of the Council of Maryland for thirty-two years. Carter now settled down, proved an intelligent though not aggressive manager, and by virtue of his family connections obtained membership on the Virginia Council. In the year 1761 he moved into Williamsburg, taking a house with handsome furnishings near the Governor's Palace. After living in Williamsburg for ten years he returned to Nomini Hall. The hospitable life at this estate, where annually there were consumed over 27,000 pounds of pork, twenty beeves, and miscellaneous supplies in proportion, is described by the tutor, Philip Fithian, in his valuable *Journal*.

The Fitzhughs, Byrds, and Carters were only several of many aristocratic families in the tobacco plantation area closely knit by friendship and intermarriage. The composite effect was a society dominated by the great clans, these three plus the Randolphs, Harrisons, Wormeleys, Digges, Nelsons, Lees, and others. The plantation gentry of the Chesapeake region assumed clear form about the time of the coming of William and Mary to England, and reached the zenith of its splendor about the time George III inherited the throne. The Cavalier tradition notwithstanding, only a handful of the plantation gentry could claim origin in the landed aristocracy of England; the founders of the great families along the Chesapeake were, in general, of substantial middle-class English stock. Enterprise, not ancestry, was the essential ingredient for the earning of substance and prestige in the New World.

In their hospitality, drinking, gaming, horse-racing, and dancing the tobacco planters in many respects appeared to concentrate on the pleasures of this world. Indeed there were inherent qualities in tobacco planting and marketing which encouraged a sort of hedonism and devil-may-care attitude. Plantation life was, by definition, rural living and much of it was of necessity monotonous. Thus the social events, when they came, were accepted with all the more enthusiasm; the days of dreariness must have their compensation. Then, subtly the Negro's concern with the day rather than the morrow seeped like a drug into the consciousness of many of the men along the rivers. Most of the plantations were self-sufficient in terms of elementary animal needs of food and shelter. The bread, the meat, the timber were all a part of the established routine. Come market glut or bookkeeping knavery there would be neither starving nor freezing, and accounting time seemed a long way off. Months, if not years, would elapse before the planter knew where he stood with his merchant if the hogsheads were shipped on consignment. The tobacco planter had in him enough of the frontiersman to be incurably optimistic, and enough of the English landed gentry to desire a high standard of living. The combination often meant piling debt on debt. And if he were in debt, it was neither dishonor nor novelty; he had more than likely inherited English creditors from his father.

Yet with all these external evidences of frivolity and love of pleasure, no quality of the gentry in the tidewater regions was more marked than the serious acceptance of public responsibility. No school of leadership was more creative than the colonial tobacco plantation. Although consistently outnumbered by the small planters, the men of property took as their natural right positions of authority in society, religion, and politics. They dominated the parish vestries, county courts, local militia, Governors' Councils, and obtained a large number of seats in the lower house of the colonial assemblies. They played the role of the English county squires, whom they instinctively imitated, but with qualities added by the American experience. The planters were managing large enterprises; they must account for the health and labor of many servants. As lords of their little domains they developed an almost unassailable momentum of independence in spirit, sometimes degenerating into starchy hauteur, more often maturing into easy dignity. Looking to Europe for market and supplies, they cultivated a breadth of view which overcame provincialism inherent in otherwise rural life. Power they had, to be sure, but power almost invariably controlled by a stewardship to the private conscience of a gentleman. And a gentleman owed the state the best of his talents. Furthermore, the man of one hogshead [3] and

---

[3] A planter was commonly designated in terms of the number of hogsheads he annually produced. For example, Grigsby in his *Virginia Conven-*

the village clerk walked as best they could in steps of the great men; thus the whole society was seasoned by the civic spirit of the colonial gentry. A generation trained in the responsible natural leadership of the plantation area was to serve the nation with conspicuous success during the American Revolution and early national period.

By mid-eighteenth century, on a slightly contracted scale the characteristic tobacco-planting society had pushed above the fall line. At the time of the Revolution a traveler could stand on a hill in the Virginia county of Albemarle, look about him and see plantations every four or five miles, clusters of buildings in the distance giving the appearance of tiny villages. Each plantation had its dwelling house, kitchens, smoke house, tobacco houses, and scattered Negro cabins. There were the inevitable peach and apple orchards for the equally inevitable fruit brandy. Closer examination showed many of the "mansion houses" to be unpainted frame structures, with wooden shutters and wooden clay-lined chimneys, and lacking both glass and plaster. Others, holding more closely to the genteel tradition, were painted, lathed and plastered within, and had window glass and neat brick chimneys. They were all in the timber district, and the meandering fields were divided by rail fences so zig-zag in design that the New Englanders developed a saying for a man in liquor: he was making Virginia fences.

TOBACCO MERCHANTS OF BRITAIN

The planter shipped his hogsheads to some merchant in Britain, who, in turn, forwarded to the planter the textiles, tools, and countless other items expected by the New World from the Old. This was the consignment system.

tion of 1788 referred to gouty and charming William Grayson as "fond of society, and whether he appeared at the fireside of the man of one hogshead, or in the aristocratic circles of the Colony, he was ever a welcome and honored guest."

At its best the relationship between American planter and the British merchant was softened by the relaying of gossip, inquiry as to mutual acquaintances, and the friendly exchange of gifts. But complaint often drowned compliment, low prices brought on sullen moods, and touchy planters resented gratuitous advice, explicit or implied.

Friction was inevitable between the agricultural and trading communities. Furthermore, the tobacco planter characteristically ran into debt. Early in the reign of George II about two-thirds of the Virginia planters were so enmeshed that they could not change factors. Thomas Jefferson, who owed Glasgow and London firms some nine or ten thousand pounds sterling at the outbreak of the Revolution, in recalling the "peculiarities in the tobacco trade" remarked, "These debts had become hereditary from father to son, for many generations, so that the planters were a species of property, annexed to certain mercantile houses in London." Further comments on the British tobacco merchants were written by Jefferson from Paris in 1786, when he was counseling the shrewish Mrs. Lucy Ludwell Paradise, who had proposed that her husband borrow enough money from one merchant to pay the other creditors. Mrs. Paradise had inherited from her father, Philip Ludwell III, lands along the James River from which hogsheads of tobacco were sent to London, where the Paradise family then lived. Yes, convert all his debts into one, advised Jefferson, but "upon condition that the person giving him this credit shall be satisfied to receive annually his interest in money, and shall not require consignments of tobacco. This is the usual condition of the tobacco merchants. No *other law* can be more oppressive to the mind or fortune, and long experience has proved to us that there never was an instance of a man's getting out of debt who was once in the hands of a tobacco merchant & bound to consign his tobacco to him. It is the most delusive of all snares. The merchant feeds the inclination of his customer to be credited till he gets the burthen of debt so increased that he cannot throw it off at once, he then begins to give him less for his tobacco & ends with giving him what he pleases for it, which is always so little that though the demands of the customer for necessaries be reduced ever so low in order to get himself out of debt, the merchant lowers his price in the same proportion so as always to keep such a balance against his customer as will oblige him to continue his consignments of tobacco. Tobacco always sells better in Virginia than in the hands of a London merchant. The confidence which you have been pleased to place in me induces me to take the liberty of advising you to submit to any thing rather than to an obligation to ship your tobacco." [4]

With engaging uniformity the planters agreed that when the British consignment merchants sold the leaf the price was never as high as that ruling in open markets. William Byrd of Westover wailed that Alderman Perry, "that hungry magistrate," trimmed tobacco prices twenty-five per cent. The estimate cannot be discounted as simple literary license when George Washington is heard judging that in four years out of five his tobacco shipped on consignment brought lower prices than were quoted in the home market. The pattern in American thought was well set: the honest, hard-working planter, and to borrow a phrase used as early as 1628 by the Virginians, the "unconscionable and cruel merchants." On the other hand the merchant saw the planter as a spendthrift and wastrel, quick to borrow, slow to pay, gifted with rare ingenuity in discovering flaws in merchandise and never satisfied with the most generous prices. In truth, abundant carelessness and some slipperiness could be proved by both

[4] The totality of the condemnation is explained first by Jefferson's recent and humiliating visit to England, an experience made notable by George III's frigid reception and by the clamorings of the merchants for payment of their pre-war debts, and second by the necessity of making his point absolutely clear to the temperamental Mrs. Paradise, whose eccentricities are still current legend in Williamsburg, where she spent her last years.

sides. As a matter of fact merchants cheated their own government more than they did the planters, but persistent defrauding of His Majesty's customs by false weights invited the further crime of swindling the colonials.

Some British traders, of course, participated in outright smuggling, and others—this group included several of the leading merchants—bought leaf from waterfront gangs, thus conniving in "socking," as was the slang expression for stealing tobacco from ships and wharves. About fifty tons of tobacco were socked in one year at the port of London; sixteen tons were recovered. The most characteristic frauds were effected under the rule allowing drawbacks or refunds of duties for tobacco re-exported to the continent. Some merchants used light weights in listing imports and heavy weights in reporting exports. (The running in of light hogsheads was called *Hickory-puckery*; the reporting of heavy hogsheads for exportation, *Puckery-hickory*.) Other merchants actually shipped tobacco, obtained the drawback, then re-landed the leaf.

Aware of this mercantile legerdemain and deciding that political expediency demanded a reduction of the land tax, which weighed heavily on the country gentry, Robert Walpole, First Lord of the Treasury and Chancellor of the Exchequer, introduced in the House of Commons on March 15, 1733, his excise scheme, providing for bonded warehouses in which imported leaf tobacco could be stored without the payment of duty until it was withdrawn for domestic use. Naturally there would be periodic inspections on the premises of dealers and manufacturers by excisemen to insure that all tobacco had been duly withdrawn from a government warehouse. The terms of the proposed act followed a plan suggested in 1732 by the Virginia Assembly and printed as *The Case of the Planters of Tobacco in Virginia*. Suspecting the merchants of sharp practices, the planters had outlined their grievances and a system of remedies, sending as their commissioner to

London John Randolph.[5] It is possible that the Virginians moved in a spirit of retaliation, for a recent Parliamentary act, passed presumably at the request of the merchants, facilitated the collection of debts in the New World.

The tobacco merchants, whatever their shade of morality, professed to find fault with the excise, and the Opposition, led by Pulteney, persistently seeking some means of discrediting Walpole, joined the mercantile group. The *Craftsman* and other anti-Walpole journals blazed away, but the distinguishing feature of the attack was the Opposition's incitement of the mobs that assembled at the doors of Parliament and in the avenues of the house crying against the excise.

The debates are usually counted among the most dramatic in Parliament's history. All England was tense. Rumors of armies of excisemen and of the death of English liberties filled the land, circulated by enemies of the ministry. Walpole saw his majorities decrease, realized that he had overestimated the loyalty of the landed gentry and underestimated the ingenuity of the mercantile group, especially the tobacco merchants of London, and decided to withdraw the bill.[6] Whereupon hysterical celebrations swept over the land. Only after three days could the vice-chancellor and proctors calm the students at Oxford. But the mob outside Parliament heaped insults on Walpole when he went towards his carriage, pressing upon him and cursing him. The excise battle goes down in history as the classic example of arousing the mob for political purposes.

The consignment system, involving direct relations between American planter and British merchant, became

---

[5] Incidentally, John Randolph, brilliant representative of the famous Turkey Island family, was at this time knighted. The ceremony probably represented Walpole's sympathy with Randolph's particular mission as much as a recognition of his undoubted ability. He was the only Virginian so honored in the colonial period.

[6] One member of the Commons who usually supported Walpole but who turned against him on this issue was Micajah Perry, Alderman and one-time Lord Mayor of London, chairman of an association of London tobacco merchants formed in 1727.

less feasible as population and tobacco culture moved into the piedmont, far from streams navigable by ocean-going craft. By the time of the American Revolution perhaps not more than a fourth of all the tobacco shipped from Virginia was marketed by consignment, the system persisting among the well-entrenched tidewater planters who produced an extra-quality leaf. To meet the new situation caused by the westward migration of the plantations and to serve the small planters who usually sold to their wealthier neighbors or to itinerant traders, English and Scotch mercantile firms sent resident factors, often junior partners or younger men, to set up stores at convenient places. These agents, paid an annual wage in addition to bed, board, and other expenses, accumulated ship-loads of tobacco and distributed the usual plantation merchandise. Many of the resident factors had some legal training, a preparation especially appropriate because an important assignment was the collection of debts. According to tradition, one of the promises extracted from the young men was that they would not marry American girls, it being feared that such an attachment would create too much friendliness and concern for the planter and accordingly lessen loyalty to the principal of the firm! In addition to these salaried factors, there were independent storekeepers operating on a ten per cent commission, in no wise restricting their business to one firm of British merchants.

The Scotch merchants were especially strong in the back-country, Londoners and English outport merchants having established themselves in the tidewater section during those days before the union of 1707, when the men north of the border were outlawed from the traffic. But now the merchants of Glasgow in particular moved into the tobacco regions and before the Revolution boasted that the wharves of their one city received about half the entire shipment of hogsheads sent to Britain from America.

Virtually all the store goods were sold on a credit basis,

with payment made once a year when the factor bought
the tobacco from the customer at the prevailing price.
Among the various account books was one, a small ledger
called the "pocket-book," in which the sums due the store
were transcribed. This the storekeeper carried on all public occasions, such as court days, so that his customers
might be tactfully informed as to their standing. Another
special volume kept by every storekeeper was the long tobacco book, recording the movement of individual hogsheads. Each cask was identified by a special *mark* and
number. The mark represented some particular design
chosen by the planter, perhaps a single letter or a combination of letters interwoven, a crow's-foot, or whatever
whimsy suggested.

The dismaying experiences of an agent newly-arrived
from England is the theme of the satirical verses entitled
"The Sot-weed Factor . . . By Eben. Cook, Gent.," published first in 1708 in London, one of the lustiest poems of
that generation and an ever-present pin prick for the bub-
bles of romanticists. The sot-weed (tobacco) factor came
to Maryland and

> Intending there to open Store,
> I put myself and Goods a-shore.

It was the beginning of a nightmarish mixture of cackling
hens, croaking frogs, plaguish "Muskitoes," greasy meals,
wild Indians, sluttish maids, drunken planters, wrangling
lawyers, and ignorant judges. On the Eastern Shore he met
a planter.

> With this sly Zealot soon I struck
> A Bargain for my English Truck,
> Agreeing for ten thousand weight
> Of Sot-weed good and fit for freight,
> Broad *Oronoko* bright and sound,
> The growth and product of his ground;
> In Cask that should contain compleat,
> Five hundred of Tobacco neat.

But "This damn'd pretended Godly Knave" absconded with the English merchandise, and the sot-weed factor, failing to obtain justice in court, took ship for home, laying on the land an elaborate thirteen-line curse, which concluded:

> May Wrath Divine then lay those Regions wast
> Where no Man's * Faithful, nor a Woman chast.
>
> * The Author does not intend by this, any of the *English* Gentlemen resident there.

Leaf sales were simplified by inspection laws designed to guarantee the quality of the exported staple. The statutes embodied extensive governmental control, a principle inherent in the mercantile philosophy of that time but heretofore directed principally at urban pursuits and shipping. The Virginia Assembly, in August 1619, when this the first legislative body on the continent was no more than a few days old, passed an act requiring the inspection of tobacco and the burning of the leaf of poor quality. There were periodic renewals and modifications of the statute, and beginning with 1640 Maryland made a brief experiment with similar legislation, but enforcement all during the seventeenth century was casual and London factors never ceased to complain of the unmerchantable character of the leaf. After passing through an exhausting trial by depression, the Virginians in 1730 were in a mood for desperate remedies. Even the large planters, who had obtained a royal veto of a former act, now welcomed the statute setting up an effective method of inspection. Superimposed on a pattern of public warehouses (or "rolling houses" as they were called) established earlier, the inspection system provided that no leaf could be exported unless it had been examined and approved by official inspectors. The inspectors, bonded to insure the proper performance of their duties, burned unmerchantable tobacco; for good tobacco they issued warehouse receipts, the so-called "tobacco notes," which were negotiable instruments.

After the Virginia act of 1730 became effective, Marylanders painfully saw their merchants moving across the Potomac to purchase the now definitely superior Virginia leaf, and realized that half-hearted attempts to control the quality of the staple would no longer suffice. But their inspection act was delayed for almost a generation by insistence of debtor, tax- and tithe-payer that a scaling down of obligations payable in tobacco should be linked with the statute for improving the staple. After the general situation was aired extensively in the pages of the *Maryland Gazette*, creditors, officers, and clergy in 1747 finally consented to a reduction of their fees and the act was passed. It was similar to the Virginia statute, though the inspectors were appointed by the governor from a slate nominated by the parish vestrymen and church wardens instead of by the county courts, and the tobacco notes were regulated in more detail.

If they subscribed to the inspection laws, North Carolinians could legally sell their tobacco in Virginia after 1730, and soon almost all of their hogsheads were sent to Petersburg and other Virginia markets for sale. In the year 1754 North Carolina passed an inspection act somewhat like that of its northern neighbors.

The inspection laws improved the whole procedure of marketing. They made possible the sale of a hogshead by a simple exchange of the tobacco note, certifying a specified quantity of merchantable leaf. The statutes, in requiring shipment in hogsheads rather than in bulk, ended a long and complicated argument on that score, but they were less successful in establishing a uniform size for the hogshead. Indeed the variant size of the cask is the despair of any student attempting to use tobacco statistics. Because most of the marketing charges were computed at so much per hogshead rather than per pound, the containers were continually being enlarged. The ancient custom of the wharves was to count four hogsheads as a ton. Once the cask was built to contain about five hundred pounds, but by the late colonial period the hogshead averaged almost twice that weight.

THE PARSON'S CAUSE

In the Chesapeake region tobacco had been a standard of value and a medium of exchange long before the effective inspection statutes. Debts were contracted in terms of tobacco; taxes were payable in the cured leaf. Merchant and mechanic, midwife and minister, all took their fees in tobacco. When the maidens arrived at Jamestown in 1619, the bachelors and widowers redeemed their brides through tendering a hundred and twenty pounds of Virginia leaf.

The use of tobacco as a medium of exchange was a natural development in a primitive community where coin was scarce, and virtually every man grew tobacco, the most vendable of New World products. And once the custom of payments in tobacco had been established, it clung through momentum of habit and inflexibility of statute even in sections where the production of tobacco as a market crop was no longer profitable. The staple was patently something less than a perfect currency device. As the leaf was then packed it was perishable, not readily divisible, and not as portable as coin. In the earliest days the leaves were of markedly uneven quality; debtors notoriously saved their worst for payment of what they owed. And of course the value of tobacco in terms of sterling fluctuated from year to year. The debtor whose bond was in tobacco pounds found it convenient to pay when tobacco was plentiful and prices low; naturally he developed fine excuses in times of short crops, and in the leanest years he had the help of stay laws. Furthermore, the average planter could be expected to have quantities of salable tobacco only during the regular market season; thus tobacco debts usually fell due in the winter or spring.

The most notable difficulties over the payment of offi-

cials in the staple occurred in the case of the clergy of the
Anglican Church, established by law in all three of the
tobacco colonies. The Dissenters, it should be remembered,
reluctantly paid their levy no matter if the minister were
of the best quality; the low income, large parishes, and
uncertain tenure offered by colonial vestries attracted too
few of the best. The sporting parson was enough in evidence to discredit the average clergyman, honest if un-
talented. Paid in produce, the ministers of necessity
watched the market with concern less fitting a chancel
than a counting room. One unhappy gentleman in a Maryland parish wrote to his bishop, "Tobacco, our money, is
worth nothing, and not a Shirt to be had for Tobacco this
year in all our county." As Hugh Jones commented in
1724, "The Establishment is indeed Tobacco," noting also
that parishes remained vacant because of the poor quality
of their leaf. Some parishioners showed shameful ingenuity in saving the worst and trashiest tobacco for their
ministers in the days before the markets were effectively
regulated. One eighteenth-century bit of advice to the
clergy threatened with difficulty in the collection of highest quality leaf was, "the best way to get sweet-scented
Tobacco has been declared by some to use sweet-scented
Words." Assemblymen of Maryland periodically initiated
measures to reduce the annual allowance of forty pounds
per poll, as established in 1702, forcing the clergy into
defensive lobbying.

The controversy in Virginia over this uncertain currency
led to the famous Parson's Cause, raised the question of
the royal veto, and carried Patrick Henry into prominence
as a defender of American rights. In the year 1755 the
tobacco regions suffered from a drought, and the Virginia
Assembly, fearing the scarcity of tobacco, provided that
debts and fees payable in the staple could be satisfied during the succeeding ten months by payment in currency at
the rate of two pence per pound, at the option of the debtor.
This piece of agrarian legislation was the first Two Penny

Act. In 1758 came more bad weather; the Assembly passed an act dated September 14, 1758, similar to that of 1755, this to last for one year.

As anticipated by the Virginia legislators, tobacco was relatively scarce and the market prices rose to three times that specified in the commutation act. In contrast to their general acquiescence in the first Two Penny Act, the clergy, each due 16,000 pounds of tobacco per year, almost to a man resisted this statute. Their arguments were simple and direct: When the market was glutted and prices fell, not a word was said about shifting the tobacco payments to currency on an equitable basis. It was not fair, so they said, to penalize them when tobacco prices were low and then refuse to grant them the advantages of a recovery in the market. On August 10, 1759, an Order of Council was obtained by the clergy declaring invalid the Two Penny Act of 1758. The clergy now contended that the ruling made the act invalid from the time of its passing; the Assembly preferred to interpret the decision as effective from the date of the Order of Council, when, incidentally, the Two Penny Act had almost expired by its own terms.

Among the various suits brought by the clergymen for recovery of their lost salary was one instituted in the County Court of Hanover by the Rev. James Maury, a dignified gentleman of Huguenot descent. It was Mr. Maury's bad luck that Hanover County, in the piedmont section immediately west of the fall line, had recently become the hotbed of southern Presbyterianism and one of the centers of the Great Awakening. The preacher Samuel Davies attracted an enthusiastic following before leaving in 1759 to become president of the College of New Jersey, later known as Princeton. Despite the popular feeling of indignation at the clergy's stand in this matter of the Two Penny Act, the November Court sustained the contention of Maury's attorneys that the act had been invalid from the time of its passing. The only question remaining was the exact amount due Mr. Maury, presumably the difference between his tobacco payment actually received on the two-pence basis and the true market price. This question was to be decided by jury at the December Court.

It was at this December Court that America's greatest orator discovered his own power. To the seemingly hopeless case Patrick Henry, twenty-seven years old and comparatively unknown, was called in defense of the tithe-payers. Fond of his gun, his fishing-rod, and his violin, he knew more of human nature than of Coke upon Littleton. Careless in dress and cheerful in disposition, he had earned a reputation for indolence as he studied the moods and opinions of the plain farmers, whose dialect he adopted as his own. Patrick Henry's mother was a Presbyterian, having come under the influence of Davies, but his father was a vestryman of the Established Church.

The usual court day crowd was enlarged as rumor spread that something special would happen. Scotch merchants, great planters, small farmers, and from nearby parishes no less than twenty ministers who considered this a test action were all there. Mr. Maury and his counsel were fretted at the list of jurymen; there were several known Dissenters. In the private words of the old aristocrat, the jury came from "the vulgar herd." Now Maury's counsel was none other than Peter Lyons, the leading lawyer of that section and later president of the Virginia Court of Appeals. Sensing the hostile feeling of his audience, Lyons left his narrow statistical argument dealing with prices and markets, where presumably the case would lie, and attempted to compliment the character of the clergy.

Henry began his plea with hesitancy and awkwardness. His own father, who presided over the court, shrank into his chair and the visiting clergymen glanced one at another in gestures of triumph. Then the young lawyer measured up to the opportunity, proving himself master of the art of arousing the passions of his hearers. In the words of one of his listeners, "he made their blood to run cold, and their hair to rise on end." He refused to be bound by any narrow view of the case, summarized the nature of the compact between king and people, declaring the law of 1758 a good law which could not be vetoed consistent with the compact. The king, said Henry, instead of being a father had now become a tyrant whose bad acts deserved no obedience. At these strong words the murmur of "Treason! Treason!" could be heard, but Henry paused not a moment in his argument.

Then he proceeded to review the character of the clergy, "rapacious harpies," who "would, were their powers equal to their will, snatch from the hearth of their honest parishioner his last hoe-cake, from the widow and her orphan children their last milch cow! the last bed, nay, the last blanket from the lying-in woman!" As the audience was rising to the spirit of the moment, the visiting clergymen thought it undignified to listen to this tempest of phrases and retreated from the courtroom. Henry concluded by picturing the chains on the neck of any people who could not make their own laws, and recommended that the jury, which was bound to award some damages to Mr. Maury, grant only a nominal fee.

In something less than five minutes the jury reached a verdict of *one penny damages*, and chance spectators would have thought it election day as the excited people carried Henry about the courtyard on their shoulders. Belatedly smitten by his sense of conscience or caution, he sought out the discomfited Mr. Maury and, according to the latter, apologized to him, confessing that his whole purpose in the case was to gain personal popularity! For all practical purposes the clergy of Virginia had lost their case. When the Rev. John Camm, indignant commissary, appealed to the Privy Council, that body, wearied of the situation, found some technical excuse for refusing to grant relief.

The Parson's Cause, as the case was popularly known, was one of those several events of the period immediately

after the French and Indian War pointing to the American
Revolution. Basic threads of Henry's argument reappear
twelve years later in the Declaration of Independence.
But a candid examination of the facts indicates that Patrick Henry saw none of these things of the future; in this
period he gave no serious thought to independence. He
was concentrating on the immediate task before him, the
winning of his lawsuit. His denunciation of the king was
but an incident in the day's work. Yet, Patrick Henry
found himself a famous man in the back-country, and he
grew in confidence. He would soon nurture his incidental
arguments into a major thesis. And a later cry of "Treason" in Williamsburg would not disturb him. Had he not
heard the word before? And it could be stomached. There
is more than a germ of truth in Moncure Daniel Conway's
often-quoted statement that, "A true history of tobacco
would be the history of English and American liberty." [7]

In the early 1770's British tobacco imports averaged
over 100,000,000 pounds, a new high in the customs records. But the planters were unhappy. Their debts mounted
and their westward land ventures were checked by crown
officials.[8] Rebellious Boston merchants found warm allies
along the Chesapeake.

[7] In his interpretive chapter, "Tobacconalia" (*Barons of the Potomack
and the Rappahannock*. The Grolier Club, New York, 1892), Conway sees
the tobacco revenue as the key issue between Crown and Commons, the
restraints on the commerce of tobacco as the beginning of the American
Revolution.

[8] After surveying the colonial staples, Adam Smith in his *The Wealth
of Nations* (1776) concluded, "The cultivation of tobacco, however, seems
not to be so advantageous as that of sugar. I have never even heard of any
tobacco plantation that was improved and cultivated by the capital of merchants who resided in Great Britain, and our tobacco colonies send us home
no such wealthy planters as we see frequently arrive from our sugar
islands."

*1776 * 1860*

ern staples, however, was active enough to concern the British; this was one reason for concentrating their armies in the South in the last years of the war. Phillips, Arnold, and Cornwallis, applying the torch with particular thoroughness in the neighborhood of Petersburg, destroyed some ten thousand hogsheads in their Virginia venture of 1780–1781, which is sometimes called *The Tobacco War* by early nineteenth century historians.

In the year 1804 vinegary Oliver Wolcott, goaded by what he counted as the unrestrained vandalism of the Jeffersonian group—Wolcott had recently lost a judgeship in the quarrel over the Federal courts—looked back on the American Revolution and in these contemptuous phrases dismissed Virginian patriotism, "It is a firmly established opinion of men well versed in the history of our revolution, that the *whiggism* of Virginia was chiefly owing to the *debts of the planters*." First given currency in the heat of early party politics, this theory that the tobacco planters went to war with the British principally to repudiate their debts was revived in the early twentieth century by historians seeking to find in economic determinism the answer to all problems. It is undoubtedly true that the Southern planters were indebted to the British merchants for huge sums. And it is equally certain that the planters blamed British cupidity and corruption as much as their own extravagance for these debts. Of all the debtors, the Virginians were most desperately enmeshed; they owed some two million pounds sterling, about as much as all the rest of the colonials put together. Many of the first

war the ship carrying the tobacco had been captured. By common and tacit consent political and military topics were skillfully avoided until the following parlor-exchange took place. According to Thomas Anburey, an officer taken at Saratoga, "As several officers were sitting with the ladies, the conversation ran upon politics, when Miss Randolph innocently asked, 'How we came to be taken prisoners?' The officer with some warmth replied, 'Just as your tobacco was, by a superior force.' I need not tell you the distress and confusion of the young lady, as well as of the officer himself, who immediately became conscious of what he had said, and for his ill-timed violence, he forfeited all claim to the hospitality of Tuckahoe."

families were trapped in the vicious downward spiral after the Seven Years' War when deflation and an unfavorable balance of trade seemed to seal all escape. Determined to rule his own affairs, whether in his plantation, his parish vestry, or his House of Burgesses, and irked by the blunderings of George III's government, especially by those rules forbidding the land-hungry subjects from freely moving west of the mountains, the high-tempered tobacco planter found himself in the comfortable circumstance of squaring his political convictions with his economic interests. Times were hard, and even temporary relief from debt payments would be welcome. In no sense the principal cause for the absence of Loyalism in the tobacco regions, the debts owed Britishers helped convince the planters that they would do well to divorce themselves from the perfidy of the mother country.

These debts complicated the diplomatic relations between the United States and Great Britain for a full generation after Yorktown. In October 1777, the Virginians passed a law providing for the sequestration of the debts owed the British. Thomas Jefferson, Patrick Henry, Edmund Pendleton, members of the Lee, Ball, and Marshall families, and many others—in all more than five hundred —freed themselves from their debts by depositing in the state loan office about £275,000 in paper money, hardly worth one-fifteenth of that in sterling. In a somewhat similar way Maryland planters, who had as an excuse the refusal of London trustees to accept drafts based on Maryland's stock in the Bank of England, discharged debts of £148,000. For sundry reasons, perhaps the belief that the debts would be fully invalidated by the war being the most important, the great majority of the planters did not take advantage of the sequestration acts.

At the news of the exact terms of the Treaty of Paris, which provided that there would be no lawful impediment to the recovery of the debts, the planters complained that Virginia interests had been sacrificed for the benefit of

New England fishermen. The tobacco country believed that payment was physically impossible; Jefferson estimated the debts at twenty or thirty times all the money circulating in Virginia. George Mason was shocked to hear loose-thinking men bandy the scandalous question: if the debts were to be paid, "what have we been fighting for all this while?" After the signing of the treaty, state laws forbidding the return of the British merchants were modified, but the concessions were poorly enforced. William Pitt himself complained of Virginia to John Adams and refused a commercial treaty.

To the hard-pushed Virginians, British destruction of property in the tobacco regions appeared a natural cancellation of the debts owed merchants of the English and Scottish towns. But, as the months wore on, planters who had any capital showed a disposition to settle accounts. In Europe Jefferson and Adams asked the British for patience and the general foregoing of war-time interest, part of the Glasgow compromise plan. In his personal negotiations with his creditors Jefferson noted some particular circumstances which should free him from the war-time interest: The agent of the British creditors had refused good private bonds in 1776; further, by state sequestration laws Jefferson had presumably been freed of the *entire* debt; in addition, referring to Cornwallis's destruction on his Elk Island tobacco plantation, "The useless & barbarous injury he did me in that instance was more than would have paid your debt, principal & interest." [2] But Jefferson was pleading for no cancellation of the principal or of that part of the interest which he felt was justly due. "What the laws of Virginia are, or may be, will in no wise influ-

[2] "Again, Ld. Cornwallis encamped 10 days on an estate of mine at Elk island, having his headquarters in my house he burned all the tobacco houses and barns on the farm. With the produce of the former year in them, he burnt all the enclosures, & wasted the fields in which the crop of that year was growing: (it was the month of June) he killed or carried off every living animal, cutting the throats of those which were too young for service. Of the slaves he carried away thirty."

ence my conduct. Substantial justice is my object, as decided by reason, & not by authority or compulsion." This
lean prose is as characteristic a statement as can be found
in all Jefferson's correspondence.

In the new Federal Constitution, drafted in 1787, the
national courts maintained jurisdiction over cases arising
from treaties; consequently if that instrument were
adopted the debt agreement, as specified in the Treaty of
Paris, would be drawn into the new and possibly unsym-
pathetic courts. The provision was a major subject of dec-
lamation in the Virginia ratifying convention. Both Henry
and Mason reminded Virginians of this fact, but, conservative by nature, the planters were attracted by the stability
promised under the new document, and some hoped that a
stronger central government might persuade European
ministries to allow freer trade in the leaf. Yet, the Federalists won by a slender majority of ten out of 168 votes cast
in the convention, and one price of the ratification was a
forlorn hope in the shape of a proposed constitutional
amendment which, in effect, would have barred from litigation the controversial debts.

The ratification saddened many a Virginia family having nightmarish fears of the British wolf at the door. "You
will have heard that the Constitution has been adopted in
this State," wrote St. George Tucker to his stepsons, one
of whom was John Randolph of Roanoke. "That event, my
dear children, affects your interest more nearly than that of
many others. The recovery of British debts can no longer
be postponed, and there now seems to be a moral certainty
that your patrimony will all go to satisfy the unjust debt
from your papa to the Hanburys. The consequence, my
dear boys, must be obvious to you. Your sole dependence
must be on your own personal abilities and exertions."
Sure enough, the Randolph heirs were soon sued in the
Circuit Court for the District of Virginia by the estate of
Osgood Hanbury.

The suits under the Federal Constitution for the recov-

ery of the debts eventually led to the famous case of *Ware,
Adm'r* v. *Hylton*, 3 Dallas 199. Argued before the Supreme Court in February, 1796, this decision clearly indicated that the treaty with Great Britain made invalid the
Virginia laws contrary to it. Planters who had paid money
into the state loan office as well as those who had not were
liable for their debts. Other than this declaration of the
supremacy of the central government and its treaties, a
landmark in constitutional history, the most interesting
feature of the suit is that it was the first of national significance for John Marshall, lawyer. He took the losing side,
supporting the Virginians and vigorously disputing "those,
who wish to impair the sovereignty of *Virginia*"! Possibly
he meant sovereignty in terms of the year 1777, the date
of the sequestration act, but certainly Marshall's Supreme
Court verdicts represented a constitutional somersault from
his general position in the Ware case.

State as well as federal courts were giving verdicts in
favor of the British creditors, and distress in the plantation
area was extreme.[3] The golden age of the tobacco planter
was passing. Some of the old aristocratic families were reduced to poverty; the abolition of primogeniture and en-
tail undermined an important prop of the gentry; many
members of the once first-families departed the land which
they considered "worn out" to try their fortunes on virgin
soil in the West.

In Paris from 1784 to 1789 Thomas Jefferson unsuccessfully tried to improve Franco-American commerce by
freeing the French market for American tobacco from
monopolistic restrictions. In this, his major problem while
American minister to France, Jefferson's allies were La-
fayette and several liberal, middle-class merchants; his

---

[3] The state of Virginia made refunds to that fraction of its citizens which
had attempted debt cancellation by payments to the treasury during the
Revolution. Finally, by the special convention of January 8, 1802, the
United States agreed to pay £600,000 in cancellation of the claims of British
merchants. Congress appropriated $2,664,000 for clearance of the trouble-
some problem.

opponents the unrelenting and unscrupulous Farmers-
General, a group of contracting monopolists typical of the
corroding *Ancien Régime*, and Robert Morris, their American agent.

The Farmers-General arranged with Morris for the purchase of a total of 60,000 hogsheads of tobacco during the
three years, 1785, 1786, and 1787. After the contract had
run for more than a year, Jefferson wrote Adams that it
"had thrown the commerce of that article in agonies,"
that Morris had managed to force the price of the leaf in
American markets from forty shillings to twenty-two and
six pence per hundredweight, thus causing a loss to the
people of Virginia and Maryland of £400,000. Indebted
to Morris for his unstinting aid in the weariest hours of
the Revolution, Washington was dismayed by the tobacco
quarrel, one of a multitude of divaricating events in the
decade after Yorktown, but refused to take sides.

Morris himself found the contract of less profit than he
had supposed. One shipment was lost and the Farm, claiming deficiency in quality, contested payment on others.
As agent for Robert Morris, Gouverneur Morris arrived
in Paris in February, 1789, to liquidate the contract with
the Farm and to enter into other commercial ventures.
Jefferson, who had gained a nominal concession for the
independent traders,[4] maintained affable relations with
Gouverneur Morris and in person presented him to the
Foreign Office. Despairing of a successful attack on the
Farm, Jefferson turned his attention to other matters of
diplomacy and sought relaxation in contemplating the arts
and sciences of France. In the Assembly of Notables, the
false dawn of the Revolution, there was a fruitless attack
on the tobacco monopoly. It was Gouverneur Morris's
private opinion that the French nobles delayed the abolition of the tobacco monopoly as long as they could because of "hatred to America for having been the cause of

[4] Veritable crumb though it was, Robert Morris became incensed and
dramatically spoke of "bread taken out of my Mouth."

the Revolution." Not until 1792 was the Farm liquidated, to be revived eighteen years later.

FRONTIER PLANTERS AND THE "SPANISH INTRIGUE"

In the lower Mississippi Valley the French as early as the seventeenth century had hoped to produce a supply of to-bacco which would make France independent of foreign merchants. However, the French exerted no real effort to give substance to their plans until the time of John Law's *Companie d'Occident*, when M. de Montplaisir brought thirty colonists to the Natchez area to cultivate and manu-facture tobacco. There was a momentary shock with the pricking of the Mississippi Bubble, and consistent uncer-tainty because of fluctuating governmental policies. But by the middle of the eighteenth century several hundred hogsheads were annually exported from Louisiana to France. Most of the leaf came from the Natchez region on the Mississippi, some from the vicinity of Natchitoches on the Red River.

The industry was churned about in the wars and di-plomacy of the 1750's and 1760's. Though Spain acquired Louisiana proper, England in taking the east bank of the river after the Seven Years' War obtained Natchez, the best of the Louisiana tobacco districts. During the Amer-ican Revolution the Spanish conquered the British planta-tions around Natchez, and thus re-united the old tobacco regions. For a number of years the Spanish encouraged the tobacco growers and promised a good price, hoping to supply the French market and the Mexican monopoly. In the 1780's the government was willing to purchase up to two million pounds annually. The news of this guar-anteed market traveled rapidly through the United States and a goodly number of Americans settled in the Natchez district, which, by the middle 1780's, was producing about half a million pounds annually.

The production and marketing of the leaf in the Natchez and Natchitoches districts represented a combination of Virginian and Latin manners. The Natchez overseer boasted that he could produce from two to three hogsheads per hand besides provisions. Visitors to the Red River outdid this with stories of crops double that amount. In preparing the leaf for market the large planters of Natchez packed the staple into hogsheads after the fashion of the seaboard districts, but the ordinary planter there and practically everyone on the Red River put up the leaf in "carottes" (sometimes spelled carrets or carrots), rolls about four inches thick, prepared in a distinctive manner. The stemmed tobacco was shaped to the desired form, wrapped in its own leaves, covered with a cloth, then tightly pressed by a laborer who wrapped a cord round and round the bundle. To apply suitable pressure, the operator attached one end of his rope to a post, braced his foot against the stake and maintained suitable tension on the cord as the wrapping proceeded. After the carotte had dried and its shape therefore fixed, the cord and cloth were removed and strips of linnbark attached at intervals along the carotte.

In sending the tobacco to New Orleans, it was common for several planters to join together in the building of a flatboat, on which the hogsheads and carottes were packed. The staple was inspected at the public warehouse and rarely rejected, unless the planter, from neglect or ignorance, omitted dropping the customary *douceur* in the broad pocket of the inspector. The gratuity, by the way, became well-established; no one considered it bribery. It was an understood perquisite to supplement the thin salary of the official. The planter preferred to collect his proceeds as a draft on the governor or commandant at Natchez or elsewhere, for it was risky business to journey homewards jingling a bag of specie.

In the quarter of a century after the Declaration of Independence the cultivation of tobacco spread across the mountains from Maryland, Virginia, and North Carolina into the present states of Kentucky and Tennessee. There the professional hunter was giving way to the farmer, who alternated axe, rifle, and hoe, raised his provisions and had for sale salt meat, whisky, hemp, grain, and tobacco. Such was the interest in the cultivation of tobacco that in the year the Revolutionary War officially came to an end three inspection warehouses were established by Virginia law in the Kentucky district, and before Kentucky was admitted as a state fourteen more such stations were authorized. Provisions for inspection were likewise made in middle Tennessee.[5] There were evidences of a familiar tobacco economy. Citizens of Lexington, soon called the Athens of the West, turned the sheets of the *Kentucke Gazette* and, in the issue of October 18, 1788, read that there was "To be sold: For inspected Tobacco, a likely Negro Wench: Enquire of the Printer."

The settlers could cure it, prize it, and go through the routine of having it inspected, but, struggle as they might, they found it almost impossible to get the staple to market. Ginseng and whisky might yield profit after a tortuous trip via the treacherous ruts known as roads, but tobacco and grain could not. Why not put the hogsheads on flatboats and simply float them down to the sailing vessels on the Gulf? But the Spaniards would be no party to such a plan. They preferred to stifle the new settlements through their hold on the throat of the Mississippi.

Sensing the apathy and timidity of Congress, some Westerners talked of a private war against the Spanish; others of a compromise separately negotiated. A few extremists, especially in the Kentucky settlements, spoke of independence from the moribund Confederation. In Washington's judgment the danger was real.

These circumstances made possible that dark web of

---

[5] One purpose in the establishment of these Mississippi Valley inspections was to provide the Westerners with a medium for payment of their state taxes.

conspiracy and bribery since known among American historians as the "Spanish Intrigue." Taking the lead was the shadowy figure of James Wilkinson, hard-drinking veteran of the American Revolution, who entered into preliminary negotiations with the Spanish in 1787, floated to New Orleans a cargo consisting principally of tobacco, butter, and hams. As a reward for his oath of allegiance to Spain, he received in effect a temporary monopoly of all trade down the Mississippi and eventually was granted a pension of two thousand dollars per annum. Corrupt and treacherous as he may have been, there is more than a germ of truth in Wilkinson's later boast that it was he who opened the Mississippi to Western trade.

In 1788 Wilkinson dispatched down the river a fleet of twenty-five boats, some armed with swivel-mounted three-pounders, and a crew of a hundred and fifty men with a cargo of tobacco and other produce. Although he ingeniously set up his private inspection system to guarantee the quality of the leaf sent the Spaniards, an inspection later legalized by the Virginia legislature, and he charged others what appear to have been usurious transportation and handling fees, Wilkinson found his trading ventures only moderately successful. His heavy shipments were balanced by expensive gifts to Spanish officials and by the shortcomings of agents either careless or corrupt.

By now the discontent in the West was declining. The Spanish relaxed their restrictions and, under the royal order of December 1, 1788, opened the Mississippi as far south as New Orleans to all Americans on an import-duty basis. For the moment the Spanish paid good prices for tobacco, and the frontiersmen concentrated on the staple. In 1790 over a quarter of a million pounds of American tobacco were registered at New Orleans. Additional tobacco was registered at Natchez, and an unknown number of hogsheads were smuggled in.

At this time, in the year 1791 (but under date of December, 1790), the Spanish government reduced its annual purchases from a maximum of two million to an inconsequential forty thousand pounds, which, at the best possible price at the royal warehouses, would mean a bare four thousand dollars. From the Spanish governmental point of view the decision was perfectly reasonable. The warehouses at Seville were full and the Louisiana tobacco was degenerating in quality. Many planters had been guilty of fraudulent packing; the manufacturer, as like as not, in breaking a hogshead would find a wad of trash, or in opening a carotte a cypress knee where good leaf should have been. Politically this reversal of policy was unwise because it emphasized the uncertainty of economic life under the Spanish regime. It momentarily discouraged the planters of Kentucky, though they survived it. It stunted the development of the Red River region, and definitely ended the commercial production in the Natchez district, which was already complaining of favoritism shown in the New Orleans market to Kentucky tobacco.

With respect to the imports from the western United States into Louisiana, Spain retreated step by step. Finally, in October, 1795, by the Treaty of San Lorenzo Spain surrendered on the territorial question and granted free navigation of the Mississippi. The right of deposit was included, meaning that American goods could be stored in New Orleans free of duty until they were withdrawn for re-exportation. This triumph of American diplomacy deflated the Spanish party in Kentucky. Tremulous with fright, Wilkinson now begged Gayoso "in the name of God" to put his name on neither lips nor pen.

From the formal opening of the deposit in April, 1798, to its mysterious closing in October, 1802, American produce, including several thousand hogsheads of Kentucky tobacco per year, poured down the river.[6] The closing of

6 Though tobacco was the principal Kentucky export down the river in the Wilkinson days, before the end of the century it had been surpassed in importance by flour.

the deposit, together with the rumors of French acquisition of Louisiana, threw the Westerners into a frenzy of excitement. To propitiate the men beyond the mountains Jefferson in January, 1803, decided to send Monroe to Europe, and the House appropriated money for the purchase of New Orleans and the Floridas. Even before Monroe's arrival, Napoleon had decided to sell all of Louisiana, which he had quietly obtained from Spain in 1800. To the Westerner the Purchase meant that the right to navigate the river, deposit his goods, and export them was no longer dependent on the vagaries of Latin diplomacy.

The river was theirs, but not the ocean, and soon they, like their brethren in the East, saw their staples as neutral goods caught in the net of British and French regulations, or rotting at home during the Jeffersonian experiments in economic sanctions. The enthusiasm of the West for the War of 1812 is partly explained by the irritation of that section at British interference with the shipment of its staples. The treaties of Ghent and of Vienna marked the beginning of an era of relative calm in the international scene, a calm which permitted the planters of the Mississippi Valley to wage in the European markets a successful commercial war against the planters of the East. It is obvious that without tobacco the history of the early West would have been different; without the staple, the Louisiana Purchase would have been delayed.

To Kentucky and Tennessee, the original tobacco-growing states of the West, were soon added Missouri and Ohio. In the eastern part of the latter state there was produced a bright tobacco, which on the Baltimore market successfully competed with the somewhat similar Maryland Kite-foot. By 1830 the average American crop of 105,000 hogsheads was distributed 30,000 hogsheads in the Western states, 30,000 in Maryland, 45,000 for Virginia. About 1843 the Western yield annually began to exceed in quantity that east of the mountains, and the quality, once con-

sidered vastly inferior, more nearly approached the standards of the older sections. Westerners undertook to
substitute tobacco for hemp, as that industry declined.

By the middle of the nineteenth century the basic districts were three: (1) *Maryland*, with production concentrated in the Chesapeake Bay counties on the Western
Shore. The Eastern Shore, like the Virginia tidewater,
relinquished the culture of tobacco soon after the Revolution and turned in the main to wheat.[7] (2) *Virginia*, a
term which included part of North Carolina. The Virginia
district was a rough trapezoid embracing that part of the
piedmont below Fredericksburg in Virginia and above the
present city of Durham in North Carolina. (3) The *West*,
less well defined, with its center in western Kentucky and
northwest Tennessee, south Illinois, and south Indiana,
and important crops in more separated areas of Ohio and
Missouri. There were sprinklings elsewhere in the nation,
including a few hogsheads of Perique grown in Louisiana.[8]
Soon after the Revolution, upcountry South Carolina and
Georgia had adopted tobacco as a staple and introduced
regular warehouse and inspection procedure, but with the
invention of the gin the planters had time for nothing but
cotton.

[7] In the 1790's the youthful Roger B. Taney observed the decline of
tobacco culture in Maryland and decided to become a lawyer rather than
a planter. An imaginative student in his idle moments might speculate on
the possible trend of American constitutional and political history had the
Chief Justice raised tobacco rather than presided over the Dred Scott and
other cases.

[8] The tobacco produced in the Louisiana area in the colonial and early
national period was a rough article, which declined in the face of competition from that grown higher up the Mississippi Valley. It is said that
in the 1820's one Pierre Chenet, descendant of the Acadians, developed a
new process of curing, essentially a ripening under great pressure in the
tobacco's own juices. Thus the product was called in his honor Perique.
Skeptics give other explanations of the name, and insist that the process
was developed before Chenet was born. The industry centered in the parish
of St. James, the best crops being raised on the elevations back from the
river, notably on the *vachery* or cattle land known as Grande Pointe.
Perique was a strong, distinctly flavored leaf. Much of it was made into
the traditional rolls or carottes before being sold.

Most of the cigar leaf was raised outside the regular tobacco plantation districts. Its production was often combined with market-gardening or with the making of the finished product. The oldest and most important section was the Connecticut Valley, once producing chewing and pipe-smoking leaf, now concentrating on cigar leaf. (A satisfactory broad-leaf variety, imported from Maryland, largely displanted the earlier Shoestring tobacco.) In this area, which stretched some forty miles northwards from Hartford, the East Windsor tobacco farmers enjoyed special advantages because of the nearby gin distilleries with the attached "piggeries." The distillers fed the refuse grain to the pigs, and the tobacco farmers collected the valuable manure from the pig lots. Other important tobacco crops came from Lancaster County, Pennsylvania, the Miami Valley in Ohio, Mason County, Kentucky, and Gadsden County, Florida.

Primarily an export crop, tobacco of necessity had reacted to the international disturbances in the two-score years between the battles of Lexington and Waterloo. About 1790 the production of tobacco had temporarily equalled the bumper crops of the early 1770's, but not until about 1820 did the industry make permanent recovery. The once Soverane Herb was yielding to King Cotton. In 1803 statistics for the first time showed the fleecy staple as the more valuable export crop.

Yet it was impressively appropriate that Benjamin Henry Latrobe, English-born architect, in rebuilding the Capitol after the War of 1812 should make effective use of the tobacco motif in designing the capitals for the sixteen columns in the small rotunda of the north wing. Latrobe had paved the way for this excursion into American staples a few years earlier when he designed for the ground floor lobby the Indian corn columns, which enthusiastic Congressmen with more gift for alliteration than for accuracy promptly dubbed "corn-cob capitals." Even the acid

Mrs. Trollope developed a sweet tongue when commenting on the design, heralded as the American order of architecture.

A REVISION OF PLANTATION ARTS

When but a cloud the size of a hand the Western crop threw the planters of the Chesapeake into a fit of apprehension. As early as the Confederation period discerning men in the old tobacco areas looked about for remedies and clutched at desperate straws. According to William Grayson, member of the Congress from Virginia, the clause in the Northwest Ordinance prohibiting slavery had been accepted by Southern delegates, "for the purpose of preventing tobacco and indigo from being made on the northwest side of the Ohio, as well as for several other political reasons." After the introduction of cotton, slavery expansion in the lower South did not fret the Chesapeake planters; indeed, in the lean years of the 1830's the selling of their surplus slaves proved a boon to that section.[9] For the protection of their leaf markets a few calculating planters thought it would be the better part of wisdom to restrict slavery in the Western tobacco belt. As a planter of Charlotte County, Virginia, read of the tremendous crops of the West in 1843 he sadly commented, "Had Missouri been a *free* State, this result would not have happened; but her fine lands tilled by slave labor tell terribly on Old Virginia."

More important in the attempt to cope with the new tobacco areas than desultory political sniping or vain regrets was a general attempt in the Eastern sections to

[9] Such a discriminating observer as Alexis de Tocqueville, author of *Democracy in America*, considered the decline in the price of tobacco about 1830 the cause of the then current anti-slavery movement in Maryland and Virginia. In Virginia the mood found expression in the sensational debate over slavery in the House of Delegates during the 1831–1832 session, the reform forces being led by Jefferson's favorite grandson, Thomas Jefferson Randolph.

revise and improve plantation practices. As already observed, the time-honored method of cultivating tobacco was to use the same plot of land until the soil was exhausted. This practice, which invited soil erosion, depleted the soil of necessary plant-food materials, increased soil toxicity, and encouraged the growth of harmful soil organisms, was sufferable when land was plenty, but it threatened the Eastern areas with ruin when they were in competition with the virgin West, where the same method was producing large crops. In Virginia and Maryland the older "mining" techniques were challenged with remarkable success by a movement for agricultural reform emphasizing diversification, crop rotation, and the application of fertilizers. Accordingly, tobacco in the East tended to become one of several money crops, and in large areas a system of general farming gradually replaced the old single-crop type of tobacco plantation.

Considering tobacco as the symbol of the one-crop exploitive type of husbandry, agricultural reformers sometimes abused the staple itself more than that system under which it had been cultivated. Even the agrarian philosopher Jefferson, on observing the effects of too much concentration on the one staple, declared in words taken as the text of many later essays, "It is a culture productive of infinite wretchedness. Those employed in it are in a continual state of exertion beyond the power of nature to support. Little food of any kind is raised by them; so that the men and animals on these farms are illy fed, and the earth is rapidly impoverished." John Taylor of Caroline, and Edmund Ruffin, Virginians both, the two greatest agricultural leaders of the tobacco states in the nineteenth century, condemned tobacco culture for its time-consuming nature.

The efforts of these reformers and of a host of lesser lights were allied with a movement to reduce the evils of over-production but rarely linked with the Northern school which had now set out in earnest to cure the nation

of the tobacco habit. The exception was John Hartwell
Cocke, who disseminated antitobacco tracts to adults and
antitobacco medals to small boys. General Cocke, co-
founder of the University of Virginia, was a ruthlessly
logical Jeffersonian and thus found himself in his late
years a stranger in his own land when he took reform as
his watchword and adopted antislavery and antiliquor
programs as well as the antitobacco movement. Probably
because of the influence of his friend Jefferson, Cocke early
ceased raising the leaf and finally published a sweeping
denunciation of the staple under the blunt title, *Tobacco,
the Bane of Virginia Husbandry*.

In addition to crop diversification and rotation, the most
obvious change in culture in the first of the nineteenth
century was the new care given the field and barn management of the leaf. The planters of the East repeatedly
observed that their only hope of survival in the face of
competition from the new West lay in a determined effort
to excel in quality. As early as 1815 the merchants, Ellis
& Allan of Richmond, wrote to one of their correspondents,
"Since you left Virginia a very important change has
taken place in the management of Tobacco, particularly in
the condition & neatness of prising." The more exacting
husbandry drew encouragement from the critical match-
ing of price with quality, and news of fabulous prices for
special crops stirred the ambition of many planters.

Although the crop management in its basic outlines
continued the same as in the colonial period, there were
minor modifications in the field and curing-barn. The
horse-drawn plow was now commonly used in the preparation of the field. As in the eighteenth century the whole
plant was cut at harvesting time, but cropmasters now
split the stalk almost to the point where it was to be cut,
an operation which facilitated curing and also allowed the
plants to straddle the tobacco sticks, or laths, on which
they rested during the curing process.

To air-curing and fire-curing, both of which had been

used in the colonial period, there was now added the novel method of curing by flues. In flue-curing the fire was kindled outside the tobacco house, and the flues distributed the heat over the barn and carried away the smoke and fumes. The new process reduced the fire-hazard—in the open-fire method the houses and contents burned with distressing frequency—required less fuel, and allowed more accurate regulation of the curing process. Originating perhaps in a conscious imitation of the method of drying lumber in kilns, the process was used about 1820 in the piedmont region of Virginia and probably elsewhere. In 1822 Peter Minor of Albemarle County, Virginia, wrote that the "improved method . . . has begun to be adopted by some judicious planters, in this part of the country." Despite its advantages, flue-curing had only a restricted following in the pre-Civil War days. It was to come into its own with the later development of Bright Tobacco. Though in both fire- and flue-curing most cropmasters by the 1830's were using the thermometer, hardheaded individualists prided themselves on their ability to judge matters by the simple "feel" of the lower poles.

In no staple was there such a wide range in prices between the middle and better grades as in tobacco, and it took a diligent cropmaster to produce the best. Now this necessity for close supervision limited the number of hands who could be managed with greatest efficiency and tended to keep the producing unit comparatively small. Furthermore, the combination of tobacco raising with general farming discouraged large-scale operations. An analysis of the manuscript census returns for over five thousand tobacco-producing farms in the heart of the Eastern district indicates that by 1859 the average producing unit was marketing about 3,500 pounds, produced on some five or six acres. Of the major Southern staples tobacco was characteristically grown on the smaller plantations. Sugar cane, incidentally, was at the other extreme and invited the largest plantation units. It is not surprising that the slaveholdings in the tobacco regions of the upper South were as a rule less extensive than those in the lower South.

Anyone supervising the production of a crop found it an exasperating and trying experience, with recurrent crises such as flood or drought, frosts, gluts of worms and debatable niceties as when to cut and how to cure. The actual labor was tedious. The price of a good crop included aching backs and weary feet, but the crop rarely required powerful exertion. Thus the weaker hands, women and children, could be used for many of the operations. Young Negroes pranced barefooted over the finely-tilled seed bed, treading in the seeds, traditionally to the tune of a jig or corn-husking song. Even the smallest could tote water from the well to the hoe gang, or shoo the turkeys and guinea-fowls through the tobacco patch in the assault on the horn-worms.[10] Patient, plodding, the Negroes accepted a sufficient amount of training and proved well adapted to the crop, though one Buckingham County planter vowed that they would go to sleep during curing season inside the barns by the open fire, and consequently catch colds or more fatal ailments.

Overseers, employed on plantations of some size, were, in the main, ill-fitted by training or disposition for this difficult assignment. For a while a share system tempted the overseers into exploiting the soil and over-working the slaves, but the most careful masters early in the nineteenth century shifted their overseers to a salary basis. Despite statutes to the contrary, a master here and there would select one of his Negroes as an overseer, and on occasions with conspicuous success. Because of the necessity for careful supervision and the consequently smaller producing unit, slavery on the average tobacco plantation was

[10] During one season planters in Prince George County, Maryland, needing turkeys for the worming task were offering as high as twenty-five cents per month for the use of the birds. A writer in the Baltimore *American Farmer* explained, "We beg our eastern brethren to recollect, that several months intervene between the worm-killing and turkey-eating season."

less formal, more patriarchal, than that in the cotton and sugar areas. Although on the typical tobacco plantation the labor was performed by Negro slaves, it was by no means uncommon to see white men engaged in the cultivation of the leaf or in the preparation of it for market. In the western piedmont section of the Virginia District poor men from the pine ridges were hired in seasons of wheat-harvesting and hogshead-prizing. And, as good example, a sensible slaveholder might put his hand to the plow, his sons help in transplanting during the precious wet season in May, or in stripping the cured leaf. Small non-slaveholders everywhere considered it no disgrace to do their own field work.

ROLLERS, BOATMEN, AND AUCTIONEERS

Because of tradition, convenience, and statutes, the leaf tobacco was ordinarily packed in hogsheads. Acceptable cooperage was a matter of course in English trading circles; on almost every plantation someone could shape staves, plane the heads, and hoop all together in sturdy fashion. If not, professional coopers could be had in any village. The hogshead was adapted to the necessary practice of packing under pressure, the pressure executed by a succession of crude but powerful levers.[11] The heavy cylinders could be rolled about the warehouses, or swung by block and tackle on board ships. By experience planters learned how tightly to prize the leaf and the more efficient limits to size. Yet, as in the colonial period, the planters tended to make their hogsheads larger and larger and heavier and heavier, because marketing and transportation charges were usually based on a hogshead rather than a poundage basis. In the search for uniformity in charges and efficiency in marketing, state governments regulated

[11] Iron and wooden screw-presses were well known, but the average planter made his own prizing machinery on the lever principle.

both size and weight, but the law usually lagged a bit
behind custom. The Virginia hogshead, soon after the
Revolution, by statute measured a maximum of 30 inches
diameter for the head and 48 inches for length of stave,
but because of political pressure from the planters these
figures were by 1822 raised to 38 and 54 inches, representing an increase of 80 per cent in volume. Although
the variation from district to district was considerable—
the Virginia hogsheads characteristically outweighed the
Maryland casks, and usually slightly exceeded those from
the West—the average was almost a thousand pounds in
the late colonial period, a bit more than that figure in the
early national period, and about twelve hundred soon after
the War of 1812.

Now it was not impossible to roll the hogshead short
distances by hand, and warehouse Negroes amazed visitors
by their dexterity in manipulating the huge casks, instinctively sensing the center of gravity and giving to the
ounce the correct force. In times of necessity the hogsheads could even be rolled by hand considerable distances.
The British seamen in the colonial period had the rough
duty of rolling the hogsheads to the wharves, a point of
complaint as the sailors found that the planters expected
more and more of them. Indeed, this labor diffused the
false notion that the American climate was bad. The libel
was spread by English merchants made sick by too much
warm clothing and too little temperance, but, according
to Robert Beverley, "In the next place, the Sailers for
want of Towns there, are put to the hardship of rowling
most of the Tobacco, a Mile or more, to the Water-side;
this Splinters their Hands sometimes, and provokes 'em to
curse the Country." Hot and thirsty they then drink too
much water or cider or eat injudiciously of green fruit,
"and so fall into Fluxes, Fevers, and the Belly-Ach; and
then, to spare their own Indiscretion, they in their Tar-
pawlin Language, cry, God D— the Country."

But human endurance had its limits, and out of neces-

sity was born the most distinctive method of land transportation ever associated with the movement of tobacco,
"rolling." In "rolling," one or two horses were hitched to
the hogshead itself by means of shafts attached to spikes,
securely driven in the heads, and the hogshead was rolled
along on its own staves, re-enforced with hooping of strong
hickory. A tobacco roller would contrive a box-like arrangement on the shafts, throw in a side of bacon, a bit
of meal, his frying pan and axe and move off to market,
sleeping along the way. In following the watersheds to
avoid the fords, the rollers laid out meandering roads that
to this good day puzzle in their seeming aimlessness the
country visitor. If his hogshead broke down, the roller left
his combination vehicle and cargo on the highway under
special legal protection, for theft of the leaf in such circumstances was punishable as a felony. As the custom
dwindled in the nineteenth century, the roller became an
object of curious interest and, for his primitiveness, even
the butt of village humor. A common story is of the village youths who found by the side of the road a tobacco-
roller asleep and his horse staked out. The practical jokers
turned the shafts over the hogshead, pointing them in the
direction from which the roller came. After a hard day's
pull the simple roller was amazed to find himself and his
tobacco back home again!

Professional wagoners, a rough and hardy lot, counted
two hogsheads as a wagon load. Their wild appearance
and free manners terrified strangers who suddenly came
upon them. One of the arguments for improved methods
of transportation was that the wagoners would thereby be
forced to change their low and itinerant mode of life,
which invited violation of the Fourth Commandment and
consequently jeopardized their chances of salvation.

But down to the time of the Civil War, most tobacco
was carried on the inland waterways of the nation, up
and down the Chesapeake Bay, on the James and the
Roanoke, on the Mississippi and its tributaries. James

River planters invented a device by rigging two large canoes together with cross-beams and carrying on the connecting platform some five or ten hogsheads. This scheme had the advantage of allowing the canoes after the down-river trip to be separated for more efficient handling going upstream. By the early part of the nineteenth century the James and Roanoke had as the standard tobacco boat the flat-bottomed *bateau*, carrying a load of from five to eight hogsheads. Running these boats down the unimproved rivers was a hazardous undertaking; the boats frequently upset and the tobacco became classified as "ducked," an expression for the damaged article which found its way into legal terminology. And, if we can believe censorious planters, the hazard of the current was more than matched by the danger from the boatmen themselves, who thought pilfering from cargoes their right, who bought from and sold to the Negroes along the river articles of uncertain origin, and who appropriated whatever they wanted from pigsty and corn crib on the river plantations. The Negro crewmen on these boats as they steered between jutting rocks on the muddy James sang as their favorite song:

> Oh, I'm gwine down to town!
> An' I'm gwine down to town!
> I'm gwine down to Richmond town
> To cayr my 'bacca down!

On the Mississippi River most of the early shipments were in flatboats, which varied widely in style and dimensions. Known often as "Kentucky boats" the typical one was perhaps thirty or forty feet long, twelve feet broad, with sides five feet high. The bottom planks were two inches thick, side planks one and a half. The draft was only about eighteen inches with the load of forty hogsheads and crew of five. Eastern boatmen were more than matched in vigor and originality by the flat-boatmen of the Western waters, whose wild ventures have passed through the twilight of folklore on into the dusk of fiction. The villain of the piece is the boatwrecker, one of the most famous being Colonel Fluger of New Hampshire, known in the West as "Colonel Plug," who operated around Cash Creek. The hero is Mike Fink, born near Pittsburgh, whose wild river cry is an imperishable item in Americana: "I can out-run, out-hop, out-jump, throw down, drag out and lick any man in the country. I'm a Salt-river roarer; I love the wimming and I'm chock full of fight." On the Mississippi trips there was much foolish spending and carousing at Natchez-under-the-Hill and at New Orleans.

With the revolution in transportation in the second quarter of the nineteenth century, the little boats on the James were largely supplanted by the heavy canal cargo boats, operated by responsible and established companies. And the flatboats on the Western waters gave way to the river steamboats. Soon a fair amount of tobacco was taken to market by the chugging little steam locomotives. Railway facilities came to the southside Virginia district as a byproduct of the race by Petersburg, Norfolk, and Richmond to tap the Roanoke River higher and higher above the falls. But safety and speed had been earned at the price of authentic American characters. The primitive rollers, the profane wagoners, the elusive James River boatmen, and riotous half-alligators of the Kentucky gave to the trade a purplish hue never to be recovered.

By mid-century the marketing of tobacco in the Virginia district centered in Richmond, Petersburg, and Lynchburg, with less important sales at Farmville, Clarksville, Danville, and in North Carolina at Milton and Henderson. Once tobacco markets of considerable importance, Fredericksburg and Norfolk had long ceased receiving appreciable quantities of the leaf. In the Maryland district Baltimore, which developed especially attractive warehouse policies, was the principal market, with some leaf going to Georgetown and Alexandria, Virginia. Dependent on the Maryland trade, Alexandria was exempted from all Virginia tobacco inspection laws. Early in the century a fair amount of Maryland Kite-foot tobacco, together with peach brandy, was sent from the Western Shore to Philadelphia. The great and traditional market for Western tobacco was New Orleans. Soon, however, most planters, impatient at the delay in receiving their funds from distant New Orleans, began selling to nearby manufacturers and middlemen. A thriving group of Mississippi Valley dealers stemmed the leaf and prepared strips for the British trade, sometimes selling the hogsheads to foreign agents and large exporters in New Orleans. Points of local concentration included Louisville, Nashville, Clarksville, Hopkinsville, and Hendersonville. The tobacco growers of Missouri looked particularly to their own towns of Fayette and St. Louis for the disposition of their crops. With the building of the railroads, much of the Ohio River tobacco was diverted to Baltimore and to New York, some to Mobile. Coastwise shipments of tobacco were made from the gulf ports to New York, Boston, Philadelphia, and Baltimore, where it was used by domestic manufacturers or sent abroad.

The warehouse auction system of selling leaf tobacco originated in Virginia early in the nineteenth century. It followed the breakdown of the colonial method of sale, which had been a simple transference of the "tobacco note," as the combined inspector's certificate and warehouse receipt was called. About the time of the Napoleonic Wars and the attendant confusion in the staple markets of this country, many tobacco inspectors scandalously neglected their duties and passed hogsheads fit only for the trash heap. Almost as important in inducing a change in marketing was the new awareness on the part of the manufacturers of subtle differences in types and qualities of the leaf. These circumstances prompted the careful leaf dealer to examine in person or by proxy the tobacco which he was buying, when formerly he had been satisfied with the inspector's certificate and perhaps some knowledge of the reputation of the cropmaster.

A fair sampling of a hogshead of tobacco after it had already been officially inspected and re-coopered was an expensive undertaking, but the best buyers, in the first years of the nineteenth century, undertook extensive re-inspections to be certain of good quality. Better than a re-inspection, unless the tobacco had been officially examined in some inaccessible warehouse, was attendance of the buyer at the state-controlled inspection where, after a scrutiny of the official samples, the merchant could purchase from the planter then and there. According to a contemporary description, the new method, informal and without benefit of middle-men, worked as follows at Lynchburg by 1810: "One or more hogsheads are opened and a public signal is given, by the sound of a trumpet, that the gentlemen speculators may attend. As many as may be in readiness come forward. The tobacco is broken open, and each one present inspects for himself, and makes up his own private opinion of its quality. The planter must then instantly sell to one of the persons present, for if the sale be deferred, he will be subjected to another inspection. . . . But this mode of doing the business is new to the planters, and many of them are so embarrassed by it as to receive real injury."

With the conversion of the warehouses into market places, the smaller inspection stations were abandoned while the larger ones increased in size; merchants sought a wide choice of tobacco, and planters congregated where buyers were plentiful. The crowding of buyers in the warehouses, especially in the speculative years immediately after the War of 1812, made imperative some rapid and orderly sales procedure, and the auction method gradually took shape first in the East, then in the West.[12]

[12] The system of free markets and unlimited bidding was not everywhere understood. On the Clarksville, Virginia, market in the days of red tobacco, John C. Clayton, of Person County, was selling a crop. The bidding on one pile went to $40 per hundred. Honest John could not stand for this

The inspectors, whose importance had momentarily declined when buyers lost confidence in the tobacco note, grasped the new opportunity and naturally assumed that profitable task of auctioneering. They were permanently stationed at the warehouses; they had some sort of standing as public officers; and they were already accustomed to "cry," for the account of the state, waste and other types of public tobacco which accumulated at their warehouses. By the middle 1820's in Virginia it was quite common for an inspector to act as auctioneer, or commission merchant, or both. The New Orleans inspectors were held more closely to their original functions.

The term *break*, it may be observed, originating in the procedure of breaking open the caked mass of leaves for the purpose of extracting samples, continues to be employed in modern times to designate the sales at the warehouses, though there is no literal breaking, the tobacco being in a loose condition. Even before the Civil War some of the tobacco brought to the warehouses was unprized, because manufacturing establishments near the market places were able to take a quantity of the leaf for immediate processing, relieving the farmer from the laborious task of packing in hogsheads.

From time to time the men in the warehouses, both white inspectors and colored hands, were accused of favoritism, inefficiency, and even corruption. Planters charged the warehouse Negroes with petty tyranny, such as tardily and clumsily handling the hogsheads of those who neglected to make them gifts. English manufacturers were believed to procure their choicest supplies from the Negroes of the Richmond warehouses, according to William Tatham, author of the classic treatise entitled *An Historical and Practical Essay on the Culture and Com-*

---

foolishness; $15 was ordinarily considered a good price. He rushed among the bidders and told them to stop, assuring them that the tobacco was not worth $40. Ever afterwards he was known as "Forty Dollar" John Clayton.

merce of Tobacco (London, 1800). Inspectors sometimes awkwardly delivered the wrong tobacco, and it was common knowledge that they gave preference in warehouse facilities to the planters who consigned tobacco to them for sale on commission. Some of these abuses stemmed from the archaic inspection system, to which the custom of warehouse sale had attached itself. But the procedure of official inspection continued until after the Civil War, in part because the old system did maintain the state-regulated warehouses and provided insurance against fire. Furthermore the appointment of inspectors was obviously a sort of political patronage in some areas. Found in the governors' papers of Virginia is the following communication from an applicant for a Lynchburg inspectorship. "I am the Same man you Saw at the Nat Springes last Summer whoe the[y] laft at Sow mutch about Saying he had rather have the Rumtism than to vote fore a Whig governey." Governor John Letcher, to whom the earnest letter was addressed, was soon inquiring if any of the incumbent Lynchburg inspectors had voted against him.

A fraction of the crop, especially in the Roanoke Valley, was sold by means less formal than the warehouse auction system. Some planters brought their hogsheads to country merchants in payment for goods advanced during the year. In boom times shrewd buyers rode on horseback from farm to farm and purchased tobacco still hanging in the curing barns. Commission merchants might sell in their own counting rooms by private negotiation. In the East the most important challenge to the warehouse auction system occurred in Richmond, when regular commission merchants, irritated at the business usurped by the inspectors, and buyers, weary of the trek from warehouse to warehouse, organized the Richmond Tobacco Exchange in 1858. Buyers and sellers congregated in a central sales room where tobacco was sold by sample. Despite the lamentations of the Richmond inspectors, the exchange

prospered and, in 1860, erected its own building, opened
with the lavish serving of punch, which gave Richmond
wits abundant opportunities for puns concerning the *spir-
ited* trading of the day. The market procedures at New
Orleans in the middle 1840's were thoroughly revised by
a new inspection law, copying the best in the Virginia and
Maryland practices. Apparently most of the New Orleans
trading was by sample in factors' counting rooms, somewhat in the manner that cotton was sold.

The American export trade, which only slowly recovered from the setback of the Napoleonic Wars, now
centered in the north European markets, the Baltic Prov-
inces, the Low Countries, and especially the states of Germany. The British trade was still important, though re-
export business had shrunk to inconsequential shipments.[13]
The French cut their imports to less than they had used
in the colonial period. Europe had learned during the
Napoleonic Wars to grow a considerable part of its supply,
and by the middle of the century in quantity may have
exceeded the American growth. The tobacco sent to the
north European countries was furnished principally by
Maryland and the Western states. Virginia, concentrating
on supplying her local factories, had a declining proportion of the export trade, though her products were favored
over all others by the British consumers.

American planters, periodically suffering from low
prices, saw as the root of their difficulties the European
monopolies and the high duties charged tobacco. British
duties fluctuated between three and four shillings per
pound, equivalent to an ad valorem duty of 800 or 900 per
cent. Those north European countries engaged in manufacturing and exporting the finished product were usually
more reasonable. Quite as painful to the tobacco planter
as exorbitant duties was the regie system, or system of

---

13 In developing the British leaf trade in Virginia tobacco after the War
of 1812, John Allan of Richmond went to England, taking with him his
foster-son, Edgar Allan Poe. Doubtless these five impressionable years in
foreign parts contributed to the international quality of Poe's later writing.

state monopoly which characterized most of the Latin areas of Europe as well as Mexico.[14]

During Van Buren's administration tobacco planters, discouraged by low prices, held several local conventions and in Washington three national conventions to protest against European monopolies and tariffs and to urge appropriate diplomatic pressure. The planters of Maryland, suffering from especially high duties laid on their particular type of tobacco by the governments of Holland and Belgium, took the lead; the Westerners gave a measure of co-operation, but the Virginians, concentrating more on the domestic market, were lukewarm. Under the stimulus of resolutions by the various conventions and by state legislatures, Van Buren recognized the problem in a message to Congress, the House of Representatives named a special committee, at least one agent was appointed to study the matter, and various negotiations were instituted, all with inconsequential results. By vote of the final tobacco convention, meeting in December, 1840, on the heels of the log-cabin-and-hard-cider campaign, Congressman Daniel Jenifer of Maryland, favoring a system of retaliatory tariffs, won his point over the objections of Congressman Walter Coles of Virginia, who felt that serious but friendly bargaining had never been honestly tried. The talk of countervailing duties aroused the anti-tariff group of planters. Skillful propaganda on the part of agents for foreign monopolies combined with some improvement in prices caused a decline in the movement.

[14] The unrelenting French policy provoked the following paragraph by some contributor to the *Washington Union:* "France, that beautiful republic that gets more liberty at a grab than all the rest of the world, and loses it all in three days, is a touchy creature upon the subject of tobacco. Like the silver bodkin in the 'Monastery,' when held to the eye of Piercy [*sic*] Shafton, a plug of negro head will throw her into convulsions. Her kings can be exiled, her thrones burnt in the Tuilleries, her queens can be slaughtered amid a band of fishwomen, and her Directory can blot out the Sabbath; but never, oh! never, can a pound of tobacco enter '*La Belle* nation,' excepting through the Farmers General. The French nation is as changeable as an April day, but the French custom-house is but a familiar name for immortality."

[Chapter 4]

THE CHEWING TOBACCO ERA

INDUSTRIALISTS IN AN AGRARIAN SOCIETY

Before the Revolution, the tobacco smoked, chewed, and snuffed by the Americans was divided in unknown proportions between that imported from Great Britain and that manufactured in the colonies, in either the home or factory. Most of the imported product was for the aristocracy in and around the towns of the East, those individuals who wanted exact duplication of the London mode, whether it be in snuff or costume. A sizable fraction of the tobacco consumed in the colonies was of home manufacture. Planters would put aside a sufficient quantity and, after curing, a good twisting and aging made it fit for use, if one's palate were not too sensitive. Certainly the operation could be simple enough. For smoking purposes the twist was divided into small pieces; for chewing, into larger sections; for snuffing it was thoroughly dried and grated. Today the custom survives in the older tobacco sections, though a modern grower is tempted by advertisements in farm journals to mollify the leaf with prepared syrups.[1] Despite his turning from the commercial production of the crop in his later years, Washington provided that his tenant could grow tobacco sufficient for family chewing and smoking. Many careful husbandmen, even in areas where the production of tobacco as a staple was impracticable, grew enough in their gardens to satisfy themselves and perhaps a few friends.

Colonial manufacture on a commercial scale undoubtedly occurred, though the glimpses are fleeting and hazy. Certainly there was some processing for the Indian trade, for soon after Rolfe's experiments the natives bought most of their tobacco from the whites, and the Indian traders counted pipe tobacco as well as brandy, firearms, tomahawks, kettles, and blankets as major barter goods.[2] In October, 1732, William Byrd of Westover visited Major Woodford's one-man factory, described with engaging detail in Byrd's *A Progress to the Mines*. The raw material was a special hardy variety of leaf known locally as Long Green, not quite as fragrant as the usual Sweet Scented. The workman laid the stemmed leaves straight in a box, applied a screw press, then cut the leaf with a treadle-acting knife into "oblong cut," which was sifted until clean and then prized into thousand-pound hogsheads, sixty of which were filled per year. These Major Woodford sent to the English market for sale at eleven pence a pound. Colonel Cabiniss, a half-legendary character, was reported to own a factory in Mecklenburg County, Virginia, producing twists made flavorsome through pressing in an old bee gum. He generously supplied chews to his fellow-burgesses in Williamsburg.

In the late colonial period the manufacture of tobacco was undertaken with some seriousness in the larger seaport towns for sale to foreigners and sailors, the latter

---

[1] As late as 1883 a government official estimated that 28,000,000 pounds of leaf per year were consumed by the growers in the natural, unmanufactured, state.

[2] A popular trade article was the tomahawk-pipe, a combination instrument with a hatchet at one end and pipe-bowl at the other.

wanted it both for their sea stores and for smuggling abroad, or, as one narrator more circumspectly put it, "to carry as *ventures* to those places, where tobacco was heavily dutied."

We hear of snuff mills here and there, especially in the Northern colonies, but the total number is unknown. The first snuff mill of any importance in New England appears to have been that constructed and operated in the 1750's by Gilbert Stuart, father of the great painter of the same name. Stuart, a millwright and native of Perth, Scotland, came to America at the invitation of Dr. Thomas Moffat, himself a Scotch immigrant, who, observing the enormous quantity of snuff imported from Glasgow, set out to establish a local factory but failed to find a native artisan competent to erect a snuff mill. The two-story, gambrel-roofed building at the confluence of the Mattatoxet and Pattaquamscott in Rhode Island was designed with the water-powered manufactory in the lower quarters and a dwelling place in the upper. It was here that the child Gilbert Stuart, baptized Gilbert Charles Stuart presumably to attest the Jacobite leanings of the father, was born in December, 1755.[3] The snuff made from the native

---

[3] Thereby hangs a tale. In his old age Stuart, a notrious snuff-taker, was visited in Boston by Messrs. Longacre and Neagle, two young and admiring artists from Philadelphia. Neagle asked for a pinch of snuff from Stuart's great snuff box, itself an institution. As William Dunlap, the American Vasari, tells the story:

"I will give it to you," said Stuart, "but I advise you not to take it. Snuff-taking is a pernicious, vile, dirty habit, and, like all bad habits, to be carefully avoided." "Your practice contradicts your precept, Mr. Stuart." "Sir, *I* can't help it. Shall I tell you a story? You were neither of you ever in England—so I must describe an English stage-coach of my time. It was a large vehicle of the coach kind, with a railing around the top to secure outside passengers, and a basket behind for baggage, and such travellers as could not be elsewhere accommodated. In such a carriage, full within, loaded on the top, and an additional *unfortunate* stowed with the stuff in the basket, I happened to be travelling in a dark night, when coachee contrived to overturn us all—or, as they say in New-York, dump us—in a ditch. We scrambled up, felt our legs and arms to be convinced that they were not broken, and finding, on examination, that inside and outside passengers were tolerable whole, (on the whole,) some one thought of the poor devil who was shut up with the

New England tobacco was said to have equaled the Scottish varieties, the business prospered, but after awhile there was great difficulty obtaining the usual glass bottles. Under Dr. Moffat's instructions the snuff was packed in beeves' bladders. Sales dropped for this and for other reasons, and the elder Stuart moved his family to Newport.

It is known that Pierre Lorillard, a Huguenot, established a tobacco shop in New York City about the year 1760. The principal business of the establishment, situated on the west side of what was then known as the High Road to Boston, was the manufacture and sale of snuff. With Gallic shrewdness and perseverance, Lorillard developed a trade which was to remain in the hands of his family for more than a century.

During the Revolution and immediately thereafter, Americans appreciably increased their manufacture of plug tobacco and snuff, and sometimes with curious political results. William Allison and one of George Mason's sons in partnership erected a snuff factory in Fairfax County, Virginia, and the author of the Virginia Bill of Rights wrote Patrick Henry requesting help in obtaining a state tariff to protect the industry! William Pitkin, fourth of that name, an eminent jurist and manufacturer, in 1784 was granted by the General Assembly of Connecticut a

---

baggage in the basket. He was found apparently senseless, and his neck twisted awry. One of the passengers, who had heard that any dislocation might be remedied, if promptly attended to, seized on the corpse, with a determination to untwist the man's neck, and set his head straight on his shoulders. Accordingly, with an iron grasp he clutched him by the head, and began pulling and twisting by main force. He appeared to have succeeded miraculously in restoring life; for the dead man no sooner experienced the first wrench, than he roared vociferously, 'Let me alone! let me alone! I'm not hurt!—I was born so!' Gentlemen," added Stuart, "I was born so"; and, taking an enormous pinch of snuff, "I was born in a snuff-mill."

Incidentally, another great artist born in the late colonial period, John Singleton Copley, also spent his early years surrounded by the tobacco business. The boy Copley and his widowed mother lived above a tobacco shop, which she operated on Long Wharf in Boston. Then, in 1748, after she married the engraver Peter Pelham, she moved her wholesale and retail store to the upper end of King Street.

twenty-five-year monopoly of snuff manufacture in that state, with exemption from taxes for fourteen years.

In these early days Philadelphia became the great center of manufacture under the leadership of Thomas Leiper and Gavin Hamilton. By 1794 the city boasted of twenty-seven establishments employing about four thousand persons. One of the most important single establishments in the early national period was operated by James Caldwell at Albany, New York.[4] In contrast to these urban entrepreneurs there were primitive spinners throughout the tobacco country, who sold their rope-like product at so much per yard. Such was the expansion of the business over the nation that domestic manufacturing partly compensated the planters for the upset foreign trade during the Napoleonic Wars. The increase in twenty-five years may have been as much as six- or eight-fold. In 1790 Hamilton had estimated domestic manufacture of tobacco at over a million and a half pounds; soon after the War of 1812 American manufacturers were absorbing between ten and fifteen thousand hogsheads per year.

About this time, the "Era of Good Feeling," enterprising men within the tobacco-growing sections began in earnest the making of plug and twist. These manufacturers had the advantage of adjacency to raw material and of operations simple enough for the ordinary laborers of the South to perform. By 1860 nine-tenths of the "manufactured tobacco," [5] was produced within the slave states. The block of four tobacco-raising states, Virginia, North Carolina,

---

[4] This early merchant prince suffered injury in the excitement following the ratification of the Federal Constitution. He was hit on the head with a brick when, in August, 1788, the Anti-Federalists attempted to break up the procession of the Federalists, who were engaged in full-dress celebration after the fashion of that day, with Master Van Rensselaer as Bacchus carrying a silver beaker and straddling a butt of beer in a brewer's dray.

[5] When used in the census "manufactured tobacco" meant all tobacco products save cigars. In this sense the term is used in these paragraphs. In the major producing areas the term was almost synonymous with chewing tobacco.

Kentucky, and Tennessee, accounted for four-fifths of the nation's total. The Virginians in particular took the manufacture of plug and twist as their rightful vocation. Excluding the cigar industry, the single state of Virginia produced 41 per cent of all tobacco manufactured in the nation by 1840, 56 per cent by 1860. In the latter year the factories of Virginia used 76,000,000 pounds of the leaf. Next came Kentucky, with a product less than one-fourth that of Virginia. The factories of the nation, consuming about one-half the domestic crop, by the time of the Civil War were turning out almost twenty-two million dollars worth of chewing tobacco, smoking tobacco, and snuff.

Many of these factories were scattered over the countryside in the tobacco-raising districts. "Nearly every planter who raises tobacco to any extent is a manufacturer; but there are some who make a business of it, and purchase the article in the leaf from their neighbors, without prizing, at a very liberal price," wrote Joseph Martin in describing conditions in Patrick County, the heart of the Roanoke Valley. In some degree this generalization made in 1835 might apply to all the tobacco producing areas of Virginia, North Carolina, Tennessee, Kentucky, and Missouri. The country factory integrated into the plantation system, giving seasonal employment to the hands and, as suggested by Martin, the planter might gradually begin to look on his factory as his main business, the farming as the lesser endeavor. The country storekeeper easily went into tobacco manufacturing as a side line; he received the leaf in payment for goods purchased; he might sell some plug and twist to these same individuals or to his other customers. But most of the manufacturing was concentrated in key towns, leaf markets of the tobacco producing districts. Arranged in the approximate order of their importance the principal tobacco manufacturing centers of the nation on the eve of the Civil War were Richmond; Petersburg; Lynchburg; Danville, Virginia; New York (the exception to the rule); Clarksville, Tennessee; Louisville, Kentucky; Henderson, Kentucky; Fayette, Missouri; Milton, North Carolina; and St. Louis.

The manufacturers, forerunners of a new group of aristocrats, were drawn from all classes. The older small-farming class and the newly-arrived immigrants contributed the most aggressive leadership. A Negro manufacturer of local fame was Lunsford Lane of Raleigh, North Carolina, who prepared a type of smoking tobacco favored by the state legislators and earned enough profit to purchase his own freedom. As a freedman he was so persecuted by the "poor white trash" that he left to become prominent in antislavery circles in the North.

St. Louis gave few hints of its future importance in the plug business, though there were established in the generation before the Civil War several of the businesses later to grow into towering institutions. Among the early industrialists of the city were Dan Catlin, and his son Daniel. Joseph Liggett, a Londonderry man, came to St. Louis and married Elizabeth Foulks, daughter of Christopher Foulks, one of the pioneer manufacturers. A son, John Edmund Liggett, entered his grandfather's business at the age of eighteen, and, at the retirement of Christopher Foulks, became a junior partner in the firm, the senior partner being his own stepfather, a Mr. Shaw. Shaw's share was purchased by John Edmund Liggett's brother, W. C. L. Liggett, and the firm name became J. E. Liggett & Brother. One Henry Dausman purchased the brother's share and the business title was changed to Liggett & Dausman. This was the nucleus of the organization later known as Liggett & Myers.

In this period between the Revolution and the Civil War, the greatest of the New York City manufacturers were the Lorillards. Pierre Lorillard II and his brother George, under the title P. & G. Lorillord, expanded manufacturing operations to include a large snuff mill in Westchester on the Bronx River. George Lorillard died in 1832 and Pierre

A MAP of
the most INHABITED part of
VIRGINIA
containing the whole PROVINCE of
MARYLAND
with Part of
PENSILVANIA, NEW JERSEY AND NORTH CAROLINA
Drawn by
Joshua Fry & Peter Jefferson
in 1775.

To the Right Honourable, George Dunk Earl of Halifax First Lord Commissioner,
and to the Rest of the Right Honourable and Honourable Commissioners for TRADE and PLANTATIONS
This Map is most humbly Inscribed to their Lordships,
By their Lordships's
Most Obedient & most devoted humble Serv.ts Thos. Jefferys.

A COLONIAL TOBACCO WHARF

HEAD LABELS AFFIXED TO BOXES OF PLUG TOBACCO
(About 1890)

II in 1843.[6] The business was then carried on by Pierre III, who returned to the old business name of P. Lorillard. By this time, of course, the principal products were chewing and smoking tobacco. In 1860 Pierre IV, great-grandson of the founder, was admitted to the firm.

In Lynchburg, a small town of unusual wealth known as "The Tobacco City," there was Colonel Augustine Leftwich, described in 1830 by Mrs. Anne Royall as "a stout noble figure, and a very gentlemanlike man: his face is full and manly, and complexion dark, with an arched brow, and fine, full hazel eye: his manners are polished and familiar." On sunny days he walked to his factory, dressed in white and escorted by a black slave, who held over his head a great green umbrella. An out-and-out Whig, he suffered only a momentary set-back when, in 1844, he allowed his sporting blood to tempt him into contracting with dealers that they would pay him if and when Clay were elected.

The Petersburg industry, characterized by relatively large plants and an emphasis on the foreign market, was dominated by a group of industrious Scots recently-arrived. Among them were Robert Leslie, Robert L. Watson, James Dunlop, Robert Dunlop, David Dunlop, David B. Tennant, James M. McCulloch, and the three Cameron brothers, William, Alexander, and George.

Richmond was the tobacco capital of the nation, its fifty-odd factories employing 3,400 hands and producing goods valued at almost five million dollars per year by 1860. Robert A. Mayo of that city, the grandson of the Major William Mayo who with William Byrd of Westover laid out Richmond, for many years contracted with the federal

[6] In 1843 Philip Hone irreverently recorded in his diary "Tuesday, May 23.—Died this morning at his seat in Westchester County, Mr. Peter Lorillard, in the eightieth year of his age. . . . He was a tobacconist and his memory will be preserved in the annals of New York by the celebrity of 'Lorillard's Snuff and Tobacco.' He led people by the nose for the best part of a century, and made his enormous fortune by giving them to chew which they could not swallow."

government to supply the navy with plug tobacco and is credited with originating the distinctive name, Navy Tobacco.[7] A staunch Democrat, he was running for some local office when the journal of the opposing party, the *Richmond Whig*, protested that this contract with the government involved an "emolument" and thus Mr. Mayo was disqualified. This criticism invited an urbane comment from the famous *Enquirer*, "Mr. Mayo simply sells his tobacco to the United States Government and gives *a quid pro quo*—(we mean no pun)." [8]

The most famous of all the mid-nineteenth century tobacco manufacturers was James Thomas, Jr., of Richmond, who employed 150 hands and produced over a million pounds of chewing tobacco per year. Entering the tobacco business by way of the leaf trade, he first specialized in buying for the French monopoly. In the early 1830's he began manufacturing, and with notable ingenuity he adapted his product to the demand of the times. When the California rush was on, he prepared his plugs for the West Coast trade with such care that the sea-borne tobacco twice crossed the tropics without moulding, and thus he earned almost a monopoly of the California chewing tobacco trade. He was aggressive and, by way of foreshadow-

[7] The popularity of the particular plug tobacco prepared by Mayo appears to have been the cause for a special act of Congress permitting the Secretary of the Navy to negotiate for tobacco by private arrangement without having to give the tobacco contract to the lowest bidder. The act was dated August 3, 1848. To the intense irritation of the Secretary of the Navy the act was repealed in 1860. The Secretary protested that, "The sailor also should be permitted to have his favorite tobacco prepared for his use." The Navy and Mayo were protected for a little while longer inasmuch as a three-year contract had been made on November 30, 1859, for the Navy Tobacco at 19 cents per pound. Obviously the events of 1861 ended the 1859 contract.

[8] In a generation which saw nothing incompatible in its love for both classical learning and plug tobacco, punsters succumbed to inevitable temptation. Out of Philadelphia came the story of a tobacconist, enriched by his trade, who desired a motto for his carriage panel. An educated friend convinced him that "QUID RIDES" was appropriate. The crowd shouted with glee as the newly-made gentleman drove by, but Latinists held their tongues as they grasped the translation, "What are you laughing at?"

ing a type soon to come into the tobacco industry, did not believe in coddling his rivals. Yet he subsidized the struggling institution, Richmond College, and his home, nicknamed "The Baptist Hotel," was always open to visiting clergymen.

With rare exceptions the factory buildings in the tobacco district were neither distinctive in design nor attractive in appearance. The oldest structures represented stark utilitarianism and therefore had a certain forthright simplicity. The numerous factories erected in the middle of the century, however, did not rise above the general vulgarization of American architecture then blighting the land. The small country establishment, part of the plantation system, was operated in any available farm building, a vacant corncrib or tool shed, and thus had little character in its external appearance. The largest urban factories, extending fifty by a hundred feet or more in ground dimensions, and three or four stories in height, were uniform only in their rectangular plainness and imposing solely because of their size. The use of fires in the manufacturing processes and the fear of arson from an occasional vengeful Negro encouraged important tobacconists to build their structures of brick or stone. Internal arrangements varied, but any well-planned factory possessed loading rooms near the street, and a spacious central hall in which one overseer could direct the labor of many slaves. Usually there were broad, flat drying-roofs, which accentuated the box-like nature of the buildings.

The preparation of chewing tobacco, the major product of the factories in the middle period, consisted of four basic operations:

(1) *Stemming.* After the staves were removed from the half-ton cakes of tobacco, which had been tightly pressed on the plantations and broken in only two or three places at the inspection warehouses, the factory hands moistened the leaves to make them pliable. Then the stemmers deftly ripped from each leaf the coarse and harsh-flavored mid-

vein, after which the leaves were again dried. This operation was identical with that carried on by many leaf exporters, who stemmed their tobacco to reduce freight costs and import duties, and to lessen the danger of spoilage. The exporters before shipment re-prized the strips, as the stemmed tobacco was called.

(2) *Flavoring.* Next, the dippers soaked the stemmed tobacco in a black, syrupy compound of licorice and sugar, which had been cooked in massive iron kettles vigorously stirred to prevent scorching. The leaves were then placed in the open air, usually on the factory roof, to dry. To obtain a final bouquet the factorymaster prepared a fragrant concoction of rum, sweet oil, and sundry spices, which some chosen worker sprinkled on the leaves. Licorice, the most distinctive ingredient in the flavoring formula, was probably first used in the manufacture of tobacco about 1820. Though many divergent stories have arisen concerning its appearance in the tobacco factories, licorice was apparently introduced by the Heald family of Baltimore. Flavoring formulas varied widely in the manufacturers' attempts to satisfy all palates and to create new customers. In general the Yankee wanted his plug well licoriced and heavily sweetened; the Southerner preferred his chew nearer the natural flavor. Many wild rumors were circulated as to the use of ruinous acids, ranging from uric to prussic, in flavoring formulas.

(3) *Lumpmaking.* Lumpmakers, seated at benches in a large room somewhat after the manner of school children, took the flavored leaves, molded them into neat rectangular plugs of specified size, and wrapped each in a choice, unflavored leaf. The laborers used trimming knives and scales to insure correct weight, which might vary in the different brands from a few ounces to over a pound per plug. If the manufacturer desired twists instead of plugs, trained Negroes called twisters were given the flavored leaves from which they fashioned the orthodox chewing twist.

(4) *Prizing.* Once the plugs had been prepared by the lumpmakers and inspected by the overseer, they were taken to the pressroom. There prizers or screwmen, as strong as the lumpers were nimble, placed the lumps in multi-divided wooden "shapes," or pattern-boxes and, heaving and chanting as they worked, swung giant wing-screw presses with tremendous impact, forcing the plugs into proper shape and firmness. After several prizings, in the course of which the edges of the plugs were perfectly aligned and the pieces accurately fitted for the boxes in which they were to be packed, the plugs were ready for distribution among the countless lovers of the quid in domestic and foreign markets.

The screw press, the basic piece of equipment in the plug and twist factories, was not dissimilar to the hogshead prize which could be found on many plantations. In the 1850's the most progressive factories installed hydraulic presses, adapted to the manufacture of tobacco by several inventors, the most important being William Cameron of Petersburg. An occasional country manufacturer used an open-air contrivance worked by a draft animal harnessed to a long pole and driven in circles around the press. This machine had its counterpart in the horse-powered bale presses of the cotton region, and in the cane mills of the sugar areas.

In addition to plug and twist there was a variant chewing article called spun tobacco or "pigtail," made with a special spinning wheel. Smokers often filled their pipes with parings from a plug of tobacco, for the regular smoking mixtures of the time were seasoned lightly or not at all. The major mechanical operation in the manufacture of smoking tobacco was the shredding, effected by "cutting machines," hand-powered until steam was introduced for this operation the middle of the century. By way of contrast with smoking tobacco, commercial snuff, ground in mills of various types, was elaborately flavored. But in this chewing-tobacco era neither the smoking mixtures nor snuff received the choicest leaf. Indeed scrap and stems often found their way into these preparations. Though there were a few establishments which specialized in the manufacture of smoking tobacco or snuff, usually these products were made in factories devoted principally to chewing tobacco. A factory making smoking tobacco exclusively was that of Maurice Moore of Lynchburg.

SLAVES IN THE TOBACCO FACTORIES

Visitors entering one of the huge tobacco factories of the slave country noticed first of all the chant of Negro spirituals which filled the dusty air. Stemmers and lumpers, twisters and screwmen sang as they worked. They sang of Eden and of Egypt, of Adam and of Moses, of angels and of harps. From Bible and hymn book came the basic words, but each wail and chord bent with the mood of the day. Among the travellers fascinated by the slave chorus of a century ago was William Cullen Bryant, who, to catch authentic local color, came to Richmond and followed the leaf from auction warehouse to factory. At a later day he pondered the singing of the eighty men and boys in the lumpmakers' room, quoted Dr. Johnson's line, "Verse sweetens toil," and added: "Verse, it seems, can sweeten the toil of slaves in a tobacco factory. 'We encourage their singing as much as we can,' said the brother of the proprietor, himself a diligent masticator of the weed, who attended us, and politely explained to us the process of making plug tobacco; 'we encourage it as much as we can, for the boys work better while singing. Sometimes they will sing all day long with great spirit; at other times you will not hear a single note. They must sing wholly of their own accord; it is of no use to bid them do it.' "

Another literary visitor, Charles Dickens, heard the Negro chorus and liked it, though the smell of tobacco sickened him and the sight of slavery infuriated him. Even to enter a plug factory was a triumph of will-power, for he bore naseous memories of the poor marksmanship of both amateur and veteran chewers in America—"which has rather inclined me to doubt that general proficiency with the rifle, of which we have heard so much in England." When steered away from the noon-day victual room Dickens wondered if the Negroes ate as well as they sang. His visit to Virginia converted him to Southern mint-juleps and sherry-cobblers, but the great Boz remained unshaken on the subjects of tobacco and slavery.

These laborers whose hymns pleased Bryant and Dickens and travellers less famous were the Brahmins of the Negro world, treasured by their owners, humored by their factorymasters, and envied by their less fortunate cousins condemned to plowing and hoeing in narrow fields. It was best to be free, but almost as good to go to Petersburg or Richmond and work for a tobacco manufacturer. Whether at work, on the streets, on the doorsteps in the evening, or at church on Sunday, the factory slave lived in the middle of a crowd—balm for the Negro's gregarious soul. If worth his salt, a hand earned a fortnightly cash bonus to spend as he pleased. And at Christmas time he could change factorymasters if he chose. A few die-hard whites shook their heads and grumbled to the newspapers about the new-fangled ways of handling Negroes.

Indeed a new order had quietly emerged in the Upper South during the two-score years before Fort Sumter. A distinctive and liberal scheme of factory management made flexible the normally rigid "peculiar institution," to use the orthodox euphemism for Negro slavery. Every tobacco town below the Mason and Dixon Line, especially the large centers of Richmond and Petersburg, showed evidence of this studied attempt to make the laborers responsive to the exacting demands of the manufacturing routine.

Slaves were hired by factorymasters because outright purchase called for an almost unbearable outlay of cash. The price of a prime factory hand easily ran a thousand or twelve hundred dollars, an investment which cholera, a knife fight, or a sudden whim to follow the north star could erase overnight. Fortunately for the manufacturers, the farmers in the countryside discovered that they were "Negro poor"; the slaves multiplied more rapidly than did the arable acres. At the increase of hungry mouths some planters simply shrugged their shoulders and waited for inevitable bankruptcy; others compounded with their consciences and disposed of a few hands each year to the wandering Negro-traders, who coffled them for re-sale to the cotton and sugar planters; still others sought a way out by hiring a likely hand or so to nearby manufacturers of plug and twist. The system of hiring, which steered neatly between painful sale and expensive purchase, grew in popularity. By the 1850's in the largest tobacco towns approximately half the factory slaves were hired on an annual basis.

The practice of allowing the slave "to choose his own master," that is, to find his own hirer for the year, was perhaps the most radical of all innovations in management. The owner set the hire and the Negro, with much chaffing to hide his utter seriousness, bargained for his personal privileges. In this manner the tobacco industry curbed the exploitive evils otherwise inherent in any form of absenteeism. The custom received most general acceptance in Richmond, where the concession was granted both domestic and industrial workers.

By setting minimum tasks and paying the Negroes cash bonuses for all extra work, manufacturers vitalized the entire routine of production. The factory owners found it common sense to put a premium on speed and efficiency; the Negroes rejoiced in having money of their own. And good money they earned, too. A competent stemmer, lumper, or prizer expected a bonus of a couple of dollars per week; the best craftsmen collected twice that amount or more. With truth some hands boasted that on payday they pocketed as much for overwork as their owners received for their hire.

The factory hands labored under the direct supervision of overseers, or managers as they called themselves. Their presence was inevitable. The most efficient establishments employed several dozen hands, and it was impossible for one factorymaster to be everywhere at once. The overseers were young white men, some of them country relatives of the owners, ambitious to learn a new and promising business. They mixed the flavoring formulas, presided over the high desk in the lumpers' room, perhaps took a canvas-topped wagon on a peddling circuit, and, when the owners were laid up by sickness or had business elsewhere, bought raw leaf at the auction warehouse. Like their plantation counterparts, these men were prone to be jealous of their prerogatives before the slaves; the blacks knew that the overseers were but hired hands of a different color. Some of them, with an instinct for tact and firmness, prospered and graduated into the ranks of owners and substantial townsmen. Others, shiftless, intemperate, and tyrannical, demoralized the hands, infuriated the factory owners, and were sent on their way.

Even the best overseers had their troubles. They must watch for those who idled on Monday mornings and feigned sickness almost any day. A tolerant boss might wink at the palming of a few plugs for personal use; it was a different matter when a slave supplied wholesale quantities to depraved whites who ran back-alley grog shops. No factory was entirely free from insubordination. The devil would get into a Negro and, under the code, there was no specific better than a good tanning, then and there. But it was dangerous business; some Negroes would fight back. And after the mildest thrashing of a slave all went expressionless, gave neither song nor careless shout for days, while the bosses fretted at slackened production. Furthermore whippings gave the establishment a bad

name at hiring time, and, if the hands ended the year
marked or maimed, the owners might file civil suit for
damage to their property. If a thrashing were absolutely
necessary, the safer course was to register a complaint with
the city magistrate and ask that thirty-nine lashes be administered in the name of the court.

One winter day in Richmond, Ben, a slave in the Hampton factory, used bad language to Cook, the overseer, who
thereupon asked the owner of the factory for permission
to discipline the Negro. Mr. Hampton ordered Cook to
"cool off" before whipping the slave, then, on second
thought, decided to discharge the white man because most
of the hands disliked him anyway. Cook, however, petitioned the Mayor's court for redress and had the sadistic
pleasure of witnessing a verdict of ten lashes, well laid on.

More tragic was the quarrel between overseer and slave
in a neighboring factory about the same time. The overseer, nineteen-year-old William Jackson, rebuked Jordan
Hatcher for the base quality of his work in the stemming
room. The Negro's reply irritated the overseer, who picked
up a cowhide lash. Hatcher grabbed the whip, the white
man kicked at the Negro, the slave tossed him aside, found
an iron poker, and dealt him a fatal blow. The Richmond
Hustings Court declared the Negro guilty of murder, but
Governor Joseph Johnson, a Buckskin from beyond the
Alleghenies, convinced himself that there were extenuat-
ing circumstances. After a brave period of investigation he
commuted the sentence to banishment from the United
States, and defied an angry crowd which milled around
the governor's mansion.

Certain dramatic events excepted, however, man-mas-
ter relations in the plug and twist factories simply reflected
the personnel problems characteristic of any manufacturing establishment in that undisciplined era of the Industrial Revolution, regardless of climate, pigmentation, or
traditional systems of servitude. In its labor problems the
tobacco industry of the South bore quite as much resem-

blance to the textile industry of the North as to the plantation system. Many freed Negroes worked alongside the
slaves, and within the factory walls no real distinction was
drawn between the two classes.

Some of the factory slaves, after leaving work Saturday
night, their jackets jingling with overwork coin, lost
every cent to liquor dealers, gamesters, and alley-wenches.
Especially tempted was the Negro newly come from the
patriarchal life of a small plantation. But most of the
slaves learned a measure of restraint, in part because they
sat in public judgment, the one against the other, in their
church congregations.

Neither hymns nor conversions of the tobacco workers
were confined to the churches. One famous and cyclonic
religious experience occurred at the stemming rather than
the mourners' bench. John Jasper, hired slave, was busy
at his task one July morning when all of a sudden he "got
religion" with the enthusiastic approval of his fellow
workmen, who encouraged him by shouting and singing.
With the peculiar bluntness of his tribe, the overseer ordered the Negroes to stop the racket and to get along with
their tasks. At this point the factory owner, Samuel Hard-
grove, appeared. Sympathetically he listened to the young
Negro describe his heavenly vision, welcomed him as a
spiritual brother, and gave a holiday for the spreading
of the good news. John Jasper developed into a powerful
orator and the most famous slave preacher for miles
around. After the Civil War no one visited Richmond without trying to hear Jasper give his sermon entitled, "The
Sun Do Move." He had a ready wit and was credited with
turning off rhythmic phrases, such as the following list of
the great peoples of the earth:

> The Hottentots, the Huguenots,
> The Abyssinians, and the *Vir*ginians.

In factories as well as on plantations the staple, tobacco,
mellowed the institution of slavery. The rising class of

Southern townsmen through trial and error moulded the system to stir the initiative of the slave, to gain his confidence and co-operation. The success of the manufacturers was infectious and the new methods received wide acceptance. It is not strange that travellers thought slavery in the tobacco South a different thing from the labor system in the cotton South.[9]

TRADE NAMES AND WOODEN INDIANS

By the middle of the nineteenth century many shrewd manufacturers were giving to their products trade labels more distinctive or attractive than mere surnames. Cherry Ripe, Wedding Cake, Winesap, Cantaloupe, Pine Apple, Rock Candy, and Bouquet called up visions of orchard and pantry. Patriotism or politics were involved in the titles Diadem of Old Virginia, Uncle Sam, The People's Choice, and Daniel Webster. Of local legends in the tobacco district concerning brands none is better known than the naming of Lone Jack smoking tobacco, leading article produced by John W. Carroll, of Lynchburg. The most popular version explains that Carroll, who had come to Lynchburg as an orphaned youth and was in desperate straits, found himself in a card game, staking his last cent on a hand distinguished by a single jack. The bluff worked and Carroll vowed to make the card famous, which indeed he did in sending Lone Jack all over the land.[10]

[9] Furthermore, an analysis of the status of the free Negro in Virginia in the late ante-bellum period by Luther P. Jackson suggests that the demands of an expanding tobacco industry ameliorated the condition of the freedmen. On the statute books were severe laws requiring manumitted Negroes to depart the state, but their labor was needed in the factories, and they were seldom refused special permission to remain.

[10] Carroll, who enjoyed his greatest prestige after the Civil War, married the daughter of William M. Crumpton, chewing tobacco manufacturer and for awhile Carroll's business partner. Carroll, as a youth, was trained in the craft of cabinet-making. In the Crumpton family today there is a burl walnut game box, with an interesting inlaid design on top: the words, "Wm. Crumpton's—Lynchburg, Va.," four aces in the center, and a tobacco-leaf

The names were either branded with a hot iron or sten-
cilled with commercial ink on the oak, poplar or pine boxes.
False branding was as inevitable as the devil in human
nature. Always some sly operator out in the counties
thought he could gain a slight premium by indicating the
place of origin as one of the larger manufacturing centers.
More vicious was the practice of a few manufacturers west
of the mountains, where the product was in general inferior to that of the East. They borrowed not only the
address but the names of prominent Virginia and North
Carolina manufacturers.

Inconspicuous notices by retailers constituted almost the
entire newspaper advertising of the period, though manufacturers attempted to obtain favorable publicity in both
news and editorial columns. It was good business for
Gilliam & Matthews of Richmond to pay over 40 cents per
pound for leaf designed for their Winesap brand; the
transaction was reported as news. When Charles Napoleon
Bonaparte Evans, the originator of the famous North Carolina figure "Jesse Holmes the Fool-Killer" and editor of
the *Milton Chronicle*, received sample plugs from the
Samuel Watkins factory, courteously he set in type his
acknowledgment of the gift, "made of splendid leaf and
manufactured in the very best style."

The bulk of the chewing tobacco, smoking tobacco and
snuff was marketed through factors, or manufacturers'
agents, residing in the large coastal cities. The route of a
typical plug of tobacco was from manufacturer to factor
(or agent), to jobber (or wholesale grocer), to retailer, to
consumer. Economic connections were particularly strong
between the manufacturers of Virginia and North Carolina
and the factors of New York City who by 1850 were dis-
tributing one-half of all the tobacco manufactured in those
two states. Operating on a complicated plan of generous

design around the edges, all in various colored woods. It appears almost
certain that the sociable Carroll, creater of Lone Jack, made this box for
his father-in-law.

commissions and long credits, the factor irritated the manufacturer somewhat as the English merchant provoked the planter in the colonial period. Particularly in times of sectional controversy the relations between the Southern manufacturer and his Northern agent reached the blazing point. During the Panic of 1857 the Northern factor returned unpaid the acceptances drawn by the Southern manufacturer. (In normal times Richmond bankers held a million dollars worth of drafts on Northern agents.) Whereupon the enraged industrialist accused the Northerner of manipulating accounts in order to build up "fictitious" capital "with which to carry on his business [,] buy fancy stocks, shave paper, build fine houses, and drive fast teams." Goaded by an excited press, the manufacturers of Virginia and North Carolina called a convention which met in Richmond. The one hundred delegates in calmer mood declared that "nothing has been further from our purpose than to cast imputations of dishonor upon agents," but presented a calendar of reforms, and reduced commissions and credits.

Cutting across the regular channels of trade, manufacturers sent out hundreds of two-horse, canvas-topped wagons directly to the retailers of the backcountry in the cotton belt. Loaded with plug and twist, provisions and cooking utensils, the wagons rolled through the valleys and foothills, drawing up before the cross-roads stores. The drivers sold for cash, or bartered for meat, fish, grain, and other vendable produce. Not only the professional peddler but small manufacturer and factory overseer in slack seasons might venture eastwards to the coastal towns or southward into the gulf states, camping along the way. There was romance on these trips; Henry Evans Thomas of Rockingham County met his future wife while in Florida. There was profit; William T. Sutherlin of Danville cleared $700 on his first trip. Such ventures as these inspired Washington Duke some years later to undertake his peddling ventures in the sale of *Pro Bono Publico* smoking tobacco.

Exports of snuff and manufactured tobacco rose from about half a million pounds in 1800 to a million in 1815, three million in 1830, ten million in 1853 and over seventeen million in 1860. Petersburg manufacturers were particularly successful in developing strong English and Australian connections. The forward-looking Lynchburg firm of Cabell & Whitehead, in 1860, presented through their representative in Congress samples of smoking tobacco to the Japanese ambassador and his aides.

As well as the nativity of the business can be determined, it appears that the cigar-making industry was born in the Connecticut Valley, where housewife, husband, and child by the fireside rolled from the local leaf a heady article, taken by the village merchant in trade for store goods. The cigars were packed several thousand to the barrel and forwarded to the seaport towns, where they challenged the stamina of the hardiest men, waterfront laborers, sailors, and the like. About the time of the War of 1812 or shortly before, a general expansion of the business brought with it a shift from home to shop production and a larger market for the "long-nines," thin, pencil-like cigars, "short-sixes," shorter merchandise, and "supers," more nearly like modern cigars but made with a twist rather than glue to keep the leaves from unrolling. Shops such as those in Suffield, Connecticut, improved their processes and workmanship, and these better cigars became the bargaining stock of Yankee peddlers, who travelled the sparsely-settled areas and traded for skins. Some of the cheapest cigars were exported for use by West Indian slaves.

The short-sixes were distributed gratis in the taverns and grogshops to steady customers; strangers could have them two-for-a-cent. Another type of free goods in the saloons was the nondescript German- or Belgian-made cigar, fabricated of Palatine or Dutch leaves and bought by the tens of millions; over a hundred million paid duty in 1856. They were popular among the New York masses, though reputedly the most fearful product ever ignited on these shores.

The premium cigars were of Cuban manufacture. In the colonial period isolated importations occurred, such as the three donkey-loads of Havanas brought in by Major General Israel Putnam after his participation in the expedition against Havana in 1762, but not until about the time of the adoption of the Constitution were these first-class products much in evidence. They were imported in tremendous quantities by mid-century, over a hundred million in 1849, and the ambition of the American manufacturer was to duplicate the Havana cigar. In this effort he imported Cuban leaf, two to five and a half million pounds per year in the 1850's, a product originally brought into this country as an inconsequential side-line of the New York sugar importers. As early as 1810 the cigar-makers of Philadelphia, rolling about thirty million cigars per year, were using "Spanish" tobacco in one out of every ten cigars, probably putting a West Indian wrapper on a Kentucky filler. Among the first to make a "clear Havana," 100 per cent Cuban leaf, was Thomas G. Little of Baltimore, who, in 1844, was selling these for $16 per thousand instead of $3, the price of his product made with domestic leaf.

About the middle of the century the arrival of numerous proficient cigar-makers among the German immigrants and an expanding market offered by the Californians who had struck it rich by mining gold, or by mining the miners, greatly encouraged the business. For several generations every major contact with Spanish culture, whether in the protocol of diplomacy or the amenities of commerce, had stimulated the cigar habit in America. The Mexican War and the annexation of California converted thousands to this more exotic type of smoking, which, in the public mind, became associated with the idea of substantial wealth. (Furthermore, the sophomores of the land considered the cigar quite *collegiate*.) A large percentage of the output of the shops in the coastal cities of the northeast was designed for the California market and put on the sailing vessels going around the Horn. The German cigar-makers were particularly numerous in New York City, but enough of them wandered into the Valley of Connecticut to arouse the ancient Puritanism of that area by their free continental manners. All over the land there were more shops engaged exclusively in the making of cigars than ever before. Earlier in the century the manufacture of cigars had often been combined with the product of plug, pigtail, and snuff.

By 1860 the ten leading cigar-manufacturing centers were, in the order of their importance, Philadelphia, New York, Baltimore, Cincinnati, Hartford County in Connecticut, St. Louis, Hampden County in Massachusetts, Newark, Albany, and New Orleans. Hartford County, embracing the Windsor-Hartford district, and Hampden County, consisting of the Springfield-Westfield district, represented the strongly-entrenched Connecticut Valley industry. Because the business involved hand-labor and a minimum of capital, small establishments employing two, three, or four laborers could be found in almost any sizable town. Yet the industry gravitated towards the free states. Philadelphia and New York were the only "million-dollar cities"; the annual value of the product in Philadelphia was almost one and a quarter million dollars and in New York over one million one hundred thousand, with additional and important production in areas adjacent to these centers. The total for the United States was over nine million dollars with four-fifths of the sum north of the Mason and Dixon Line. Cigar making was almost, but not quite, as characteristic of the free states as the making of plug and twist was of the slave areas.

Shops selling cigars and other tobacco products were identified by the wooden Indian, a distinctive trade symbol beckoning passers-by on the streets of America in the era beginning with *Uncle Tom's Cabin* and ending with Coxey's Army. These tobacconists' figures were not always Indians; there were Scotch Highlanders, Turks, Negroes, Canadian trappers, and contemporary female favorites, notably Barnum's protégée, Jenny Lind. Nor can they be claimed as American in origin; as early as the reign of James I a black boy ("Black-more") was used in England as a tobacconist's sign. Other trades had their signs; the butcher his bull's head, the furrier his bear, and large carved watches, boots, and hats outside the shops proclaimed the services or products to be found indoors. But the popularity of the cigar-store figures, the importance placed on them by the retailer—in setting up shop tobacconists were known to invest more heavily in their Indian than in fixtures or stock—and the loving-care expended by their carvers raised them out of the common category of trade signs.

Though some figures were English-made, most were created by American craftsmen. Alien importation of the idea notwithstanding, these Indians and the similarly-contrived ships' figureheads constitute an honest vernacular art, in a sense more satisfying—perhaps because less pretending—than Powers' frigid *Greek Slave*, Mills' teetering *Jackson*, and the marble and bronze crimes of the Reconstruction era, extravagantly praised in their time. Certainly the wood carving was a priceless school in native forthrightness, as William Rush's Portrait of Joseph Wright testifies.[11] The tobacconists' figures were, of course, a people's art. The critic to be pleased was the average man possessed of a small coin and an appetite for a smoke or a chew. Successful specimens came from under the

[11] So far as is known, William Rush never carved a cigar-store Indian, but in his ship-carving he was particularly adept at Indian figureheads.

chisel of such men as Julius Theodore Melchers of Detroit, and John Jager of Baltimore.

The English fault of giving an African cast to the countenance of the Indian appears to have been corrected in the American versions. Indeed the Chicago figure, popularly known as "Big Chief Me Smoke 'Em," is supposed to have been modeled from an Iroquois chief, whose descendants for many years paid their respects to the statue whenever they visited the city. After the Civil War, figures of zinc, tin, or cast iron were often substituted for the earlier models of one-piece clear-pine construction. About 1890 public taste changed, and with the increasing congestion in the cities pedestrians were less patient with sidewalk obstructions. Furthermore, city ordinances gave more strict regulation to trade signs and the industry began to concentrate on national advertising. There is a fanciful story concerning a Yankee skipper who purchased as many of these cast-off figures as he could, loaded them on his vessel, and sailed for the South Seas, where he exchanged them for gold and ivory, the natives desiring imported gods! Whatever their disposition, most of them vanished from the streets about the time Bryan was coming into prominence, some to appear in this present generation as collectors' items.

The dominant mode of tobacco consumption during most of the colonial period was pipe-smoking. M. Durand, Fitzhugh's visitor of 1686, recorded that "Large quantities of it [tobacco] are used in this country, besides what they sell. Everyone smokes while working & idling. I sometimes went to hear the sermon; their churches are in the woods, & when everyone has arrived the minister & all the others smoke before going in. The preaching over, they do the same thing before parting. They have seats for that purpose. It was here I saw that everybody smokes, men, women, girls & boys from the age of seven years."

Soon after the middle of the eighteenth century, pipe-smoking was succumbing in social circles to the newer and more fashionable habit of snuffing. Many of the wealthy merchants and great planters affected the snuffbox because such was the mode in London. London had finally caught the style from the French. The snuffing aristocrats of the East unwittingly possessed kindred spirits in the persons of a few rough pioneers fronting the French-speaking settlements who, in a more direct way, were borrowing the Gallic custom. The European manual of the snuffbox gave infinite opportunities for the graceful waving of jewelled fingers and opened a new field of social expression quite as telling as the pout or smile of the face. A fraction of the ritual was, of course, a discipline to encourage tidiness. The custom of snuffing filtered across the channel, was accepted by English upper classes, and finally arrived in America with mannerisms diluted. Doubtless the custom was confirmed in social circles by the example of the French allies in the American Revolution.

When Alexander Hamilton pondered a suitable arrangement of excise taxes the congressional discussion made clear that snuff was for the aristocrat, that the farmer and laborer found little use for it. After some deliberation the statesmen decided that the excise of 1794 insofar as it referred to tobacco should apply only to snuff. As a revenue measure the snuff bill proved to be of no consequence, modifications, suspensions, and finally repeal marking its downward course. During the general debates on tobacco taxation, the high point was the protest registered by James Madison, leading the Jeffersonian forces. As summarized in the official *Annals of the Congress*, on Friday, May 2, 1794, Madison asserted: "As to the subject before the House, it was proper to choose taxes the *least unequal*. Tobacco excise was a burden the most *unequal*. It fell upon the poor, upon sailors, day-laborers, and other people of these classes, while the rich will often escape it. Much has been said about the taxing of luxury. The pleasures of life consisted in a series of innocent gratifications, and he felt no satisfaction in the prospect of their being squeezed. Sumptuary laws had never, he believed, answered any good purpose."

Possibly in imitation of the communal snuffbox in the House of Commons, zealous caretakers in the new government placed boxes in the halls to accommodate Congressmen and judges.

The best-known snuffing episode of the century occurred in the halls of Congress on Friday, March 7, 1834, at the height of the argument over Jackson's removal of the deposits from the Second National Bank. In support of a petition from the master builders of Philadelphia, Clay pictured an America prostrated by the President's unwise manipulation. Impulsively he turned to Vice-President Van Buren, the presiding officer of the Senate, and besought him to go to the President and tell him "of his bleeding country." Heady with his own oratory Clay conjured up a parade of despairing bankrupts, tearful widows, naked and hungry orphans. On and on he went in his rhythmic dirge, with "Tell him" as the chorus. "During the delivery of this apostrophe," reported Senator Thomas Hart Benton, "the Vice-President maintained the utmost decorum of countenance, looking respectfully, and even innocently at the speaker, all the while, as if treasuring up every word he said to be faithfully repeated to the President. After it was over, and the Vice-President had called some senator to the chair, he went up to Mr. Clay, and asked him for a pinch of his fine maccoboy snuff (as he often did); and, having received it, walked away." Thus the Red Fox pricked the bubble blown by Harry of the West, though the Philadelphians saw no humor in the situation and resolved that Van Buren should be execrated if he refused to convey to Jackson the message sent by "the honorable Henry Clay."

In the second third of the nineteenth century occurred the decline and fall of snuff, its descent from nose to mouth, in a word, its debasement from sniffing to *dipping*. The Rev. John H. Aughey, in his antislavery volume, *The Iron Furnace*, affirmed that scarcely one in fifty of the women of the Southern poor white class was exempt from the vice. More trustworthy than his fraction is his outline of the technique of dipping: "The female snuff-dipper takes a short stick, and wetting it with her saliva, dips it into her snuff-box, and then rubs the gathered dust all about her mouth, and into the interstices of her teeth, where she allows it to remain until its strength has been fully absorbed. Others hold the stick thus loaded with snuff in the cheek, *a la quid* of tobacco, and suck it with a decided relish, while engaged in their ordinary avocations; while others simply fill the mouth with the snuff, and imitate, to all intents and purposes, the chewing propensities of the men."

The chief method of tobacco consumption during the first half of the nineteenth century was chewing. Restricted in the colonial period to a few ordinary workingmen and sailors—save in the Connecticut Valley, where under the term "fudgeon" a good deal of tobacco was chewed—the habit was widely-diffused in the post-Revolutionary era. It was an almost prideful variant from dominant European modes; it is the only one of our tobacco customs which did not originate in a conscious imitation of European manners. The habit was being disseminated while Noah Webster was pleading for a distinctive American language, Benjamin Rush an American system of medicine, and the Hartford Wits an American literature. For better or for worse, chewing was an *American* trait and was recognized as a characteristic native accomplishment. One British journal referred to it as "the peculiarly disgusting American form of tobacco vice." [12]

It was symbolic that America early in the nineteenth

[12] Yet Adam Clarke of London sadly reported that kneeling for prayer had become more impracticable because of the carelessness of the tobacco-chewers of England.

century turned from snuff and knee breeches to the quid and long trousers, both once the habits of ordinary laborers. Chewing had its strongest hold on the people in the Jackson era, when the common man reigned supreme. While pipe and snuff customs had filtered down from the leaders of fashion to the common folk, tobacco chewing was a practice which, by some democratic capillary attraction, seeped from the common man upwards into the higher ranks of society. The people now had the ballot, and every statesman must needs be politician enough to identify himself with the masses. The log-cabin-and-hard-cider campaign put William Henry Harrison in office; Daniel Webster apologized publicly for not having been born in a log cabin.[13]

Tobacco chewing and its attendant expectoration did not seem out of place in a society notorious for its slovenliness in dress, frank crudity in personal habits, and bumptious democracy. The frontier did more violence to the manners of the nation in this period than ever before or after. Urbanity was lost in the woods; cosmopolitanism was a lesser variety of treason. John Melish, Harriet Martineau, and other foreigners found the squirting of saliva unspeakably nauseous, especially where men congregated in tavern, steamboat, canalboat or railway car. Charles Dickens could not keep his eyes from his fellow-travellers on the canalboat, "with yellow streams from half-chewed tobacco trickling down their chins." He added, "You never can conceive what the hawking and spitting is, the whole night through. Last night was the worst. *Upon my honour and word* I was obliged, this morning, to lay my fur-coat on the deck, and wipe the half dried flakes of spittle from it with my handkerchief: and the only surprise seemed to be, that I should consider it necessary to do so. When I turned in last night, I put it on a stool be-

[13] The political implications of tobacco habits in America have never been quite as incisive as in France, where *priser* vs. *fumer* vividly represented *ancien* vs. *nouveau régime,* and where a mid-century struggle went on between bourgeoise cigar and democratic pipe.

side me, and there it lay, under a cross fire from five men
—three opposite; one above; and one below. I make no complaints, and show no disgust." The Englishman, Charles
Mackay, had something in common with Benjamin
Franklin; each thought it a mistake for America to have
as its national emblem the eagle. Franklin would have
substituted the native turkey; Mackay the spittoon.[14]

In summary, the pipe had been the American style of
tobacco consumption throughout most of the colonial
period; soon after the French and Indian War snuff became the fashion in elegant society; in the early national
period chewing was accepted by all classes and easily led
other modes of tobacco consumption until well past the
middle of the nineteenth century, when it shared first-
honors with cigar-smoking, phenomenally popular soon
after the Mexican War. The movement of fashion made
no difference to large numbers of tobacco-users. Decade
after decade there were steady pipe smokers and the art
of snuffing never disappeared. And some used tobacco in
more than one form. Apparently no citizen of the United
States quite equaled the intemperate South American who
placed snuff up his nostrils, then stuffed shag tobacco after
it (this last feat termed "plugging"), after which he put
a coil of pigtail tobacco in each cheek, and lit a Havana
cigar. The truth of the circumstance is attested by a horrified witness, the Scottish surgeon John Lizars, who need-
lessly added that "This gentleman was . . . frightfully
nervous."

Until the time of the internal revenue laws of the Civil
War period statistics of tobacco consumption were either
non-existent or notoriously inaccurate. Yet it appears reasonably certain that in the first half of the nineteenth century there was a slight decline in the per capita consump-

[14] The burlesque approach may be seen in S. P. Avery's popular com-
pilation, *The Harp of a Thousand Strings; or, Laughter for a Lifetime*
(1858). One of the selections is "What Comes of Chawin Terbacker," the
theme being the discomfiture of a rural swain who, spitting tobacco juice,
put the fire out.

tion of tobacco, caused by three factors: (1) Women no longer consumed much tobacco. They had used great quantities of snuff, and many frontier women still smoked. Western travelers were intrigued at the sight of pipe-smoking mothers nursing their babies. It is an accepted fact that both Mrs. Andrew Jackson and Mrs. Zachary Taylor [15] smoked pipes. But no large number of women became addicted to chewing or to the smoking of cigars, the new and dominating modes. (2) The newly-arrived immigrants used tobacco moderately or not at all because of the relative scarcity of the leaf in the countries of their origin. (3) The energetic antitobacco crusade made a number of conquests among the potential neophytes and a few in the ranks of the hardened users of the herb.

REFORMERS AND THE TOBACCO HABIT

Early Puritans hopefully ventured a few statutes designed to curb the use of the leaf. In 1634 the Massachusetts Court went so far as to issue the unsocial rule that two or more persons should not take tobacco together anywhere, publicly or privately. The mid-seventeenth century legal code of Connecticut but summarized dominant opinion when tobacco users were classified with common idlers and those hunting birds for mere pleasure. Later rules concentrated on reducing the fire hazard, and by the eighteenth century the sumptuary laws of New England had either fallen into disuse or suffered outright repeal. Even Cotton Mather, in his classic *Manuductio ad Ministerium* of 1726, was not inflexible on the smoking question, though he emphasized moderation. Save for the evanescent statutes of the Massachusetts and Connecticut General Courts and inconsequential declarations of minor religious sects

15 However, the sad condition of the straw carpet in the chamber above the Blue Room was chargeable to the inaccuracy and carelessness of President Taylor himself.

(the Methodists for a time neither smoked, chewed, nor snuffed),[16] the antitobacco movement came to America only after the American Revolution, and then as the uncertain little sister of the antiliquor crusade.

Writing from Philadelphia on August 25, 1790, Dr. Benjamin Rush announced to his friend, Jeremy Belknap, that he was preparing a tract demonstrating the evils of tobacco. Three months later the essay was finished, but it was not until 1798 that it appeared in print as one section, "Observations upon the influence of the Habitual use of Tobacco upon Health, Morals, and Property," in Rush's *Essays, Literary, Moral and Philosophical*. Dr. Rush described the disastrous effect of tobacco on the stomach, the nerves, and the oral cavity. The use of tobacco was expensive, and tended to idleness, uncleanliness, and poor manners. Under the head of morals, Dr. Rush arrived at his main point, the connection between tobacco and liquor. "One of the usual effects of smoking and chewing is thirst. This thirst cannot be allayed by water, for no sedative or even insipid liquor will be relished after the mouth and throat have been exposed to the stimulus of the smoke, or juice of Tobacco. A desire of course is excited for strong drinks, and these when taken between meals soon lead to intemperance and drunkenness. One of the greatest sots I ever knew, acquired a love for ardent spirits by swallowing cuds of Tobacco, which he did, to escape detection in the use of it, for he had contracted the habit of chewing, contrary to the advice and commands of his father. He died of a Dropsy under my care in the year 1780." The tract was the first significant antitobacco document published in the United States.

For the moment the words of warning written by Rush fell on deaf ears, but they were treasured and repeated by

[16] At the first General Conference of the Methodist Episcopal Church, 1792, item seven in the directions given to the Band Societies once reading, "To use no needless self-indulgence; such as taking snuff or tobacco, unless prescribed by a physician," was abbreviated to, "To use no needless self-indulgence."

the seekers and agitators of the generation reaching maturity in the 1830's, '40's, and '50's. Bearing testimony against the leaf in this era when man was to be freed from his deviltries were such well-known men as Gerrit Smith, Horace Mann, Henry Ward Beecher, Amos Lawrence, John Hartwell Cocke, and Horace Greeley. The Virginian Cocke was a conspicuous exception to the rule that the reformers came from the North. Somehow or other a few chips from Plymouth Rock slipped into the masonry of Bremo, his famous home along the James River and Kanawha Canal and hard by a figure-eight race track. Greeley, whose opposition to what he termed "narcotic sensualism" was generated in part by an unfortunate experience with a cigar at the age of six, was unique among the reformers in that he possessed a sense of humor. It was he who coined, or at least popularized, the blistering description of a long-nine, with "a fire at one end and a fool at the other." Perhaps the three leading agitators for the abolition of the nicotine menace in the period from 1830 to 1860 were the Rev. Orin Fowler, Dr. Joel Shew, and the Rev. George Trask.

Rum and tobacco are allies, chorused the reformers in agreement with Father Rush. "Rum-drinking will not cease, till tobacco-chewing, and tobacco-smoking, and snuff-taking, shall cease," declared Rev. Orin Fowler before the Fall River Lyceum on June 4, 1833. Tobacco and alcohol were Satan's twin sons, said Rev. George Trask; the great-grandparent vices, wrote Dr. Trall. An anonymous Dante traced the descent into the hell of intemperance in these words: "They [the users of tobacco] frequent soda fountains, and from soda water get to drinking beer, and then brandy, and finally whiskey." Fowler hazarded a guess, taken by other reformers as a sort of sanctified census, that "Probably *one tenth*, at least, of all the drunkards annually made in the nation, and throughout the world, are made drunkards through the use of tobacco."

The characteristic approach of the antitobacco essayist

was first to establish his thesis that tobacco was deadly poison. He could do this more conveniently, and, it seemed to him, more effectively, by citing cases in which a drop or two of nicotine placed on the tongue of a cat or dog caused the immediate death of the animal. It was, by the way, quite an ancient test. Samuel Pepys saw a cat destroyed in this way, by "oyle of tobacco" in 1665. Then there was the common story that the Indians had insured the destruction of their enemies by dipping their arrow points in a brew of tobacco leaves.

In describing the sickening nature of the weed and the uncleanliness of smoking, chewing, and snuffing, a distressingly large fraction of the speakers and pamphleteers engaged in the holy task of slaying demon nicotine felt privileged to describe nauseous details and to use figures of speech drawn from the stagnant sewers of that undrained period. There was talk of the "black, loathsome discharge from the nose" after snuffing, the drooling mucous, the omnipresent spittle, and painful repetition of the theme that a man chewing tobacco was as disgusting as a dog re-eating his vomit. From Denmark came the often-repeated story that merchants laid down their tobacco in outhouses to make it "brisker, stronger, and more foetid." Almost to a man the tobacco abolitionists believed that stale urine was commonly used in the manufacture of the leaf. Less malodorous, but hardly less alarming, was the affirmation that much snuff was sharpened through the addition of ground glass.

The gentlemen who thought the pipe loaded with brimstone furnished an astounding list of diseases caused by tobacco. Dr. Joel Shew carefully itemized eighty-seven such ailments, the first being insanity, and the eighty-seventh cancer. In between were such deviations from normalcy as delirium tremens, epilepsy, slavering, hemorrhoids, rheumatism, gout, perverted sexuality, and impotency. Incidentally the reformers were divided among themselves as to the effect of tobacco on the procreative organs. Some, like Dr. Shew, warned that tobacco would render users impotent. Others, notably Orson S. Fowler, esteemed as an authority on eugenics as well as phrenology, thought tobacco a remover of inhibitions, an essentially erotic article: "No man can be virtuous as a companion who eats tobacco: for, although he may not violate the seventh commandment, yet the feverish state of the system which it produces necessarily causes a craving and lustful exercise of amativeness. Just as alcoholic liquors cause such amatory cravings, and for the same reason. As alcoholic liquors and the grosser forms of sensuality are twin sisters, so tobacco-eating and deviltry are both one; because the fierce passions of many tobacco chewers, as regards the other sex, are immensely increased by the fires kindled in their systems, and of course in their cerebellums, by tobacco excitement. Ye who would be pure in your love-instinct, cast this sensualizing fire from you." [17]

Naturally tobacco undermined one's morals. To illustrate the point L. N. Fowler, brother of the great Orson S. Fowler, presented the following prologue and drama: "Tobacco benumbs the affections and moral feelings, and renders love a mere passion. I knew a man, who married a fine woman. At first he was very affectionate, his moral

[17] The British students of the situation appear to have interpreted whatever data came to hand somewhat as had Dr. Shew. Mr. Turton, who seems to have specialized in debilitated authors, reported before the Royal Medical Society in 1857 the case of "an eminent author in the literary world, of the highest graphic historical writing . . . between whose lips cigar has followed cigar in endless succession." Naturally, "all marital connection between his wife and him has been suspended; that the poor woman might have been, during that period, as well banished or divorced, she has been so wholly deprived of her lawful pleasures." Furthermore, "I am informed by a gentleman, whose name I am not at liberty to mention, that a popular writer of the present day married a lady, and that immediately after his marriage he proposed separate beds, which was agreed to. But on the young bride telling her situation to her mother, the latter investigated the condition of the two partners, and learned that the husband was impotent; he, in short, had long been an inveterate smoker. A separation and divorce were immediately obtained, and the lady was married to Mr. J. M. After the ordinary time she became a mother."

feelings were active, and for a time he studied for the ministry; but imbibing the habits of chewing and smoking, he became less pious and affectionate to his wife, and by the time that he smoked thirty cigars per day, he could swear like a pirate, and abuse his wife shamefully. Not being able to endure his treatment any longer, she commenced drinking to drown her trouble, and soon put an end to her life."

Of course the literature was ornamented with countless stories of individuals whose untimely death was credited to tobacco. Napoleon's death was blamed on excessive snuffing. John Hancock died from a train of ailments induced by his swallowing tobacco juice; he was too much of a gentleman to spit just anywhere. Reformers were convinced, and repetition of the point made it appear all the more certain, that twenty thousand Americans every year were killed by the noxious leaf.

Many persons announced that they had successfully broken the habit, with consequent improvement in health. Of all the testimonials that of John Quincy Adams, a leading connoisseur of West Indian cigars in his middle twenties, was most widely quoted.[18]

Dr. Trall warned that the struggle would be hard, and that there would be desperate moments before emancipation could be achieved. Picture a man breaking himself of the habit, said Dr. Trall. "Ghosts and goblins, spooks and apparitions, haunt his brain; and snakes and serpents of all shapes, sizes, colors, forms, and lengths dance attendance around the room, each in dumb-show chanting the praises of Tobacco . . . All through the long night do these fiends of a disordered nervous system play their fantastic tricks to his torment; and as the morning dawns, the wretched victim of a miserable habit feels utterly prostrated; and although he may still be determined to per-

---

[18] His experiences roughly followed those of his father, John Adams, who confessed that he learned the use of tobacco at the age of eight when skating with the boys on the ice ponds. He tempered or ceased the use of tobacco in his old age, and expressed sympathy with the antitobacco movement.

severe in his abstinence and suffer through, he finds it almost impossible to think of anything but Tobacco; while every perverted, enraged, and rabid instinct is crying out, 'A quid! a quid! my kingdom for a quid!' " "He may feel like death, but he will not die," consoled Dr. Trall.

The literature addressed particularly to the youth of the land is best represented by a compact, plainly written volume entitled, *Thoughts and Stories for American Lads: or Uncle Toby's Anti-Tobacco Advice to his Nephew Billy Bruce*, prepared by the Rev. George Trask and published in Boston in 1852. If one may believe the testimony of the reformers, Trask's work was greatly needed, the country being crowded with precocious infants who showed perfect mastery of the arts of chewing and smoking. Joel Shew pictures babies seasoning pulls on the maternal breasts with puffs from their mothers' pipes. *Uncle Toby's Anti-Tobacco Advice* was ornamented by letters from various public men such as William Ellery Channing, Neal Dow, and P. T. Barnum.

Well-informed Americans heard of a vigorous, but surprisingly good-tempered, debate on "The Great Tobacco Question," as it was called, carried on in the pages of the English medical journal, the *Lancet*, in the years 1856–1857, by over fifty physicians divided about equally pro and con. To prove the evils of tobacco American as well as English clinical cases were presented, but to the popular mind much of this American evidence was nullified when General Tom Thumb, who happened to be in London at the time—and, of course, was considered a typical if diminutive American—pronounced the leaf "one of his chief comforts." (What Barnum, his manager, thought of this is not a matter of record.)

The last important antitobacco essay written in the pre-Civil War period was entitled, "A New Counterblast," and published in the youthful *Atlantic Monthly*, December, 1861. Prepared by Thomas Wentworth Higginson, clergyman, author, noted abolitionist and friend of John Brown, the article was a foretaste of a new type of attack, cautious and well-mannered.

In the era of the Mexican War, the gold rush of the "forty-niners" and the prosperity of the early 1850's, reformers sadly observed an upturn in the use of tobacco. One social critic as early as 1845 commented, "Even street-smoking, which was once considered too ignoble and execrable a practice for any well-bred man to perpetrate, is becoming as fashionable as almost any other folly of the times, not even the vast bustles, or 'bishops' . . . on the other sex, excepted!" And Dr. Wm. A. Alcott in 1849 certified that, "From one end of the commonwealth to the other—temperance or no temperance—it is, as it were, one mighty *puff—puff—puff.*" In 1854 Dr. R. T. Trall reported for America the highest per capita use of tobacco in the world, urchins of New York aged three to six smoking, eight to ten chewing, "And more and worse than all this: Some of the *ladies* of this refined and fashion-forming metropolis are aping the silly ways of some pseudo-accomplished foreigners, in smoking Tobacco through a weaker and more *feminine* article, which has been most delicately denominated *cigarette.*"

The antitobacco movement practically disappeared with the Civil War. And that conflict, like every other major war, made new converts to tobacco.

*1860 * 1911*

[Chapter 5]

THE NEW SOUTH AND BIG BUSINESS

IN THE LAND OF JOHNNY REB

When the Confederate States of America was organized in Montgomery, Alabama, February 4, 1861, not a single tobacco state was represented. The original Confederacy was the Cotton Kingdom; the Tobacco Kingdom hesitated and made eleventh-hour efforts to save the Union. But men in high places would have none of the middle-ground talk. Then followed Fort Sumter, and on April 15, 1861, Lincoln's call for troops. The tobacco district split along its seams: Virginia, North Carolina, and Tennessee went with the new Confederate States of America; Maryland, Kentucky, and Missouri wavered but ultimately declared their loyalty to the Union.

In terms of normal tobacco poundage, it was almost a fifty-fifty division of the Tobacco Kingdom. Thus while cotton was scarce behind the Union lines, fair crops of tobacco continued to be raised. In and around New York City factories were built to supply the Northern markets once served by the Virginians, and the industry was considered sufficiently stable to suffer the extremely high excise taxes plastered on the finished product in 1862. Because of the blockade of the Southern coast, New York City became the great export market and headquarters for European buyers, most of whom had once resided in New Orleans. In the Mississippi Valley, Louisville profited by the closing of the more southerly market towns and by the opening of the Louisville and Nashville Railroad. It became the center of the tobacco trade for the West; for the fiscal year ending November 1, 1864, Louisville warehouses sold over 63,000 hogsheads of tobacco. During the conflict Kentucky succeeded Virginia as the leading tobacco-growing state.

In the South, both Confederate and state governments attempted to restrain the growth and manufacture of tobacco. The Confederate Congress in March, 1862, passed a joint resolution, "recommending the planters of the Confederate States to refrain from the cultivation of cotton and tobacco and devote their energies to raising provisions." Yet the Confederate crop of that year may have been half the bumper yield of 1859. The wave of optimism sweeping over the South during the plant-bed season of 1863 meant still larger plantings, and this despite warnings from responsible officials that the war would be long and foodstuffs scarce.

The State of Virginia on March 31, 1863, passed an act "to limit the production of tobacco and increase the production of grain." Subsequent Senate and House resolutions scored the use of labor in the manufacture of tobacco, and recommended that the levies for work on public defenses should be applied first to those Negroes in the tobacco factories.

Governmental remonstrances did not cure the tobacco-planting habit. During the spring and early summer of 1864, according to a Northern soldier, both south of the James River "and in the territory stretching from the Wilderness to Cold Harbor, immense quantities of tobacco were found in the various stages of curing. The drying-houses were full of it." Southerners, however, considered the crops planted in 1864 and in 1865 as short, and anyone who could find on his farm a few odd hands of the leaf could barter them with the merchants for needed supplies.

Tobacco entered comparatively little into the actual fiscal operations of the Confederacy. After the act of April 21, 1862, authorizing the exchange of bonds for cotton and tobacco, had been in effect for over eight months, the Principal Clerk in charge of the Produce Loan Office announced "No purchases of tobacco, under the act of April 21st, have been made until very recently, for the reason that a large portion of the tobacco-planting region and the principal points where it is deposited, have been either invaded or have been under constant threat of invasion by the enemy."

There are haunting phrases from a report made by an obscure Commissioner of Taxes which ring in the ear whenever one is plagued with questions concerning the fall of the Confederacy. A tax-in-kind was levied by statute on tobacco crops. But the Commissioner of Taxes plaintively reported that "A serious obstacle has been encountered in the effort to secure the tax on a large amount of tobacco stored in the public warehouses of Virginia," and proceeded to explain the inspection system and the obligation on the inspector to deliver the tobacco specified in the warehouse receipt. Yes, according to section 15 of the tax law tobacco was enumerated and the Confederate States government was supposed to have a lien, "but the difficulty is to be found in the fact that the lien cannot be enforced, without coming in direct conflict with a law of the State," for by Virginia statute the tobacco inspector was bonded to deliver the full poundage specified in the warehouse receipt. The Committee on Confederate Relations of the Virginia Senate was good enough to review the situation, but, with the concurrence of the Senate, on November 2, 1863, decided that the state statutes were "essential to the protection of the planter" and refused modification of the law. This menace of state sovereignty was obviously a fundamental weakness of the Confederacy.

A matter of minor diplomacy during the Civil War was the status of the leaf tobacco in Richmond which had been purchased by foreigners. The Confederate government passed an act authorizing the destruction of staples and supplies when such action was necessary to prevent their falling into the hands of the enemy, and the consuls representing the foreign interests were in a fright lest the leaf belonging to their nationals or to their governments be burned. When Richmond was threatened in May, 1862, and army officials impressed a hundred or so Negroes and a goodly number of wagons to gather the tobacco in central places where it could be readily fired if necessary, the consuls employed as their attorney an individual described by J. B. Jones (famous keeper of the *Rebel War Clerk's Diary*), as "Mr. Myers, the little old lawyer." With specious phrasing Myers argued that destruction would redound to the benefit of the Yankees by increasing the price of the tobacco they had stored in Missouri, Kentucky, and Maryland! Whatever the reasons, Judah P. Benjamin, Secretary of State, permitted the consuls to collect their tobacco in special warehouses protected by their own flags. M. Alfred Paul, French consul at Richmond, succeeded in the spring of 1864 in getting a few hogsheads shipped on a British freighter convoyed by French men-of-war.

A number of the tobacco warehouses and factories of Richmond were commandeered by the provost marshal of the city after the First Battle of Bull Run and used as prisons. The best-known and best-hated by its inmates was a brick structure at the corner of Twentieth and Dock Streets, originally built by the wealthy manufacturer John Enders but occupied at the outbreak of the war by Libby and Sons, ship chandlers. This building, known as Libby Prison, was used for the confinement of commissioned officers. It became badly crowded, and food ran short, especially during the winter of 1863–1864 after the failure of exchange plans. There were sensational escapes and desperate Union cavalry raids for the purpose of releasing prisoners.[1]

In all American wars there have been three factors accentuating the tobacco habit: (1) absence of family restraints, (2) indulgence by way of escape from the fatigues of military life, and (3) quickened imitativeness accompanying the massing together of people. During the Civil War to these factors were added special circumstances in both the Northern and Southern armies. The soldiers did a large part of their fighting in the tobacco country and could pick up a crude but usable article for nothing when they saw fit. As one Northern soldier, John D. Billings, reported, "Every soldier who had a liking for tobacco helped himself as freely as he pleased, with no one caring to stay his hand. But I believe that the experts in smoking and chewing preferred the black navy plug of the sutler, at a dollar and a quarter, to this unprepared but purer article to be had by the taking."

And, a most interesting development, during the last of the Civil War the Confederate government by act of its Congress decreed that regular tobacco rations be granted the soldiers. Though tobacco rations had been issued in the United States Navy for some years, it appears that this was the first time regular tobacco rations were supplied at government expense to an American army. In August of 1861 Abraham Watkins Venable, a member of the House of Representatives from North Carolina, failed in an attempt to persuade the Confederate Congress to issue tobacco as part of the soldiers' rations. A new bill to supply tobacco to the army was introduced in the Senate March 24, 1863. Almost a year later, February 17, 1864, it became law.

---

[1] Libby Prison was taken down and shipped to Chicago for the World's Fair in 1893. Later a part of the wall was used in the construction of the Chicago Coliseum.

The Senate had hidden the bill in the Committee on Finance until the General Assembly of Virginia presented resolutions on the subject. The act reads as follows:

CHAP. LXXI.—*An Act to provide tobacco for the army.*

The Congress of the Confederate States of America do enact, That there shall be furnished to every enlisted man in the service of the Confederate States one ration of tobacco, under such regulations as the Secretary of War may establish.

APPROVED February 17, 1864.

The quality of tobacco issued was not always good, complaints from the army reached Congress, and the House of Representatives set on foot an investigation regarding the rumored "unsound and worthless tobacco . . . supplied to our soldiers."

Johnny Reb had to put up with many substitutes, but a considerable fraction of the time he had genuine tobacco, and this during periods when the Yankee was running short of such supplies. In those intervals of fraternizing, which the indignant officers on both sides were never able to prohibit, the standard swap through the picket lines was Southern tobacco for Northern coffee. Southern officers were not included in the tobacco ration plan; those who liked their tobacco bought it for themselves. Many were fond of the fashionable cigars, when they could be procured.[2] Cigars played an incidental role in one of the

---

[2] Laurent Marcellin Joseph de Give, Belgian consul at Atlanta, reported under date of November 15, 1862, while on a visit to his home government: "Tobacco like everything else has got into the hands of the speculators; today you must pay for the better brands a dollar and twenty-five cents instead of thirty-five cents, the former price. Cigars are out of reach."

Civilians outside the tobacco area often suffered from the scarcity and high prices of the chewing and smoking material. There were various ways to remedy this situation, including an approach to army men if they were in the neighborhood. According to a letter from Captain Charles M. Blackford, on October 25, 1863, there came to Longstreet's headquarters in Tennessee a lively old woman in silk dress and bonnet. "After she had breakfasted she informed the general that the object of her visit was to get him

famous accidents of the Civil War. It is well known that just before the battle of Antietam General Robert E. Lee's order to General D. H. Hill, dated September 9, 1862, and explaining in part the Confederate plans, fell into General George B. McClellan's hands. The document, wrapped around a bunch of cigars, had been dropped by a careless Confederate officer and picked up by a Union soldier. It would be easy to exaggerate the importance of the discovery of Lee's orders in the subsequent military reverses suffered by Lee, but difficult to overestimate the significance of the battle itself, considered by Lincoln as an appropriate occasion for issuing the Emancipation Proclamation.

THE BIRTH OF THE GOLDEN CALF

After Lee offered his sword to Grant at Appomattox, General Joseph E. Johnston surrendered to General William T. Sherman the last Confederate Army east of the Mississippi River, the interviews between the two generals taking place at the Bennett farm, about six miles northeast of the wood-and-water stop on the North Carolina Railroad known as Durham's Station. Their first meeting occurred on April 17, 1865; the final conference, April 26, 1865. These days of armistice tried the souls of the civilians in the countryside, who until the last moments of the war had escaped the major armies. Taught in the lusty school of marching-through-Georgia-and-South Carolina, Sherman's bummers were peculiarly adept at foraging, and the Confeds had talents of their own. One suspects some exaggeration in the Southern tradition of a silver service in every Yankee knapsack, but it is certain that the sties, cribs, and barns suffered from the bored and hun-

to give her a little tobacco to smoke. Her pockets were filled with 'Lone Jack' and she was sent home in an ambulance." Lone Jack was the famous smoking tobacco put up by John W. Carroll of Lynchburg. During the war Carroll continued his profitable business.

gry men of both armies. Simply as a matter of course smokers and chewers picked up whatever tobacco could be discovered.

The hamlet of Durham's Station was a sort of neutral ground, an every man's land, where blue and gray uniforms could be seen mixed indiscriminately as the men swapped yarns and horses, held running and target contests, and reinforced their private stocks of smoking tobacco by joint visits to Green's tobacco factory, a two-story frame building about a hundred yards from the station. By the time the armies dispersed, the looters had cleaned out the establishment in which had been stored a large quantity of the granulated leaf, ready for shipment.

There is no evidence that John Ruffin Green made any serious effort to protect his stock of tobacco. Perhaps he knew it would be useless to try to guard his property against the youthful vandals, and markets and profits were problematical in the immediate aftermath of Lincoln's assassination. And might not some Yankee official confiscate the whole supply on a basis of Green's not having paid the United States excise tax? Although he did not realize it, before his eyes there had taken place a scheme of "free samples" which might have been capitalized at many thousands of dollars. Within a few weeks letters scrawled by men more accustomed to the trigger than the pen came addressed to the postmaster, the station agent, or other officials. They were out of that Durham tobacco and wanted more. From whom could they get it? This was the day of triumph for the new Bright Tobacco, lighter in color, milder in taste, the climax of man's groping for relief from the tongue-biting qualities of the original dark leaf.

John Ruffin Green had processed a little smoking tobacco on a farm near Durham's Station, suffered from a fire, and moved into the village about 1860. There he began manufacturing the granulated article with the particular idea of selling to the young University sports from

Chapel Hill, who, after their teeth-rattling hack ride of twelve miles, had time on their hands as they waited for the train. He had built up a fair business when the calamities of war descended on his factory in April, 1865. With the subsequent revival of his trade, he adopted a brand name, choosing as his label the name of his town, now usually shortened to Durham. Pleased by the bull's head on the jars of Colman's Mustard, manufactured in Durham, England, and impressed by a very fine breeding animal owned by a neighbor, Green adopted as his trademark the Durham Bull, a happy inspiration in a still predominantly rural society and for a product designed for male purchasers.

Green's accomplishments were three-fold: he initiated a quality product when the usual granulated article was of trashy and inferior leaf (the notable exceptions being the Lynchburg brands, Carroll's Lone Jack and Moore's Killikinnick), he created a famous trademark, and finally, before his death in 1869, he took into partnership William T. Blackwell, who had been a merchant and tobacco peddler. There were lesser figures that moved in and out of the business, but the important fact is that Blackwell purchased Green's interest from the Green estate—reputedly $500 was the value placed on the Bull trademark—and in the year 1870 admitted as a partner Julian Shakespeare Carr, son of a Chapel Hill merchant. In building their great institution Blackwell and Carr developed methods of mass production keyed to their larger sales, they defended their trademark, and they advertised their wares. Over a long period of years the Bull Durham factory adopted the latest machines for shredding the leaf, for packing the granulated mixture in the bags, for making the bags, and for labeling.

Blackwell and Carr engaged in historic litigation to protect their brand and trademark. They triumphed in the federal district court, the decision clearly affirming Blackwell's right to the Bull and restraining imitators. The famous case decided in the state supreme court in 1875 involved judicial comparison of Blackwell's Genuine Durham Smoking Tobacco, adorned with a full-view bull, and a label by Wesley A. Wright, The Original Durham Smoking Tobacco, illustrated by some beast's head. Unhappily for the plaintiff in this case of William T. Blackwell v. Wesley A. Wright, the judges saw a sharp distinction between the words "genuine" and "original," toyed with the idea that the head of the animal pictured on Wright's tobacco might be an ox instead of a bull as far as they could tell! Accordingly they decided that there had been no infringement on the Blackwell rights. Blackwell and Carr were successful in subsequent state litigation, thoroughly defeating their most persistent antagonist in the North Carolina courts, John H. McElwee, who had the boldness to borrow the word "genuine," use the full view of the bull, and copy the name Durham despite the fact that the tobacco was manufactured in Statesville!

In advertising the Bull to the public, the firm scattered over the land testimonials of approval from prominent men, senators and clergymen. Even Alexander H. Stephens lent his name to the cause. According to figures given out by the Blackwell Company, in one year in the early 1880's the firm spent $100,000 for advertising in the country newspapers, about $50,000 with the metropolitan dailies, and distributed as premiums clocks costing $60,000. The president, Julian S. Carr, announced "Yes, sir; as long as I have a dollar to spare, I will invest it in advertising." His was the first great advertising campaign carried on by an American manufacturer of tobacco.

The picture of the Bull was spread by sign painters all over this country, and even in Europe and the Orient. Some of the American displays were sensational panels eighty by one hundred feet. Any new design quickened public interest, and the rural editors freely commented on the work of the commercial wielders of the brush. The greatest of the painters in the 1880's was a North Carolinian, J. Gilmer Koerner, whose *nom de plume* was Reuben Rink.[3] Only in Durham did the Bull have sound effects. The Blackwell factory of brick and stone, "the shrine of all pilgrims to Durham," in the words of a contemporary chronicler, was ornamented by two pictures of the Durham Bull. "An interesting feature, also, of this establishment is a steam whistle, so constructed that it imitates the bellow of a bull. The imitation is so perfect that a stranger would be slow to detect the deception. It is said that it costs $6 each time this bull whistle bellows. It can be heard a distance of thirteen miles."

The establishment became the largest smoking-tobacco factory in the world. In 1869 there were perhaps a dozen employees, in 1884 about nine hundred. Bull Durham became a definite part of the American scene, as attested by the mellow blending of fact and fiction about the product. A standard part of the cowboy's costume, if we may believe what we are told, was the tag from a sack of Bull Durham hanging from his shirt pocket. And with the popularity of the home-made cigarette (again, if tradition may be accepted), the classic feat of the cowboy was to roll his cigarette with one hand while controlling a mettlesome pony with the other!

In the 1880's the firm was changed from partnership to corporation, Blackwell left the company, and modifications took place in the title. But Julian S. Carr held a steady rein, and grew in wealth and in charity. One youth he helped educate was an Oriental, Charles J. Soong, who, on his return to China, became a leading merchant. Soong is best remembered as the father of Madame Chiang Kai-shek and of Madame Sun Yat-sen.

[3] Koerner's bulls were hardly more amazing than his own residence in Kernersville (as the village finally spelled its name), a square brick structure embracing the usual residential rooms plus furnaces, smokehouse, woodhouse, wagonhouse, hayloft and stables, all capped by a Gothic roof. In the house were murals, famous throughout the countryside.

As factories in Durham multiplied, all forms of tobacco were produced. Smoking brands such as Sitting Bull, Pride of Durham, and Duke of Durham tagged along after Bull Durham. The incessant theme in the village was tobacco. On damp days the odor settled in every nook and cranny. In such an atmosphere was revived the doctrine of nicotine therapy. The Clingman Tobacco Cure Company of Durham presented cake and ointment for the relief of bunions, snake-bite, scarlet fever, lockjaw, and other ailments.[4]

The new town was fairly bursting with hustle, bustle, and energy. Durham was not ashamed to be known as the Chicago of the South. Passionately devoted to trade and enterprise, the village grew rapidly, perhaps too rapidly to consolidate on all fronts. Durham was self-made, thus self-confident. The old planter class had little or nothing to do with the miracle of Durham's Station; once yeomen and peddlers and little merchants did. Sedate Hillsboro and scholarly Chapel Hill looked down or held their aristocratic noses at the bumptious village whose golden calf was a Durham Bull, and this at a time when no lady and no gentleman in a lady's presence would even use the word b-u-l-l.[5] It was no place for those who wanted culture, said its critics, and when Durham offered $50,000 toward establishing the Baptist Female Seminary, the representatives of that body could not stomach the thought of exposing young ladies to the crudities of the town and chose more effete but mellowed Raleigh. Angry Durhamites then and there determined to bring Trinity College to their town, despite the fact that for the moment Raleigh appeared to be winning the contest for that school also.

In the quarter of a century from Abraham Lincoln to

[4] The prime mover was General Thomas L. Clingman, the Congressman, soldier, and amateur natural scientist, who once fought a duel with Yancey of Alabama.

[5] Not until the free and easy manners of the post-World War I period did parlor-opposition to the word decline. Nineteenth century euphemisms, according to H. L. Mencken's survey, included cow-creature (or cow-critter), seed-ox, cow-brute, and Jonathan.

Benjamin Harrison, another lusty tobacco town emerged in the North Carolina piedmont, Winston, growing up on the edge of the sedate Moravian village of Salem. As Durham was particularly noted for its smoking tobacco, Winston became famous for its "flat goods," the term applied to the tightly-compressed plugs. By 1872 Winston had a population of some three or four hundred, and sundry village enterprises including Major Hamilton Scales' small plug factory, which had been started in a Liberty Street carriage house two years earlier. During that year, 1872, two significant developments took place: the railroad reached Winston and in an old stable Major T. J. Brown opened the first leaf sales warehouse. Whereupon the farmers increased their crops, warehouses and factories multiplied, and the town expanded. The greatest names in Winston tobacco history were Hanes and Reynolds.

A North Carolinian by birth, Pleasant Henderson Hanes served as a courier in the Confederate army. It was prophetic that even during the lean days of the war the teen-age youth kept his horse plump and his haversack at least partly full. The conflict ended, he dealt for awhile in leaf tobacco then, in 1870, he became a salesman, traveling in covered wagons over the whole South. Soon in Winston he organized his own firm, P. H. Hanes & Company, an enterprise which his brothers joined. By the late 1880's the firm was recognized as Winston's largest, employing over three hundred hands and annually producing almost a million pounds of flat tobacco, including the leading brands of Missing Link, Man's Pride, and Greek Slave. The firm sold out to the R. J. Reynolds Tobacco Company in 1900. Hanes invested his money in the manufacture of men's underwear and became famous in that field.

Richard Joshua Reynolds, better known simply as R. J. Reynolds, was born in Patrick County, Virginia. His father Hardin W. Reynolds, one of the three or four largest slave-holders in the county, was both planter and manufacturer, a combination in no wise unique in the late ante-bellum period.[6] At the end of the war Hardin W. Reynolds resumed manufacturing at the home place, and R. J. Reynolds, after a period at Emory and Henry College, went on the road to sell the finished product. He would pack a two-horse wagon with tobacco, and drive through southwest Virginia and on into eastern Tennessee and Kentucky, selling, bartering, swapping. Even the horses, wagon, and harness went if the bargain were good enough. The husky, fine-looking youth of seventeen matched wits with the best traders of the back country, sharpening his mind on this hard whetstone of experience. After a short while in a Baltimore business college he returned to Patrick County, for an interval took charge of the home factory, then, in 1875, moved directly south across the state line to Winston and set up shop for himself. His earliest business was principally the making of twist on a contract basis for jobbers, using the jobbers' tags and brands. Two brothers joined him, the firm became incorporated, and eventually was known as the largest manufactory of flat goods in the world. Even his great admirers admitted that Reynolds possessed a rough, unpolished personality, but he was forceful, decisive, and unexcelled in business acumen in his chosen field, save by James B. Duke.

Durham, Winston, and sundry lesser North Carolina manufacturing centers including Reidsville, threatened to upset the applecart of the Virginians, bred on the colonial tradition that the North Carolinians were ne'er-do-wells. In North Carolina the theme was innovation: new tobacco towns, new tobacco people. In Virginia there were many links with the ante-bellum days.

---

[6] Tax and census schedules show that Hardin W. Reynolds by 1860 owned 33 slaves over twelve years of age, reported personal property valued at $24,900, had title to 18 tracts of land scattered over the county, and was operating a farm appraised at $11,500 and consisting of 2300 acres, 500 of which were improved. He practiced a diversified agriculture; his tobacco crop was considerably less than it had been in 1850. His factory, employing on the average 14 hands when in operation, used annually 25,000 pounds of the raw leaf (some three times the amount of his own crop), an increase over the operations reported for the 1850 census.

THE OLD GUARD AND NEWCOMERS

If the tobacco industry were typical, it appears that the manufacturers in the upper South found themselves and came to terms with reality more quickly than did the farmers. The manufacturers readily accepted the new economic order. But this was not strange. They needed the strength of economic freedom. In pre-Civil War days the tobacco manufacturers had profited in part because they moulded the institution of slavery to give it something of the labor-incentive of a free society. On the farm new labor systems had to be worked out with the fall of slavery. There were painful adaptations. But the handling of free labor in the factories of 1870 was not much different from the management of the hired slaves of 1860, with their overwork bonuses, their Christmas holidays, and their privilege of choosing-their-own masters.

The tobacco manufacturers of Virginia put heart in a people badly needing encouragement. Many of the industrialists were survivors of the ante-bellum period. William T. Sutherlin, leading manufacturer of Danville in the days of slavery, joined his name with that of Robert E. Lee in the famous letter sent to General W. S. Rosecrans in 1868 explaining the reaction of the South to the war settlement. In the economic and educational rehabilitation of the Dan Valley, Sutherlin worked tirelessly.

Somewhat like the Durham smoking tobacco, the Lynchburg pipe mixtures, notably Maurice Moore's Killikinnick and John W. Carroll's Lone Jack, became well-known to the soldiers during the war, and benefited by the ensuing national demand. While the conflict was going on and immediately thereafter Moore wisely translated his granulated tobacco into real estate.[7] But before long a calendar

[7] The recorded deeds of April, 1866, attest the barter character of two transactions undertaken by Moore: the consideration in one instance being

of difficulties, including the pirating of his brand by far away rivals, caused him to retire from business. In the course of time the word Killikinnick (or Killikinick) was used as a generic term, applied to any kind of granulated smoking tobacco. With the cessation of hostilities John W. Carroll found his money worthless. He moved into the old Crumpton factory and spread his brands over the world. At his death in 1898 he was supposedly worth almost a million and, to quote the Lynchburgers, "There was not a dirty dollar among them."

James Thomas, Jr., the dean of the Richmond manufacturers in the ante-bellum period, came out of the war in better financial condition than most. At the news of the firing on Fort Sumter, he had rushed large quantities of tobacco to foreign markets and deposited the proceeds with his London correspondents, the old tobacco house of J. K. Gilliat and Company. During the war he operated a factory in Danville. With Horace Greeley, Cornelius Vanderbilt and others, he signed the bail bond which released Jefferson Davis from Fortress Monroe in 1867. His dyspepsia made him nervous, so nervous that he only put his mark on the bond; another wrote his name. Thus was born the foolish rumor that the great Southern industrialist was illiterate. The Gilliat funds aided him in the trying post-bellum days. He now took less active part in his business, deputizing to young men many of the details. His old firm became known as Thomas C. Williams & Company. At the time of Thomas' death in 1882, he was reputedly the wealthiest citizen of Richmond. His nephew, the prominent tobacconist Dr. Richard Archibald Patterson, served as surgeon during the Civil War. After Lee's surrender Patterson resumed the manufacture of tobacco, creating several popular products, one being a high-grade smoking plug, which he named Lucky Strike. Family tradition

"Ten thousand pounds of Smoking Tobacco," in the other, "Thirteen thousand pounds (Killikinnick) smoking tobacco."

holds that the original casing was based on a formula used by Dr. Patterson in a cough syrup.

By 1870 Richmond's "big four" were Alexander Cameron, James B. Pace, J. G. Dill, and P. H. Mayo. The Scottish family of Camerons, well-established in Petersburg before the Civil War, had extended its operations to Richmond, where Alexander Cameron took a leading part in rebuilding the industry of that devastated city. By 1870 Alexander Cameron & Company was statistically the greatest in Richmond, employing 350 hands. The plant under the business title Wm. Cameron & Bro. was the largest in Petersburg, hiring 390 laborers. In Richmond still another company was organized, Cameron & Cameron, which soon concentrated on smoking tobacco, cheroots and cigarettes. In the early 1870's the Camerons set up operations in Australia, establishing factories at Melbourne, Sydney, Adelaide, and later at Brisbane. William Cameron in 1886 sold out to his brothers. George Cameron took charge of the Petersburg interests, Alexander Cameron had his headquarters in Richmond, and Alexander Cameron, Jr. went to Australia, succeeding William J. Young, William Cameron's protégé, as local manager of the business. Down to the time of the creation of the American Tobacco Company, it appears that the combined Cameron properties represented the largest tobacco manufacturing enterprise operated by Americans. Captain P. H. Mayo headed the firm of P. H. Mayo & Bro. Tobacco Company and carried on the tradition established by his father, Robert A. Mayo, creator of navy plug. J. G. Dill, aided by his brother Adolph Dill, prepared a brand, Dill's Best, plug and cut-plug, which became world famous.

More portentous than the survivors of the ante-bellum period and, in the light of subsequent events, more significant than the manufacturers established immediately after the war, was Lewis Ginter. Born in New York City, Ginter had established himself as a merchant-importer in Rich-

mond in the 1840's. He served with distinction in the
Confederate army and after his parole in 1865 went to
New York, where his brokerage firm, with many others,
failed in the Black Friday crash of 1869. Returning to
Richmond, in 1872 he entered into partnership with John
F. Allen, under the style John F. Allen & Company, for
the manufacture of chewing tobacco, smoking tobacco, and
cigars. Here he showed a brilliant sense of packaging and
salesmanship, relics of his earlier mercantile days. The
firm went into cigarette manufacture in 1874 or 1875,
apparently the first Richmond concern so to do. The cigarettes won honors at the Centennial Celebration in Philadelphia, 1876. So impressive were the cigarette displays,
prepared by this firm and others, that some writers have
thought that the Philadelphia exposition marked the birth
of the cigarette as well as of the telephone! As his business
prospered, Major Ginter devoted much energy to philan-
thropy and civic improvement. In 1888 the establishment,
now known as Allen & Ginter, was producing 2,000,000
cigarettes per day.

Despite individual triumphs in Virginia and the retention by that state of national supremacy in tobacco manufacturing through the decennial census returns of 1880,
the Old Dominion never recovered that proportion of the
nation's business which it controlled in the slavery days.
Indeed, the value of the tobacco produced by the Virginia
factories in 1890 was slightly less than the 1860 figures.
For four years the Civil War had freed the makers of plug
and twist behind the Union lines from Virginia competition. And now to the south of Virginia, Bright Tobacco
offered manufacturing opportunities not missed by energetic Carolinians; to the north, urban markets and immigrant labor invited new enterprises; to the west, the
Burley leaf encouraged the entrepreneurs of the Mississippi Valley, especially those in Cincinnati, Louisville, and
St. Louis.

In time St. Louis became the great center for the manu-

facture of plug tobacco. The Daniel Catlin firm, one of the
ante-bellum establishments, received incorporation in 1876
as the Catlin Tobacco Company, and was known as the
leading tobacco house of the city. The Liggett company,
also established before the Civil War, operated under the
name Liggett & Dausman until the year 1873, when
George S. Myers bought Dausman's share, changing the
name of the business to Liggett & Myers. Then John Edmund Liggett's son, Hiram Shaw Liggett, entered the
business. Newer to the ranks of the great St. Louis establishments was the Drummond factory. About the beginning of the Civil War James T. Drummond, of Scottish
ancestry, invested in a small factory at Alton, where he
was soon joined by his brother, John Newton Drummond.
Then the business was moved to St. Louis. Another new
plant was that of Paul Brown, which finally reached truly
mammoth proportions. When seventeen years of age Paul
Brown began working in a tobacco factory. Next he, like
Reynolds and Duke, engaged in the itinerant trade, selling
tobacco from a wagon. Eventually he moved to St. Louis,
where he built one of the greatest plug factories in the
country, putting on the market the Standard Navy and
other popular brands. Under the general classification of
manufactured tobacco (meaning that cigars and cigarettes
were excluded) Missouri increased its proportion of the
nation's business from 9 to 27 per cent during the decade
of the 1880's, and displaced Virginia as the first tobacco-
manufacturing state of the Union.

In the quarter of a century after Appomattox, the makers of chewing and smoking tobacco were doing more
than creating and then satisfying the tobacco hunger in
millions of American jaws. Those manufacturers below
the Mason and Dixon Line were doing more than proving
the vitality of the New South, important as was that affirmation. The manufacturers of the nation were furnish-
ing the substance of the most absorbing American dream
in the 1870's and 1880's, the progress from rags-to-riches.

The men of St. Louis and Richmond, of Winston and Durham, were exhibits in testimony of the gospel of wealth in the gilded age. Dozens of characters, in good Horatio Alger, Jr. fashion, began in poverty and achieved at least a modest plenty, in some cases great fortunes. The story was better than Carnegie's career from a bobbin-boy to multi-millionaire, for there were more of these little tobacco-Carnegies. In hack and surrey on the streets of the tobacco towns rode men who started out peddling tobacco from covered wagons. And subtly the success of these townsmen filtered throughout their society, and there was obviously a growing self-confidence in those centers where the manufacture of tobacco was a distinctive and dominating vocation. A few manufacturers never outgrew the manner of the haggling wagon-trade, but they were in the minority. And it was the rule rather than the exception for them to develop philanthropic interests with age and wealth. To the year 1890 neither the farmers nor the public had particular complaint regarding the manufacturers. They were hardworking, aggressive, charitable, and freely mingled with the people from whom they sprang. There were still many separate businesses. The farmer could not point to any one corporation which dominated the leaf market; the consumer could not single out any one great manufacturer who arbitrarily set the prices of the finished product.

However, by 1890 a fair amount of concentration had taken place in the tobacco industry. Patrick County, Virginia, provides the classic example of the disappearance of the little enterprises from village and countryside. This was the county of small manufacturers described by Joseph Martin in 1835.[8] There were 18 establishments as late as 1850; 7 in 1860; still 7 factories by 1870. By 1880 Patrick County had only one tobacco factory, that of Green Penn, and it could scarcely be called small, employing 60 hands during its operating season. There had been

[8] See above, page 79.

many of these little establishments before the Civil War, it will be recalled, and revivals were attempted after the conflict. But they did not long survive the competition offered by the larger businesses, and the embarrassment presented by the new internal revenue laws.

For a half-dozen or more years after the Civil War the ex-Confederates attempting to operate small country factories treated the revenue laws with scant respect. Those in remote corners, like their cousins distilling a few barrels of apple brandy, felt that their enterprise was none of the government's business. Some of the "blockaders" in spots not quite so inaccessible did the inspector the courtesy of forging his stencil marks or used over and over again the same revenue stamp.[9] Occasionally a realistic officer, concerned over holding his job when stamp sales were totted, would threaten the rural plug makers with a raid unless they bought ten dollars worth of stamps every quarter. Even the most conscientious manufacturer far from the stamp office found the purchase and accounting an oppressive burden. With improvements in methods of collection, the total revenue went up markedly, reaching over $34,000,000 by 1873, almost $52,000,000 by 1902.

A special subdivision of the trade, the rehandling establishments, had become more important by 1890. These were the concerns which sorted the cured leaf, sometimes stemmed it, and put it in good keeping order for the domestic or foreign trade. Both rehandler and manufacturer who bought his own leaf were soon to benefit from the development of adequate re-drying machines.

The typical factory adopted new machinery, new methods, and new motive power, and became larger. There was more metal and less wood in the presses, more hydraulic and less hand power in the press rooms. A proc-

[9] In the post-bellum period the term *blockader* was used in referring to the illicit maker of tobacco or whisky. There can be little doubt that the word was a carry-over from the Civil War period when a blockader was one who ran the naval blockade and thus circumvented the federal government.

ess was developed to avoid the dangerous open-air drying of the manufactured leaf. Steam power was now generally employed, and by 1890 a few of the modern plants boasted of electric motors.[10] Yet, particularly in the old Virginia area, the labor though now free carried on much the same as formerly in the plug and twist factories, and their characteristic singing continued. The Negro workers in the stemming rooms, prize rooms, or lumpmaking rooms were likely to greet a visitor with a spiritual. So popular was the factory chorus that it became a standard part of the state fairs. Large crowds came to the booths, where laborers demonstrated their ability to sing as they carried on the regular factory operations. Before the turn of the century some establishments were to revolutionize their organizations by introducing automatic plug machines.

More significant than size or mechanization was the new and aggressive attitude of these middle-sized institutions toward obtaining the customer's business. By 1890 the old leisurely days of merchandizing were gone. The manufacturer became alert, and experimental. His major task was to woo and wheedle the retailer and the customer. He showed new concern for trademarks, and the chewing plugs now carried tin or paper tags bearing the name of maker and brand. He adopted highly-colored lithographed "head labels," which were pasted on the tops or heads of the rectangular wooden boxes of chewing tobacco. This popular art represented various themes: flowers, animals, historical events and persons. A few frank egotists insisted that their own pictures be fixed in the labels; proud fathers might send to the lithographer a portrait of some son or daughter to be incorporated in a label. Indicative of a new trend was the girl motif, slightly scandalous for the times but only rarely running to the nudity soon characteristic

[10] After 1890 industrial chemistry offered the trade glycerine as a casing agent to preserve moisture, and saccharin as a sweetener especially valuable for the flavoring of the Bright plug, not as absorptive as the more porous Burley leaf.

of the cigar-box art. Most of the barn-side displays of chewing tobaccos were decent enough, but Homer Croy recalls a Mail Pouch advertisement insufferably suggestive. Bull Durham set a fancy pace for general advertising, both outdoor and in journals, and the new cigarette manufacturers of the 1880's were venturesome. The industry as a whole, however, was no major element in newspaper and periodical advertising, not even approaching the soaps and baking powders.

Though the manufacturers might congregate in local trade organizations,[11] there was much reckless competition in the late 1880's. To establish a new brand the jobber must perforce be given an allotment of tobacco; the retailer presented with a clock or stepladder for every five caddies sold; the jobber's agents and retailer's clerks gently bribed; the consumer awarded a dinner pail or a pocketknife if he saved a certain number of plug tags. These promotion schemes demanded as much or more skill than the process of manufacture, and twice the worry. No wonder that the survivors were usually men trained for years as skilled salesmen.

As though their resources were not sufficiently depleted after the premiums, rebates, and bribes had been distributed, about this time the manufacturers engaged in price wars, which were exhausting and ruinous. Leading plug manufacturers formed trade associations to prevent price cutting among the jobbers, the most important organization being the Manufacturers' and Buyers' Association of the United States. In 1890 there were rumors of a proposed plug combination headed by Lorillard. That year in fact saw the formation of the American Tobacco Company.

[11] The average tobacco town had its local trade association, the Tobacco Association, which included a Manufacturers Board and a Tobacco Warehouse Board. The Manufacturers Board was more successful in fixing the maximum wages to be paid the factory workers in the town that they were in enforcing a fair-trade price at which the finished articles would be sold.

W. DUKE & SONS

Washington Duke belonged to the independent, small-farmer class, the backbone of the ante-bellum South. He and his sons hewed their own wood, drew their own water. In the year his red-headed son, James Buchanan, formed the American Tobacco Company, the grim old man pondered his own early days and ventured the honest boast, "I have made more furrows in God's earth than any man of forty years of age in North Carolina." As a young man he had little in common with the slaveholding plantation group. He owned one houseservant, a girl named Caroline, but no field hand. In the middle of the Civil War, the middle-aged widower was called into the Confederate forces, first performing guard duty then serving in the artillery. After the collapse of the Confederacy, Washington Duke was lodged in Libby Prison in Richmond, then taken to New Bern, where he was paroled. On foot he plodded the one hundred and thirty odd miles to his children.

Duke surveyed his well-looted farm near Durham and took stock of himself and his property. The single coin in his pocket was a fifty-cent piece obtained from a Yankee soldier in exchange for a souvenir five-dollar Confederate bill. His livestock consisted of a pair of blind mules; his farm equipment one ancient wagon. But in one of the outhouses was a quantity of cured Bright Tobacco. Unlike the slaveholding planters, he was not forced to include in his post-war adjustments a new system of labor.

Supplies must be obtained somehow or other, and men were packing their pipes more persistently than before the war. Father and sons examined the tobacco and found it mellowed with age. In a small log barn they beat it out with a grain flail, sifted it through a sieve, packed it in muslin bags. Then, by way of compensation for his lack of a classical education, Washington Duke labeled his product *Pro Bono Publico.* Hitching his mules to the wagon, Washington Duke set out on a peddling trip, bartering or selling his tobacco, and camping along the way. From eastern North Carolina he brought back bacon, sugar, and coin. Other journeys were equally successful, and Duke resolved to keep his "factory" going in conjunction with his farm operations. A log building twenty by thirty feet was erected, then operations were transferred to an abandoned residence, then to a new frame structure built for the purpose. The business was growing. In 1866 the factory produced 15,000 pounds; in 1872, 125,000.

The two younger boys, James Buchanan and Benjamin Newton, or Buck and Ben as they were called, sons by Duke's second marriage, helped on the farm, in the barn, and in the factory. It was a dawn-to-dusk, hard-working, hard-trading life, which left its mark especially on the youngest, James Buchanan. He relished those moments of idleness at the mill while looking at the great water wheels and waiting for the corn to be ground, but moments of idleness were scarce, and holidays even more rare. In the treks over the countryside in a covered wagon with his father he learned the art of good trading, ripened his judgment and developed an instinct for speedy decisions. Perseverance, economy, caution in general were lessons taught by his father, but daring and hard-headedness at the right time he learned for himself. There are reflections of the story of James B. Duke in Elizabeth Pickett Chevalier's novel, *Drivin' Woman* (1942).

Brodie, uninhibited son of Washington Duke's first marriage, joined his father and half-brothers for two or three years, then decided to strike out for himself. Accordingly he moved to the nearby village of Durham in 1869, and set up shop in a two-room establishment on Main Street. Five years later, to diminish the problem of shipping, the hard rock on which many of the country factories were breaking, Washington Duke and his two younger sons shifted their operations from the farm into Durham and together the four Dukes built a roomy three-storied factory with a false front and a genuine bell tower. Within this building, however, for three or four years Brodie Duke carried on his operations on one side of a partition, Washington Duke and the younger sons on the other. W. Duke & Sons was the title, for the two boys were full partners now. It was soon obvious to all that the youngest, Buck, was the most dynamic character of the four.

Needing extra capital for expansion, the Dukes in 1878 sold to George W. Watts of Baltimore a fifth interest and a partnership in the firm for $14,000. Two years later Washington Duke disposed of his share to Richard H. Wright, though before very long Washington Duke returned to the business and in the course of time Wright sold out his share. But all the competitors in town were left far behind by the manufacturers of Bull Durham. James B. Duke had the good sense to acknowledge this fact. "My company is up against a stone wall," said he. "It cannot compete with the Bull. Something has to be done and that quick. As for me, I am going into the cigarette business."

As early as 1854, it will be recalled, Dr. R. T. Trall accused New York society ladies of smoking cigarettes, but the habit developed slowly in America. It took the encouragement of British example to create the necessary momentum. Yet the new smoke was nicely tuned to the nervous, high-speed, urban civilization coming to dominate in America. In Northern cities domestic production started in the 1860's and soon spread elsewhere. By 1880, in addition to Allen & Ginter there were two tobacco factories in Richmond making cigarettes, E. T. Pilkinton & Company, and Oliver & Robinson. Production in all American factories in that year amounted to only a little over half a billion cigarettes, most of which were manufactured in New York City.

Thus, although the cigarette had only a tenuous hold

on the American public, its production was by no means a new thing, even in the South, when, in 1881, James B. Duke introduced its manufacture to W. Duke, Sons & Company. As superintendent of the cigarette department the Dukes employed one of the pioneer cigarette-rollers in the United States, J. M. Siegel, a Russian Jew, who had learned the craft in the government factories of Kovno. He had worked in London; then he came to New York and rolled cigarettes for Goodwin & Company. He and his brother David, who was soon chosen to supervise the cigarette manufacture of W. T. Blackwell & Company (the makers of Bull Durham), trained local artisans in the manner of rolling cigarettes.[12] An important leader in the labor force at the Duke plant was Moses Gladstein, who had learned the trade in Kiev, Russia, emigrated, then worked for awhile with the cigarette-manufacturing firm, Kinney Brothers, of New York City.

In their operations the hand workers used tobacco about the same as that put up for pipe smoking, except that instead of being granulated the leaf was shredded in a so-called "long-cut" to insure easier rolling. The usual system in the factories was for several laborers to gather around a table (somewhat as the workers at their lump-making tables in the plug factories), and to work on individual marble squares, deftly rolling the cigarettes, which were pasted with a mixture of flour and water. A roller completed some 2500 or 3000 per day, but in most factories the day began early and lasted late.

The Dukes made their boldest stroke for new business in 1883, when Congress on March 3 voted to reduce the cigarette tax, effective July 1. They promptly cut their prices in half and received a certain fraction of orders at the new rate even before the lower schedule went into effect. Their packs became the cheapest on the market.

[12] The Siegels, J. M. and David, withdrew from the Duke and Blackwell establishments and set up for themselves, producing an article sold under the name Cablegram.

Sensing that the future belonged to those who could most effectively employ labor-saving devices, the Dukes acquired on a royalty basis the Bonsack cigarette machine, invented by young James Bonsack of Virginia. The Dukes and Bonsack's mechanic, William T. O'Brien, improved its operation, and when set up in Durham in 1884 it made 120,000 cigarettes per day, approximately fifty times the rate of hand rollers, and only three machine-tenders were needed. There were other cigarette machines, but the Bonsack proved the best of the early attempts, and the Dukes were the first to produce the machine-made cigarettes on a large scale.[13] The immigrant cigarette rollers of Durham complained, as had displaced hand workers for a century. Most, either from weakness or from philosophy, soon reconciled themselves to the new order and returned to the North. Some stayed in Durham, establishing a mercantile group. Among the latter was Moses Gladstein.

The Dukes were determined that no surplus stock would accumulate in their warehouses. Well before the coming of the Bonsack machine the Dukes had developed a talent for selling cigarettes. Or was it Edward Featherston Small who made the market for the cigarettes? One school of thought, of which Small himself was the center, held that, in a sense, Small was the creator of the Duke fortunes. Small, once described by the company as "our able & fearless lieutenant," was about as smooth a drummer as could be found in any hotel lobby between the Great Lakes and the Rio Grande. For example, after finding Atlanta lukewarm to his goods, Small threw aside the Indian motif in his advertising, and scattered over the city pictures of Madame Rhea, the then popular French actress, with her arm on a pedestal containing a box of Duke's cigarettes. Druggist Joe Jacobs decided to order over three-quarters

[13] A Bonsack machine was used in the Allen & Ginter factory in Richmond before the Dukes acquired their model. The Blackwell concern of Durham soon obtained a machine. By 1884 there were fourteen Bonsack machines in operation, seven in Europe and seven in America.

of a million cigarettes. According to Small, Henry W. Grady of the *Constitution* offered him ten dollars for Madame Rhea's letter of authorization.

Out in St. Louis, when retailers ignored him and dashed off to wait on the ladies, Small advertised for a saleslady and chose a petite widow, a Mrs. Leonard. Whereupon the newspapermen presented him with thousands of dollars worth of free publicity regarding the first and only lady selling cigarettes.[14]

In the home office the dominant mood was a fierce determination to develop the market, to keep out encroachers, and to get the competitor's business if possible. But there were moments of fun. Even Washington Duke's sobriety was occasionally leavened by touches of humor. The most famous story in connection with this facet of the elder Duke originated during a trip to Europe. In some castle he claimed the privilege of sitting in a chair reserved for the nobility by explaining that he was the Duke of Durham! There were masculine jests when Small wrote of his employment of the thin-lipped and red-headed Mrs. Leonard. Her photograph caused great excitement around the water bucket and gourd dipper in the factory office. An office letter, presumably written by Watts, went out to Small with this report: "The photograph of Mrs. Leonard just received; she has made a mash on both Mr. W. Duke and Capt. Link. You need not be surprised any day to have one or both of these gentlemen reach St. Louis

[14] But Small liked good living, and his expenses went up. Though his major district was now in the West, he wanted to keep his family in Atlanta, using expense money for his trip back home. One day when he and James B. Duke were on a pleasure trip to Coney Island, Duke abruptly told him to move his family to Cincinnati. Small's reply, as he later recorded it, would have incensed the city fathers of Cincinnati. "The devil I will! I won't raise my children in that smokey town." This was in the year 1888. Small left Duke and started working for Allen & Ginter. When Allen & Ginter shortly thereafter merged with the Dukes and others to form the American Tobacco Company, Small left the cigarette business, though he kept his belief that he had created more cigarette customers than any man living.

to succeed you. We think the old gentleman would leave
today but he is not certain whether or not she is a widow.
(W. Duke says it don't make any difference whether she
is a widow or not.)" Captain Link, "the old gentleman,"
was Isaac N. Link, who, in 1881, sold his smoking brand
Dime Durham to the Dukes and entered their services as
bookkeeper.

Realizing that the cigarette was, first of all, an urban
smoke, James B. Duke in 1884 established a branch in
New York City, where he took a cheap room, toured the
tobacco shops and jobbers' offices to talk with clerks and
customers. He set up a loft factory on Rivington Street not
far from the Bowery, and entered on a daring system of
advertising and premiums. For the moment Major Lewis
Ginter, of Allen & Ginter, was the acknowledged genius
of cigarette advertising; his reputation was world-wide.
Rival cigarette manufacturers put into the packages puz-
zles, maps, and pictures of rulers, boats, flags, actors and
actresses in numbered sets. Of course the collectors attempted to finish out their sets of cards. Allen & Ginter
distributed a fancy colored booklet showing various types
of architecture, ranging from the Egyptian Temple of Kom
Omboo to the various state capitols. But the Temple of
Kom Omboo hardly had the appeal of the folding album
in color entitled, "Sporting Girls," distributed by W. Duke,
Sons & Company in exchange for 75 certificates, obtained
only through the purchase of 75 boxes of cigarettes. However, the bulk of the advertising by cigarette cards was
"educational."

American factories produced over a billion cigarettes in
1885; by 1890 two and a half billion. Five major firms
competed for the cigarette business. Out in front now was
W. Duke, Sons & Company, with plants in both Durham
and New York City. Next came Allen & Ginter of Richmond. The Kinney Tobacco Company of New York City,
W. S. Kimball & Company of Rochester, New York, and
Goodwin & Company of Brooklyn followed in that se-

W. Duke & Sons

TOBACCO--HAND CULTURE AND TREATMENT.

ABOUT 1880

1. SOWING SEED
2. HILLING
3. TRANSPLANTING
4. LAYING BY AND TOPPING
5. WORMING AND SUCKERING
6. CUTTING AND STICKING
7. HOUSING
8. STRIPPING AND TYING
9. PACKING

quence. The fervid rivalry in cigarettes ran parallel with the competition in other types of tobacco products.

Great combinations were appearing in many different fields; the immediate cause in most cases was to escape ruinous competition. The classic combination was created by John D. Rockefeller and his associates, who brilliantly but ruthlessly mastered their competitors and by 1882 controlled 90 per cent of the nation's oil. Enthusiastic imitators sprang up. Before 1890 there were formed the cottonseed-oil trust, the linseed-oil trust, the cordage trust, the lead trust, the whisky trust, the sugar trust, and others. The industrialists basked in the prevailing laissez-faire philosophy, and read approvingly Andrew Carnegie's freshly-published *The Gospel of Wealth* (1889).

THE TOBACCO EMPIRE

In the middle of the "fierce trade war" of the late 1880's, to use the Supreme Court's description of the rivalry in cigarettes, James B. Duke, who was spending about $800,-000 per year on advertising, proposed that the five leading cigarette firms combine. Allen & Ginter held out for awhile, but representatives of all the concerns eventually agreed to form the American Tobacco Company, incorporated in New Jersey under date of January 31, 1890. The corporation was capitalized at $25,000,000 and assumed the properties of the merging companies. Tangible assets were $5,000,000, of which $1,825,000 was represented by notes of the stockholders. Although the appraisal of goodwill and brands is a controversial matter, the Bureau of Corporations estimated overvaluation at $12,500,000. Stock was allotted: $3,000,000 preferred and $4,500,000 common to Allen & Ginter; the same to W. Duke, Sons & Company; $2,000,000 preferred and $3,000,000 to Kinney Tobacco Company; $1,000,000 preferred and $1,500,000 common to W. S. Kimball & Company; the same to Goodwin & Company. James B. Duke, who had just passed his thirty-third birthday, was elected president.

The officers welded into a unit the supervisors, buyers, and salesmen of the constituent companies, promoting talented and loyal men, discharging others. Rigid cost accounting was introduced, jobbers' profits were cut, leaf was bought from the farmers rather than from dealers and speculators. The new organization purchased exclusive use of the Bonsack machine for a period of years. Many old tobacco firms were bought; some were closed, their former owners having promised in the sales agreement not to re-enter the business for a specified number of years. The combination was immediately profitable, even on a basis of the inflated capitalization. Earnings for the first year exceeded $2,500,000, and the nation began to speak of the "cigarette millionaires."

At the time of the chartering of the American Tobacco Company in 1890, the merging companies controlled about nine-tenths of the nation's cigarette manufacture, and something less than a tenth of the smoking tobacco. Twenty years later the group of men headed by James B. Duke had extended its operations to include approximately four-fifths of the entire industry, save cigars.[15] Purely for purposes of convenience the history of the combination may be divided into eight phases.

(1) *The plug-tobacco war and the formation of Continental.* The American Tobacco Company originally controlled only an inconsequential fraction of the plug business, which at that time was the most important branch of the industry, save cigar making. The leading plug firms were Liggett & Myers, Lorillard, and Drummond. American soon entered this field, buying among other companies the National Tobacco Works of Louisville. In 1893

---

[15] By 1910 the proportion of the annual output controlled by the combination was: plug 84.9%, smoking 76.2%, fine cut 79.7%, snuff 96.5%, cigarettes 86.1%, little cigars 91.4%, cigars 14.4%.

Duke approached rival plug manufacturers but failed to bring about a consolidation. In the plug-tobacco war which soon developed, American ran up its share of the plug business to a fifth of the national total, but the campaign cost over $3,000,000, a loss which it could sustain only because of its profits on the cigarette business. After American bought the two St. Louis plug establishments, Drummond Tobacco Company and Brown Tobacco Company, various competitors, with the conspicuous exception of Liggett & Myers, fell into line. Lorillard was bought out, but Pierre Lorillard was allowed to retain separate corporate organization of his firm. In 1898, under the auspices of the American Tobacco Company, the Continental Tobacco Company was formed, primarily to handle plug tobacco. The American Tobacco Company passed the Drummond and Brown companies on to Continental, as well as such old firms as P. H. Mayo & Bro. James B. Duke was elected president of the new organization, and American tobacco men were in a majority on the board of directors. In January, 1899, the American Tobacco Company bought the old and important Catlin Tobacco Company in St. Louis, makers of fine-cut and smoking. Catlin received $550,000 and retired.

(2) *The threat by Union and entrance of the financiers.* Then the American-Continental companies saw their position threatened by a lusty grouping of tobacco firms called the Union Tobacco Company, organized in 1898 by the financiers Thomas F. Ryan, P. A. B. Widener, A. N. Brady, W. C. Whitney, Thomas Dolan and others. They had managed to buy National Cigarette and Tobacco Company, the only independent cigarette manufacturer of any importance, to purchase most of the stock in Blackwell's Durham Tobacco Company, manufacturers of Bull Durham, and to obtain an option on Liggett & Myers, the major independent plug producer and largest single plug plant in the United States. After pondering this menacing spectacle, James B. Duke, head of the American-Continental

group, came to terms with Ryan and associates. Accordingly, in 1899 the American Tobacco Company bought the Union Tobacco Company, and Continental bought Liggett & Myers. O. H. Payne figured in the syndicate managing this last transaction. These deals marked the entrance into the combination's management of Wall Street financiers. They began to assume directorates vacated by the original organizers of the American Tobacco Company. The old cigarette men, Ginter, Kinney, Kimball, and Emery (Emery had owned Goodwin & Company), dissatisfied with the program of expansion, were selling out. In the year 1899, the Reynolds firm at Winston was reorganized, two-thirds of the stock going to Continental. Reynolds explained to sympathizers, "Sometimes you have to join hands with a fellow to keep him from ruining you and to get the under hold yourself."

(3) *American Snuff*. The American Snuff Company, formed in the year 1900, was essentially a merging of the snuff business of American and Continental, the Duke-led organizations, with George W. Helme Company and the Atlantic Snuff Company. The last-named corporation was itself a combination formed in 1898.

(4) *A new American Tobacco Company*. In 1901 a holding company, Consolidated Tobacco Company, was created under the laws of New Jersey.[16] In the light of the Northern Securities Case, Consolidated appeared illegal; therefore Consolidated, Continental, and American in 1904 merged into a new company with the old basic name, American Tobacco Company.

---

[16] Duke, Brady, Payne, Ryan, Widener, and Whitney were accused of manipulating the exchange of Consolidated bonds for the apparently less profitable common stock of American and Consolidated in such a way that they now had majority control of Consolidated, and therefore of American and Continental. According to their critics, they revised the corporate structure in order to garner most of the new and tremendous profits soon to come with reduction in internal revenue duties and the maintenance in general of the old prices for the finished products. American and Continental shareholders who had accepted bonds vowed that they had been deceived by the "insiders," privileged to see trends much better than they.

(5) *The cigar business.* Because of the use of hand labor and the possibility of creating efficient small organizations with little capital, nothing approaching monopoly took place in the cigar industry. Nevertheless it was a business of great importance; by 1904 the value of cigars manufactured in this country equaled 60% of the total value of all types of manufactured tobacco. In New Jersey in the year 1901, American (this the older company), Continental and a large manufacturer, Powell, Smith & Company, formed the American Cigar Company, which became the greatest single manufacturer of cigars in the United States. Yet it never controlled more than one-sixth of the cigar manufacture of the nation.

(6) *United Cigar Stores.* In 1901 the American Tobacco Company acquired a controlling interest in the United Cigar Stores, created by the brothers George J. and Charles A. Whelan to operate retail outlets of a modern character.

(7) *Foreign markets.* The combination controlled almost 100% of the cigarette export business, which by 1900 equaled approximately a third of the entire domestic production. Most were very cheap cigarettes, sent to the Orient. Tobacco factories were built or purchased in Canada, Australia, and Germany. The American Tobacco Company in 1899 by acquiring Murai Brothers Company (Limited) began cigarette-making in Japan, but soon, 1904, the Japanese government established a monopoly and purchased the plants. At one time about 20,000,000 pounds of American leaf were being exported annually to be manufactured in these establishments abroad. Handicapped by the high British duties on manufactured tobacco, Duke decided to buy a factory within Great Britain, and to manufacture and sell within the tariff walls. Accordingly, in September, 1901, Ogdens, Ltd., an important Liverpool corporation, was purchased. Thirteen frightened British manufacturers scurried to merge their resources into one huge corporation, The Imperial Tobacco Com-

pany, for the purpose of defending their markets from the Yankee invaders. Imperial encouraged the islanders to buy-British, while Ogdens advertised and distributed premiums in American fashion. The trade war went on for a year, at the end of which time a peace was negotiated. The American company was to have the United States and Cuba to itself; Imperial, the United Kingdom; a new corporation, British-American Tobacco Company, was to take over the general export business of both. In this last-named corporation the Americans were to own two-thirds of the stock, the British one-third.

One of the most valuable assets obtained by British-American was the person of James A. Thomas, the cigarette-missionary from North Carolina. In 1888, as a twenty-two year old Rockingham County boy, Thomas had been packed off to Australia, on a salary of $53.33 per month and expenses, to match the products of Motley, Wright & Company against the goods of the Camerons and others. After several years of success he returned to the United States, accepted employment from Liggett & Myers, and again went to the Orient. As the corporate changes took place in this country, Thomas moved into the American Tobacco Company, thence to British-American. As company manager of British-American for India then for China, he blended American aggressiveness with concessions to Oriental manners, and won great markets.

(8) *Miscellaneous properties.* The combination pushed into the corners of the tobacco trade, producing by 1911 about 95% of the licorice paste made in this country, making bags for smoking tobacco, manufacturing boxes and numerous incidental items for the trade.

In the development of the great industrial empire, James B. Duke showed an uncanny aptness in picking clever men from the companies purchased. Percival Smith Hill, Philadelphian managing Blackwell's Durham Tobacco Company, went with Duke when his firm was taken over by American. Duke soon made him vice-president, in charge

of sales. In the course of time Duke also obtained the
services of Percival S. Hill's son, George Washington Hill.
From the Hills, father and son, from the Dulas, and
from many others Duke received that single-minded de-
votion to the American Tobacco Company which he
wanted. R. J. Reynolds was another type. He was assured
that he could continue to run his own business, and he
took that promise with aggressive seriousness. The Winston firm had its own brands, its own blends. After 1905
there was not a representative of the American Tobacco
Company on the Reynolds board. When the Reynolds firm
entered the smoking tobacco markets with its great Prince
Albert trademark, there was friction with the supposedly
dominant organization. Whatever the details, it is certain
that Reynolds had been left enough liberty of action to
strain at the leash. The Reynolds firm, when announcing
to its salesmen the news of the Supreme Court decision of
1911 dissolving the combination, began its circular, "News
of Freedom . . . In keeping with the spirit of '76—the
Court declared that the American," etc.

But ill-humor inside the corporation was nothing as
compared with the antagonism outside. Competitors,
whether frustrated by price wars or by their own out-
moded methods, cursed the trust; organized laborers hated
the company for its open-shop policy; leaf speculators and
dealers saw their profits disappear as the company adopted
direct buying from the farmers; farmers claimed that the
company dictated prices because of its monopoly position,
and that prices were ruinously low; investors vowed that
"insiders" milked the ordinary stockholders in the shifting
corporate organizations.

Key individuals saw their investments pyramid in won-
drous fashion. The stock received by the firm of W. Duke,
Sons & Company, in 1890, had a par (and market) value
of $22,000,000 by 1908. Furthermore, by that date divi-
dends had totaled $16,732,500. Thus the market value of
the securities and accumulated dividends on the stock by

1908 totaled nearly $39,000,000, a sum 156 times the value of the Duke interests in 1885, 557 times the value of those interests in 1878.

In terms of money and markets, the companies headed by James B. Duke had achieved amazing success. The formula was (1) aggressive leadership backed by vast capital, (2) the most up-to-date machines, (3) the most modern devices of salesmanship, and (4), at times, the most primitive techniques of meeting and destroying competition. Most of the tobacco men had learned competition in the rough school of the 1880's. Strategy included local-price cutting, the development of "fighting brands" which were given away or sold at a loss, secret control of so-called "independent" concerns, special consignment agreements involving discrimination by dealers against competitors, the obtaining of promises from former competitors not to re-enter the tobacco business. Most important of all was the simple method of buying rival firms. The Supreme Court, in that famous sentence which depresses the grammarian and tantalizes the economic historian, declared, "Indeed, the history of the combination is so replete with the doing of acts which it was the obvious purpose of the statute [the Sherman Act] to forbid, so demonstrative of the existence from the beginning of a purpose to acquire dominion and control of the tobacco trade, not by the mere exertion of the ordinary right to contract and to trade, but by methods devised in order to monopolize the trade by driving competitors out of business, which were ruthlessly carried out upon the assumption that to work upon the fears or play upon the cupidity of competitors would make success possible."

Of all the curious turns in this hostility to the tobacco combination none is more paradoxical than the fact that the most violent opposition appeared to come from the farmers. Of all groups convinced that their interests ran counter to those of the combination, the agrarian group probably had the least valid reasons for concentrating the blame for its plight on the trust.[17] But an angry spirit on the part of the farmers was quite understandable. For a generation they had suffered from general deflation, from high interest rates, from high railroad rates, from high warehouse charges, and often from overproduction. They had seen new wealth and new comforts in the city, while their position remained at best static, at worst one of actual regression. It was a period of rural inferiority feeling, and the farmers were shamed to hear that the hick-farmer was the butt of jokes in the city vaudeville. The farmers had vainly sought relief in the Granger movement, the Farmers' Alliances, and Bryanism. When the tobacco farmers rebelled, the storm center was the Black Patch region of Kentucky.

[17] Henry Seager and Charles A. Gulick, Jr., in their *Trust and Corporation Problems* (Harper & Brothers, 1929), do not hesitate to condemn the combination as grievously negligent in its obligations to various groups, including the shareholders and the buying public. "But it seems to us that other evidence presented by the Bureau of Corporations makes its conclusion on the combine's domination of the price of cigarette leaf extremely questionable if, indeed, it does not overthrow it." Further, "From these facts it seems to us only fair to conclude that, although there were doubtless instances in which the growers of particular types of leaf or growers in given localities were paid lower prices than unrestrained competition would have established, the extent and effectiveness of the trust's power to dictate prices to the producers of its chief raw material have been 'greatly exaggerated.' "

[Chapter 6]

THE AGE OF CONFLICT

NIGHT RIDERS VERSUS HILL BILLIES

In the Nabb schoolhouse neighborhood of Caldwell County, Kentucky, there lived an inconspicuous tobacco farmer, Robert L. Hollowell, his wife, Mary Lou, and their eleven-year-old son, Price. One night early in May, 1907, they were awakened by a volley of shot fired by forty men who were closing in on the house. The child begged that his mother, already wounded by glancing shot, be harmed no more. But she was pushed down and kicked. Then she fainted. Robert was stripped, beaten with buggy whips until the blood ran, and warned to leave the state. Robert had refused to join the Dark Tobacco District Planters' Protective Association, and Mary Lou had testified to the grand jury against the Night Riders, the militant wing of the Association.

The Hollowell affair was one incident in the tobacco war which raged for several years during the first decade of the twentieth century, coming to a focus in the western tobacco district of Kentucky and Tennessee, the area known as the Black Patch. In essence the turmoil originated in the low prices the farmer was receiving for his tobacco, a situation which he blamed on the tobacco trust and foreign monopolies. The Association and the Night Riders saw as their enemies not only the monopolies but the Hill Billies, those farmers who would not join the Association.

In time-honored cadence the struggling tenant farmers sought remedy from the price decline by adding another thousand hills and another child to work them. Thus the crops were over-large, and sometimes the quality poor. But the growers counted these as nothing compared with the operations of the buyers. No matter what the published prices, the farmers in some districts swore that the actual average was only two cents: three cents for ordinary leaf, two cents for lugs, and one cent for trash, or "Three, Two and a Cussin'."

Grasping at straws, the farmers petitioned Congress to repeal the special tax of six cents per pound levied on the cured natural leaf, vainly hoping that they could thereby revive the planter-to-consumer business which was of some importance before the tax was first levied in 1872. A bill to abolish the tax passed the House but died in the Senate Finance Committee, bossed by Senator Nelson W. Aldrich, chairman.

The farmers in the western district of Kentucky and Tennessee gathered five or six thousand strong at Guthrie, Kentucky, in September, 1904, to form the Dark Tobacco District Planters' Protective Association. The leading spirits were Felix G. Ewing, called the "Moses of the Black Patch," and Charles H. Fort, president of the Association. The plan was to re-dry the tobacco, then sell it directly to the manufacturers by sample. In the campaign for signing up the growers, Colonel Joel Fort, President Fort's brother known as the "Tennessee Warhorse of the Black Patch," presented to appreciative audiences rip-roaring, hair-raising, side-splitting performances, denouncing the trust, promising better things through the Association, and ridiculing the Hill Billies.

Naturally these Hill Billies were wooed by the buyers for the American Tobacco Company and foreign monopolies, who refused for some time to do business with the Association. As members were signed up by the Association, a record was kept of the farmers who refused to join. At the September, 1905, meeting of the Association a Dr. David A. Amoss suggested that only those business and professional men who supported the farmer in this struggle should be patronized. Thus life in the Black Patch was being split asunder.

The high prices offered the Hill Billies by buyers caused so many Association farmers to break their contracts that for awhile in 1905 it seemed as though the Association would perish. Then a Tennessee wing of the Association, calling itself the Possum Hunters Organization, resolved to visit and warn non-member farmers and agents of the American Tobacco Company. When Congressman A. C. Stanley urged the Association to stop the "night riding," the militant members dropped the name Possum Hunters and called themselves Night Riders.

Eventually about ten thousand men joined the Night Riders, who organized formally in 1906 as a secret fraternal order under the name The Silent Brigade or The Inner Circle, with passwords, challenges, and signs. Blindfolded initiates swore a solemn "Blood Oath," and then learned the ritual of identification: An exchange of whistles, two long and one short. Then, *Sentry*, "Who goes there?" *Answer*, "The Seven Wonders." *Sentry*, "I wonder."

For the sake of appearances the Association officially condemned the Night Riders, but there was, of course, an intimate and interlocking relationship. According to former Night Riders the commander-in-chief of the order was this Dr. David A. Amoss, who had spoken at the 1905 meeting. In his late forties when he founded the order, he was of solid, stocky build, with a florid face, square brows, deep eyes, and a free-growing moustache. He was exceedingly popular in his neighborhood, and took a leading part in his church, often supplying in the pulpit and giving especially well-liked funeral orations. He believed his cause was morally right, since the law allowed no ordinary recourse against the buying monopolies.

The first open exhibition of the power of the Night Riders occurred in the early morning of December 1, 1906, when a small army of masked men captured the town of Princeton, Kentucky, and destroyed two factories. On December 7, 1907, Hopkinsville, Kentucky, was taken. In this raid, the high-water mark of Night Rider activity, the Riders burned a tobacco factory and a large warehouse operated by independent tobacco dealers and agents of the Italian Regie. A pursuing posse from the town shot and killed one young man of the Night Riders. Dr. Amoss suffered a scalp wound.

Many Hill Billies had their plant beds scraped, their barns burned, and their homes shot at. In the raid on Eddyville, Kentucky, February 16, 1908, the Night Riders wore out twelve buggy whips in beating twelve men, four white and eight Negro. The whites had spoken against the Riders, and the Negroes were lashed as a sort of warning to all other colored people in the community. The worst whipping given to any man by the Night Riders was administered one Henry Bennett, an independent dealer of Dycusburg on the Cumberland River who had publicly denounced the Riders. They visited him the night of February 3, 1908, tied him to a tree, beat him with thorn limbs, shot off part of his right ear, and roweled him with a steel spur. In Metropolis, Illinois, two years later he was buried under a stone lettered "Killed by the Night-Riders." Metropolis, the refuge of many of those whipped or threatened, became known as the Night Rider Refugee Colony. Minor activities of the Night Riders lasted from 1906 on into the year 1909, but the most active years for whippings, warnings, scrapings, and destruction of property were 1907 and 1908.

The Hill Billies had no organization to correspond in strength and discipline with that of the Night Riders. Ben H. Sory of Adams, Robertson County, Tennessee, an agent for the Italian Regie, led the opposition to the Association for awhile and earned the title, "King of the Hill Billies." A local leader was one Henry Wilson, known as the only Hill Billy who actually shot it out with a Night Rider. He moved from the countryside into Princeton and took some job with the Henrietta Opera House. On the night of March 26, 1908, after the evening performance of the burlesque show, "Isle of Spice," Wilson saw Orbie Nabb, a Night Rider, coming up the steps. Actually it appears that Orbie had a date with one of the burlesque girls, but Wilson thought he was coming after him, pulled out his pistol, killed the Night Rider, then fled the state.

The Night Riders and the Association seemed to be having it all their way by 1908. The American Tobacco Company and foreign agents were buying from the organized farmers at over eight cents per pound average, and the Association was handling nine-tenths of the 100,000,000 pounds produced the previous growing season in that part of the Black Patch where it was operating. In general, the Night Riders controlled the state courts in the tobacco district. The only persons convicted in the state courts of destroying plant beds had been two Hill Billies, tenants of the Hollowells who had been beaten in May, 1907.

Then judicial lightning struck. The Night Riders were astonished to discover that they were now defendants in the federal courts. It was the Hollowells again! After the Night Rider episode of May 1–2, 1907, they left the state and, on the advice of John G. Miller, Sr., a leading attorney, settled in Indiana, establishing residence in Evansville. On March 2, 1908, in the federal courts Miller filed suits for the Hollowells against thirty Kentuckians. When, in the United States Circuit Court at Paducah in April, 1908, the case came to trial, the defendants displayed an amazing collection of alibis. The outcome was a hung jury. Judge Evans called for a new trial and impaneled a jury from distant sections. The new verdict awarded damages to Robert Hollowell.

Many suits were instituted by victims of the Night Riders, and these federal suits must be considered the major reason for the decline of Night Riding. Among other factors were better leaf prices and the efficient use of soldiers in both Kentucky and Tennessee. Furthermore, federal prosecution of the tobacco trust had begun, and Kentuckians finally forced the repeal of the six-cents tax on natural leaf in 1909. The provision was part of the Payne-Aldrich Tariff Act. The Planters' Protective Association suffered from dissensions among its leaders, and from the desire on the part of its membership to sell by loose leaf auctions. The decline in membership was perceptible in 1909; by 1915 the Association was dissolved.

In the attempt to remedy the price situation, blamed on the American Tobacco Company and foreign buyers, cooperatives were formed elsewhere, happily with less violence than in the Black Patch. Some of these cooperative efforts were instituted under the sponsorship of The American Society of Equity, which had been organized in Indianapolis, December 24, 1902, for the purpose of improving the prices of all agricultural products. Several of the independent growers in the Blue Grass were whipped and their barns painted with pictures of gallows. Zealous organization men were charged with at least one murder. George Graddy of Woodford County, whose tobacco barn had been burned by the Burley Night Riders, determined on protective measures. He planted dynamite around a new barn, but a drove of hogs rooting about beat the Night Riders to the dynamite; seven pigs were blown up.

In the Eastern districts various organizations were formed to cope with low prices. The most vital society in the Bright Tobacco area was established under the leadership of Samuel C. Adams, who, with a program of redrying and storage for sale to the American Tobacco

Company, instituted an organization eventually going under the title The Mutual Protective Association of the
Bright Tobacco Growers of Virginia and North Carolina.
In the course of time this association declined, partly because of the attack on Adams by leaf dealers.[1] Internal
friction, distaste for violence, suspicion that officers were
making too high salaries, opposition by the combination,
higher prices and the fact that anti-trust suits had begun
all contributed to the disappearance of the pools.

"BLOOD MONEY" AND THE TRUST-BUSTERS

The arch-enemy of the American Tobacco Company on
the Atlantic seaboard was Josephus Daniels of Raleigh,
Democratic leader and editor first of the *State Chronicle*
and later of the *News and Observer*. Daniels believed that
the combination was manipulating prices to the misery
of the farmers. Furthermore, the Dukes were Republicans
and the Republicans, supported by the Negroes and allied
with the Populists, elected Governor Daniel L. Russell in
1896. In his hammering campaign against the American
Tobacco Company, Daniels was aided by Colonel John R.
Webster of *Webster's Weekly*, Reidsville. When Washington Duke, more sensitive to criticism than were the sons,
was in Raleigh one day on a Sunday School picnic, he
stopped by the *State Chronicle* to cancel his subscription
because of this unrelenting censure. Daniels asked him
into his office and they talked for about an hour. According to Daniels, writing many years later: "And then almost in a whisper Mr. Duke said, 'I am just talking to
you now; I don't want you to say anything about this. I

[1] One of the most important phases of the attack on the American Tobacco Company was the opposition from leaf dealers or speculators, middle-
men who had made good profits in the pre-1890 era but less as the American
Tobacco Company did its own buying. Indeed it has been suggested by a
recent and competent scholar, Dr. Nannie M. Tilley, that the clue to much of
the rural opposition to the American Tobacco Company was the leadership
offered by disgruntled leaf dealers.

wish Buck had never put us into the company and that we could carry on our business like we used to do it. We were making lots of money and did not have any criticism."

The Dukes, Washington, Benjamin, and James Buchanan, even in those early days had become the principal support of the little Methodist institution in Durham, Trinity College. Some of the anti-American Tobacco Company sentiment found expression in opposition to Trinity College and its policies. In 1894 there came to the presidency of Trinity College a dynamic young South Carolina minister, John C. Kilgo. Washington Duke was particularly fond of Kilgo, who seemed more like one of the circuit riders of his youth than a college president. Kilgo was forced to fight against the accusation that his institution was fattening on "blood money" wrung from suffering farmers, and that the school was profiting from the cigarette evil.[2] In his term of academic office there were two great controversies associated with Trinity College which bear on the story of the tobacco corporation and of the Dukes: the Kilgo-Clark Controversy (or as it is sometimes called the Kilgo-Gattis Controversy), and the Bassett Affair. It should be noted here that the principal characters, Kilgo, Clark, Gattis, Webster, and Daniels were all Methodists.

The Kilgo-Gattis lawsuit, which was for many years in the courts, grew out of antagonism between Kilgo on the one hand and Judge Walter Clark on the other. Judge Clark charged Kilgo, among other deeds, with opposing the silver men (this being in the bumptious 'nineties) and of sycophancy towards the Dukes, of visiting Washington Duke and in a public speech saying in substance, "My Lord Duke, Give Us Money and Your Name Shall Be

[2] Kilgo himself was very fond of tobacco. Concerning his love for the leaf the following story is told: On one of his trips to South Carolina the president of Trinity was approached by an old lady thoroughly opposed to the use of tobacco. "I understand you use tobacco," she said. He answered, "Yes, Sister! I smoke it, I chew it, and if you know of any other good way to use it, tell me!"

Exalted Above All Names." Clark also accused Kilgo of
having had a bad reputation in South Carolina. The trustees pronounced the charges unfounded. Because the Rev.
Thomas Jefferson Gattis had been cited as Clark's authority for the statements as to Kilgo's South Carolina reputation, Kilgo made a speech treating Gattis severely,
including references to "a pious smile, a religious walk,
and a solemn switch of the coat tail." Whereupon Gattis
sued Kilgo and three trustees, including Benjamin N.
Duke, the trustees having printed the speech as part of
their proceedings. The Kilgo-Gattis suit started in 1899
and ended only in 1905 with the dismissal of the case.
For a long time in North Carolina any alumnus of old
Trinity would get fighting mad at the taunt, "Eruditio et
Religio et Cherooto et Cigaretto," a perversion of the motto
of Trinity College, born in the fertile legal mind of the
Honorable Cyrus B. Watson and presented by that gentleman in sarcasm during the celebrated Kilgo-Gattis Controversy.

Large in the annals of academic freedom is the Bassett
Affair, which can only be understood in the framework
of the circumstances already outlined. John Spencer Bassett, Professor of History at Trinity College, turned his
inquiring eye not only to the Southern problems of the
past but to those of the present. For the October, 1903,
issue of the newly-founded *South Atlantic Quarterly*, published at Trinity College, he wrote an essay entitled, "Stir-
ring Up the Fires of Racial Antipathy." In his article he
had occasion to remark, in commenting on the various
classes of the freedmen: "A man whose mind runs away
into baseless optimism is apt to point to Booker T. Washington as a product of the negro race. Now Washington
is a great and good man, a Christian statesman, and take
him all in all the greatest man, save General Lee, born in
the South in a hundred years; but he is not a typical negro.
He does not even represent the better class of negroes."

The Raleigh *News and Observer* made sensational presentation of the article, claiming that Southern leaders had been slandered. The Lenoir *Topic* referred to Trinity as having been "tobacconized, Kilgoized and republicanized." According to *Webster's Weekly*, "Our point is that Duke's money has made it possible for Trinity's teacher of history to fling defiance in the face of Southern ideals and call on the young men of the South to forsake the faith of their fathers and worship at the shrine of a negro."

The college community in general, while professing no agreement with Bassett, affirmed his right to say what he thought. Bassett submitted his resignation to the board of trustees, but members of that body, particularly Benjamin N. Duke, had been hearing from wise men, who indicated the rare opportunity for proclaiming the gospel of freedom of speech. "God help us all to a little courage," wrote Walter Hines Page, alumnus of Trinity College. Furthermore the board of trustees was in no mood to be impressed by any criticism led by the *News and Observer* and *Webster's Weekly*. Accordingly the trustees refused to accept Bassett's resignation.

Opposition to the American Tobacco Company was voiced on occasion by muckrakers and Progressives. Ray Stannard Baker, in his series, "The Railroads on Trial," (*McClure's Magazine*, 1906) took time out when explaining what the Southern Railway had done to Danville, Virginia, to condemn the American Tobacco Company as being partly responsible for the hardships of the town and surrounding country. "The tobacco trust keeps the price just high enough to tease the grower into continued production, but not high enough to yield him any appreciable profit beyond the bare payment for his labor." As to financing, "And no trust has watered its stock more notoriously than the tobacco trust. It is today earning dividends on enormous amounts of paper securities." But the Dukes caught only a sprinkling of birdshot from the muckrakers. Armour, Morris, and Swift had the siege guns of Upton Sinclair; Rockefeller, Rogers, and Flagler were forced to bear with Ida Tarbell.

"The history of the Tobacco Trust is, perhaps, the most amazing in all the chronicles of high finance," said Albert J. Beveridge in the Senate on May 14, 1909. The speech was the beginning of a dramatic attack on the American Tobacco Company, one phase of the insurgency under Taft. This revolt eventually split the Republican Party, and thereby insured the election of Wilson in 1912. While the revenue measure later known as the Payne-Aldrich Tariff was being debated, the Senator from Indiana reviewed the recently-published Report of the Commissioner of Corporations on the Tobacco Industry and decided that the tobacco trust was exploiting the people and, in effect, defrauding the government, principally because of the concessions made to the tobacco manufacturers in the revenue bill of 1902. In carefully-prepared speeches presented to the Senate in May and in June, 1909, Beveridge proposed amendments to the pending revenue bill which would increase the tobacco tax and make illegal the distribution of coupons, a device successfully used by the American Tobacco Company in fighting its competitors.

His bill, said Beveridge, would increase the revenue by almost $21,500,000. "But this amendment does more than provide this needed revenue; it corrects an injustice to the American people, which has lasted for nearly eight years." He blamed much of the excessive profits of the American Tobacco Company, "perhaps the most compact and effective private monopoly in existence," on the prophetic vision of the financiers with reference to the revenue bill of 1902. "In 1901–2 this increased tobacco tax [authorized in 1898] was removed, *but the short-weight packages of tobacco were continued by the very law that removed the tax.* Nor did the manufacturers restore the larger packages of tobacco after the tax had been removed; neither did they reduce the price." In effect, said Beveridge, the public continued to pay the tax, which in the eight years would have amounted to over $184,000,000, but the tax went to the tobacco trust. And it was at this same time, 1902, Beveridge reminded his hearers, that the anti-coupon provision in the Dingley Act had been removed.

With bland good-humor Beveridge refused to allow either the temperate questioning of La Follette or the heckling remarks of "Pitchfork Ben" Tillman to lead him into charges of corruption against the Congressmen of 1902. Beveridge's amendment was severely mutilated before its inclusion in the revenue measure. The anti-coupon provision was eliminated, the increase in taxation was much less than that proposed, and the size of the package was further reduced. The reduction in the size of the package, complained Beveridge, took the new tax off the trust and put it on the people.

The legal proceedings under which the properties of the American Tobacco Company were to be distributed had already been instituted under Beveridge's close friend, Theodore Roosevelt. On July 19, 1907, the government began suit against the American Tobacco Company as primary defendant, five accessory defendants, and fifty-nine subsidiary defendants, charging them with combination in violation of the Sherman Anti-Trust Act. The special prosecutor was James C. McReynolds from Tennessee. Duke claimed that he never bought rivals in order to do away with competition, that he had created no monopoly, that his purchases were investments. He had wanted a complete line of tobacco products. He personally thought foolish the secrecy surrounding ownership of the so-called independents, but he had never given false information as to ownership of businesses. He had simply told people it was none of their business. The Circuit Court decision of November 7, 1908, while holding most of the defendants guilty, pleased neither side. Both appealed to the Supreme Court, where the case was argued January 3, 4, 5, 16, 1910, and then reargued January 6, 9, 10, 11, 12, 1911, before the verdict was given on May 29, 1911. Chief Justice White read the verdict, judging the Company a combination in restraint of trade and therefore a violation of the Sherman Anti-Trust Act of 1890.

The legal historian finds this case and the slightly earlier Standard Oil Case of special significance in the history of constitutional law for their promulgation of the "rule of reason" in the interpretation of the Sherman statute. The Court held that the act was designed to prevent *unreasonable* combinations in restraint of trade. The "rule of reason" excited reformers who believed the Sherman law was being interpreted into a jelly. Taft commented that "the phrase 'the rule of reason' brought out the condemnation of everybody of demagogic tendencies prominent in politics . . ."

The Court ordered a dissolution and a restoration of competition, leaving the Circuit Court of Appeals in New York to manage the details. Associate Justice Harlan not only objected to the "rule of reason" theory as a gloss on the Sherman Act, but wanted the Supreme Court itself to prepare the details of the dissolution of the tobacco corporation. The reorganization was planned in a series of conferences attended by representatives of the Court, the attorney general, and the tobacco company. The formal decree of the court was issued November 16, 1911. It seems paradoxical that it was Duke himself who sketched many of the key plans for reorganization. But it was a difficult problem, this unscrambling the egg. Finally established were sixteen successor companies to handle the property of the old American Tobacco Company. There were four large general competing companies: a corporation was to continue under the name, American Tobacco Company; Liggett & Myers Tobacco Company and P. Lorillard Company would be set up; the R. J. Reynolds stock would be released. Other properties were relinquished and competing companies were established in the tin foil, licorice paste, and snuff fields.

Attorney General Wickersham and President Taft approved the plan, but McReynolds vigorously opposed the arrangement. Louis D. Brandeis and Felix H. Levy, representing the independent manufacturers, argued that by virtue of common ownership of stock in the successor companies the twenty-nine individual defendants would have effective control of the successor companies; that the successor companies were too large and dominant within their specialties; that the United Cigar Company should be divided. Efforts to persuade the Supreme Court to review the decree failed, for the two parties to the suit, American Tobacco Company and the Department of Justice, were satisfied. Josephus Daniels was furious at the type of decision given, and printed the name of the approving Attorney General, Wicker*sham*.

The case became something of an issue in the presidential election of 1912. Beveridge never made a better speech than the keynote address to the psalm-singing convention of the Progressive Party. "It was not a convention at all. It was an assemblage of religious enthusiasts. It was such a convention as Peter the Hermit held. It was a Methodist camp meeting done over in political terms," wrote the *New York Times* correspondent. Beveridge asked, "What good does it do the laborer who smokes his pipe to be told that the courts have 'dissolved' the Tobacco Trust and yet find that he must pay the same or a higher price for the same short-weight package of tobacco?" And Roosevelt, nominated by acclamation, declared that the carrying out of the dissolution of Standard Oil and American Tobacco was a farce. "There never was a more flagrant travesty of justice . . ."

The Democratic platform of 1912 condemned the way the dissolution was enforced. Wilson was favorably impressed by McReynolds' refusal to agree with the Attorney General in the final settlement of the tobacco case. Although Wilson supposedly had never heard of the Tennessean before this development, he decided to select him as Attorney General in his own cabinet.

THE LITTLE WHITE SLAVER

In the quarter of a century between the surrender at Appomattox and the formation of the American Tobacco Company the cry against tobacco was reduced to a whisper. To be sure, there were occasional stones flung at demon nicotine. Every now and then some crossroads pope issued a bull against John Rolfe and his evil works, and, as in an earlier period, the anti-liquor forces engaged in sporadic tobacco sniping as a sort of extra-curricular activity. John B. Gough, the reformed drunkard and famous temperance lecturer, would pull from his pocket a square of tobacco, smell it as though it were a fragrant rose, cry out, "Ah, you black devil, I love you," and fling the plug away. The only notable attack was launched in 1868 by James Parton, who paused in his manufacture of biographies long enough to deliver his sentiments on *Smoking and Drinking* in three essays: "Does It Pay to Smoke?" "Will the Coming Man Drink Wine?" and "Inebriate Asylums." As Godkin's *Nation* pertly remarked, Parton, as usual, was more interested in his writing than in what he was saying, he did not know much about his subject, "and we confess to having a fear that, whether he knew much or little, he would still talk on with equal courage." [3] John Fiske, the historian and philosopher of later fame, then in his twenties, made the liveliest rebuttal in a little book which he titled, *Tobacco and Alcohol. I. It Does Pay to Smoke. II.*

[3] *The Overland Monthly* was particularly irritated by Parton's "impertinent falsehood" in alleging that woman counted tobacco her rival in man's affections. "Shocking as it may seem to Mr. Parton, the young Prince of the maiden's vision generally comes to her dreams driving a fast horse and smoking a cigar." To prove the point Bret Harte's journal cited nicotine evidence in Charlotte Brontë's *Jane Eyre* and *Villette*.

The Coming Man Will Drink Wine. Fiske's saucy comments were reviewed with some approval by Charles W. Eliot, about to be offered the presidency of Harvard, despite his youthful age of thirty-five. Eliot, by the way, took a middle-ground stand on the tobacco question some forty years later.

"All hostility to tobacco seems nowadays to be concentrated on cigarettes," remarked *Harper's Weekly*, August 12, 1905. It was a statement which would have been true fifteen years earlier, and many years later. The greatest warrior in the anti-cigarette campaign was Lucy Page Gaston, a gaunt midwestern crusader, who, after a period of training on the official W.C.T.U. publication, moved over into the anti-tobacco movement in the 1890's, then practically unorganized. Concentrating on Chicago, she displayed tireless and ingenious generalship. In imitation of the cold-water armies of a previous generation, children wore pins, sang songs, disported banners, lined up for parades, preached sermons to their elders, jeered at smokers, and, with a belligerency born of righteousness, even snatched the burning brands from the mouths of sinners. Though aimed primarily at the use of cigarettes by boys and young men, the campaign reached hardened adults, spread into wider and wider circles, and threw momentary fright into the tobacco interests as city council and state legislature yielded to reform pressure and passed ordinance and statute forbidding sale of cigarettes to minors and in some cases to adults.

Domestic consumption of cigarettes actually showed a regular downward trend during the years 1897–1901 inclusive, a decline generally credited to the anti-cigarette legislation as well as to increased taxation. James B. Duke later admitted that he was then afraid the paper cigarette would be destroyed. He took out insurance in the form of purchasing several establishments manufacturing the all-tobacco cigarettes, or little cigars as they were more often called. And this threat of unfavorable laws was one

reason why he resolved to obtain for the American Tobacco Company a larger share of the nation's plug business.

In sundry cities free cures were offered penitent suf-
ferers. The program appears to have been a combination
of a wholesome diet, a mouthwash of silver nitrate solution, and gentian root for chewing when the tempter was
near. Some gentlemen of the Chicago press, smelling a
good story, posed as cigarette victims anxious to mend
their ways. They went through the "clinic," and had for
their pains a deathly sick spell when they returned to their
cigarettes! Among the most widely advertised patent medi-
cines was No-to-bac Remedy, which boasted one of the
popular business slogans of the day, "Don't tobacco-spit
your life away." [4]

Clergymen, educators, and businessmen could be found
in the groups applauding Miss Gaston and her crusade.
In that most famous of all attempts to explain the social
gospel, Charles M. Sheldon's novel, *In His Steps*, the editor, Edward Norman, decided to purge his newspaper of
tobacco as well as whisky advertisements. Of the church
groups, foremost in recorded condemnation were the
Friends and the Methodists. At their yearly meetings the
Friends made frequent but not intemperate references to
this "evil of great magnitude," and monthly meetings were
urged "to labor in a spirit of love with their members who
use or grow tobacco." At the general conference of 1900
in Chautauqua tobacco was censured, and some of the
Friends were concerned lest tea-drinking also became a
vice. At the general conference of 1902 in Asbury Park,
the grant of public money for use in research concerning

---

[4] Students of the muckraker movement will remember the following lines
on advertising in Upton Sinclair's *The Jungle:* "It was quite touching, the
zeal of people to see that his health and happiness were provided for. Did
the person wish to smoke? There was a little discourse about cigars, showing
him exactly why the Thomas Jefferson Five-cent Perfecto was the only
cigar worthy of the name. Had he, on the other hand, smoked too much?
Here was a remedy for the smoking habit, twenty-five doses for a quarter,
and a cure absolutely guaranteed in ten doses."

growing and curing tobacco was condemned. Most perspicacious, in those days of Horatio Alger, Jr., was the superintendent of the anti-tobacco commission, who at the general conference of 1910 in Ocean Grove asserted before the Friends, "It is my belief that the economic argument should be urged against tobacco. The American boy cares less about the color of his lungs or the action of his heart and cares more about his chances to make money and his 'getting on' socially among his comrades and with his employer."

The General Conference of the Methodist Episcopal Church (North) held at Cincinnati, May 1–28, 1880, resolved that preachers seeking admission to the conference were expected to answer in the affirmative the question number 19, "Will you wholly abstain from the use of tobacco?" Apparently there had been attempts to administer this prohibition even before that date. The contrasting opinion of northern and southern branches of the Methodists on the tobacco question in the Reconstruction Period has been suggested as the real reason for the failure of reconciliation attempts in that denomination immediately after the Civil War. A prominent Southern Methodist explained to Moncure Daniel Conway, "Those Northern Methodists forbid their preachers to smoke, and are engaged in a general crusade against tobacco. That is our Southern staple, and our churches are largely supported by it." But the Southerners gradually moved nearer the Northern position. By 1910 the Committee on Temperance recommended to the General Conference that applicants for the preaching position be "urged to abstain" from the use of tobacco. Thus the way was prepared for the 1914 Conference which, in effect, adopted the Northern Methodist rules prohibiting candidates for the ministry from using tobacco.

Even the great found that they could not escape some stand on the tobacco question. One day Mrs. Carry Nation, who shares with George Washington (or rather with

Parson Weems) the honor of making famous the lowly hatchet, walked into Miss Gaston's private office and was amazed to see on her walls a picture of Theodore Roosevelt. Mrs. Nation said he was a cigarette smoker; Miss Gaston refused to believe it; Mr. Roosevelt's secretary, on receiving a request for information, vowed that TR never touched the weed. Perhaps the fact that Roosevelt on occasion pocketed a gift cigar may have caused the false reports.[5] Like Roosevelt, Woodrow Wilson abstained from the use of tobacco, but, curiously enough, while president of Princeton he had earned a reputation as a great tobacco chewer! In speaking extemporaneously Wilson once referred to the distinctive and individual flavor of rural opinion, generated and expressed around the hot stove at the country store, where there was talk and checkers and chewing tobacco. Consequently he received through the mail many samples of tobacco and in the newspapers much erroneous publicity.[6]

Despite the efforts of the reformers in the period from the Civil War to World War I, annual per capita consumption of tobacco turned sharply upwards, moving from something less than five pounds (some estimates run to less than three) to almost seven. Use of the leaf was, in general, restricted to adult males. However, elderly housewives in mountain coves and piney-land creek bottoms smoked clay pipes as their mothers and grandmothers had done before them. Also Bohemian ladies flourished special small-sized cigars, and a few daring maidens puffed cigarettes while waiting their turns at croquet. Immigrant

[5] As Theodore Roosevelt recorded in his *Autobiography*, "On one occasion one of my prize-fighting friends called on me at the White House on business. He explained that he wished to see me alone, sat down opposite me, and put a very expensive cigar on the desk, saying, 'Have a cigar.' I thanked him and said I did not smoke, to which he responded, 'Put it in your pocket.' He then added, 'Take another; put both in your pocket.' This I accordingly did. Having thus shown at the outset the necessary formal courtesy, my visitor . . ." etc.

[6] As to the presidents, Grant was a great user of tobacco, Cleveland was a famous chewer, McKinley was very fond of cigars. Taft smoked for awhile but is supposed to have stopped.

and Negro women used some snuff; factory girls of New England enjoyed the powder compounded with winter-green and other flavors.

Demand for snuff increased under the advertising stimulus of the American Snuff Company. Long before the turn of the century snuff, applied between gum and cheek, had become merely a variant form of chewing tobacco, and, with the spread of *dipping*, manufacturers flavored some brands of snuff like plug. Chewing tobacco in the orthodox forms reached its peak per capita consumption in the year 1890, then retreated before numerous ordinances against indiscriminate spitting.

The swing to smoking tobacco during and immediately after the Civil War was perhaps the most sudden change in tobacco habits during the last half of the nineteenth century. This movement can never be accurately charted because of inadequate statistics for the early part of the period. Undoubtedly the more general distribution of the friction match contributed to the popularity of the pipe and the cigar. The cigar was accepted as the symbol of wealth, substance, and solidity, traits triumphant in the gilded age. The American paid more actual cash for his cigars than for all the rest of his tobacco. In the year 1904 each dollar received by the American tobacco industry from sales represented 2 cents for snuff, 5 cents for cigarettes, 33 cents for chewing and smoking tobacco, and 60 cents for cigars.

DRUMMERS AND CIGAR MAKERS

On the American scene there loomed that distinctive character, the cigar salesman, the best of whom, when on the road, were great showmen. Some wore high silk hats and frock-tail coats. Most sported double-breasted vests, across which flashed lodge emblems on massive gold watch chains. The cigar drummer entered the dark little tobacco shop, grasped the hand of the dealer, slapped him on the back, and passed along the latest stories. The heavy accordion-type sample case was unstrapped, specimens redolent of vanilla and rum rolled under the nose, a couple cut open to prove the genuine long filler. Then salesman and retailer proceeded to the important part of the business, the premiums that went along with the cigars: so many pictures of actresses and prize fighters as display cards, a wall lighter, cigar cutters, and matches, not to mention a mantel clock if the order were sizable. He served a necessary purpose in that stage of cigar merchandising, this hearty animal with his sample case, and he gave to his employer value received for his twenty or twenty-five dollars per week. Representing the larger manufacturers and jobbers, the drummer tried to break down the customary loyalty to a local product, for each city ward usually had its own small cigar manufacturer, who depended on neighborhood patronage.

In the late nineteenth and early twentieth century, cigars were manufactured in central shops, in tenement houses, and in scattered small enterprises where the shop owner was a principal laborer. The dividing line between the various types was not always clear, but certainly the average establishment during this era was of modest proportions. The labor was largely manual, the capital required was small, and new businesses could be readily set up. The better-known brands were, naturally, produced in those establishments large enough to invest in a bit of advertising. Dozens of men gathered in the central shops, creating a distinctive sort of industrial life. In a large room these craftsmen, many of them foreign-born, worked around their tables. They joked and laughed and read. There was good fellowship, good talk, good singing, and some serious reading aloud by one of the fellows with a clear voice. For his part the reader could claim toll from his listeners, in order that his piecework pay would not suffer.

Into this industrial-fraternal atmosphere came a sociable young man of Dutch-Jewish ancestry, who with his parents had left the city of his birth, London, and come to the United States in the middle of the Civil War. Acutely aware of man and nature, his senses tingled with appreciation for the things of this earth. "I loved the touch of soft velvety tobacco and gloried in the deft sureness with which I could make cigars grow in my fingers, never wasting a scrap of material. Body, senses, mind, and heart were thrilling with the wonder of life." So recalled Samuel Gompers. He found the shop life agreeable and informing. He became president of his local trade union.

As a union man and as a humanitarian, Gompers in the 1880's was disturbed by the lot of immigrant cigar makers, who, especially in the Bohemian district in the East Side of New York City, suffered from typical sweated conditions. According to the Danish-American journalist and reformer, Jacob A. Riis, writing in his classic volume, *How the Other Half Lives*, first published in 1890, the tenement of the Bohemian quarter was "made the vehicle for enforcing upon a proud race a slavery as real as any that ever disgraced the South." Probably most of the Bohemians of New York were cigar makers. As Riis described the situation, "The manufacturer who owns, say, from three or four to a dozen or more tenements contiguous to his shop, fills them up with these people, charging them outrageous rents, and demanding often even a preliminary deposit of five dollars 'key money'; deals them out tobacco by the week, and devotes the rest of his energies to the paring down of wages to within a peg or two of the point where the tenant rebels in desperation."

The ash-barrels in Seventy-first and Seventy-third Streets, filled with tobacco stems, attest the work. The smell filters into the hallways. ". . . every room here has its work-bench with its stumpy knife and queer pouch of bedtick, worn brown and greasy, fastened in front the whole length of the bench to receive the scraps of waste."

Some rollers had struck and obtained $4.50 per thousand. "Asked how long he works, the man says: 'from they can see till bed-time.' Bed-time proves to be eleven o'clock. Seventeen hours a day, seven days in the week, at thirteen cents an hour for the two, six cents and a half for each!"

Of course the organized cigar makers, working in the central shops, wanted to wipe out this tenement sweated labor, for humanity's sake and for their own protection. Posing as a book agent, Samuel Gompers tramped the dark hallways of the tenements until he learned the truth. He urged a young man in the New York Assembly to sponsor a bill doing away with the sweated industry in the tenements. As recounted by Gompers, Theodore Roosevelt "told me that if the conditions described really existed he would do everything in his power to help to secure the passage of the bill. Although he was what we called a 'silk stocking,' his aggressiveness and evident sincerity appealed to me."

One of a committee of three appointed to investigate the conditions in the tenement houses, Theodore Roosevelt found conditions which provided a turning point in his ideas about society and government. Actual investigation shocked the young silk stocking. In Roosevelt's words, "These conditions rendered it impossible for the families of the tenement-house workers to live so that the children might grow up fitted for the exacting duties of American citizenship." Some quarters were quite satisfactory. "In the overwhelming majority of cases, however, there were one, two, or three room apartments, and the work of manufacturing the tobacco by men, women, and children went on day and night in the eating, living, and sleeping rooms —sometimes in one room. I have always remembered one room in which two families were living. On my inquiry as to who the third adult male was I was told that he was a boarder with one of the families. There were several children, three men, and two women in this room. The tobacco was stowed about everywhere, alongside the foul bedding, and in a corner where there were scraps of food. The men, women, and children in this room worked by day and far into the evening, and they slept and ate there. They were Bohemians, unable to speak English, except that one of the children knew enough to act as interpreter."

Roosevelt championed the proposed legislation, and spoke to the Assembly on the evils of turning homes into workshops. Finally passed in 1884, the law was declared unconstitutional in 1885 by the state Court of Appeals, which propounded one of the most shameful sentences in the long history of the American courts. "It cannot be perceived how the cigar maker is to be improved in his health or his morals by forcing him from his home and its hallowed associations and beneficent influences, to ply his trade elsewhere."

Admitting that the judges were "well-meaning men," Roosevelt declared that "they knew nothing whatever of tenement-house conditions . . ." "They know legalism, but not life. . . . It was one of the most serious setbacks which the cause of industrial and social progress and reform ever received." This experience was the beginning of Theodore Roosevelt's education as a reformer, and gave him a lasting suspicion of the courts. And these doubts led naturally to his idea of popular recall of judicial decisions, part of his Progressive program which made it impossible for many of his old friends to rally round the Bull Moose group.

But changing tools and machines did what men's consciences would not. By the end of the century new techniques in the manufacture of cigars rendered less feasible the fully handmade article in the cheaper lines. To quote the words of the New York State Tenement House Commission, appointed by Roosevelt in 1900 when he was governor, "Through the invention of a machine called the suction table, the manufacture of cigars is being gradually removed into factories; and it is the opinion of those best acquainted with the trade, that it will soon disappear from the tenement houses."

New tools were, indeed, creating a change in the industry. At first the equipment was quite elementary, consisting of a board, a knife (known as a "Cuban blade"), and a gauge for measurement. The basic operations were four: (1) making the "bunch" the inner, central part of the cigar, of *filler* tobacco; (2) rolling the *binder* leaf around the bunch, giving the cigar its shape; (3) placing the *wrapper* or outside leaf on the cigar, an operation of particular importance because the sales depended largely on appearance; and (4) finally pasting the head and cutting the cigar to the right length.

The changes that occurred by way of new equipment may likewise be divided into four parts: (1) the *cigar mold* was introduced. This was a labor-saving device, a wooden arrangement in which bunches were pressed. The mold multiplied the productivity of the laborer by approximately two. By 1880 the molds were generally accepted. (2) Then came the *bunch-making machine*, first hand-operated then power-driven. It prepared the bunches for the mold and could utilize short filler or scrap. (3) A *stemming machine* was introduced about 1890. (4) Also about 1890 there came the *suction table* to aid the roller in cutting the wrapper. Despite all the new tools and machines, many cigars were made wholly by hand, virtually all were made partly by hand, and a long-filler, power-driven bunch machine was yet to be invented. The cumulative effect of these developments in tools and machinery was to diminish the importance of the skilled craftsman, who naturally but fruitlessly fought the innovations.

The labor organizations of the cigar makers indirectly dictated the major trends in American trade unionism for more than half a century: from them came the men, Strasser and Gompers, and the ideas, realistic day-by-day programs based on a federation of skilled craftsmen. Local societies were common in the 1850's, especially in the northeast, but not until 1864 was the national organization born. The National Cigar-makers' Union (in 1867 re-named the Cigar-makers' International Union of America) barely survived the Panic of 1873. In the year 1877 Adolph Strasser, German cigar maker earlier identified with socialism in America, was elected president. Leader of the local union in New York City at that time was Samuel Gompers. Before the year was out the union was defeated in a great strike in New York City directed against the then growing menace of tenement-house production. Strasser and Gompers reorganized their union on English models, and formulated plans which meant, in essence, acceptance of the capitalistic system but improvement of labor's place in that system. The Knights of Labor, centralized, idealistic, and unskillful, showed mushroom-growth but mushroom-strength, and fell from its own weaknesses and the rivalry of the Strasser-Gompers groups. In 1879 Strasser called for a federation of all trade and labor unions, and presented a calendar of concrete reforms. In 1881 the federation was formed, soon strengthened and renamed the American Federation of Labor. Gompers led the A. F. of L. for almost forty years. Membership of the Cigar-makers' Union itself rose from less than 4,000 in 1880 to 44,000 in 1910, though the organization never enrolled more than half those eligible.

A period of cut-throat competition in the 1880's and 1890's was succeeded about 1900 by numerous mergers of cigar manufacturers. As noted in connection with the story of the American Tobacco Company, the American Cigar Company was formed in 1901 but it never controlled over one-sixth of the national output.

Though cigar manufacturing was distributed over all the nation, Pennsylvania and New York took and held the lead. Ohio, Massachusetts, Illinois, New Jersey, Maryland, and California produced considerable quantities. A number of Cuban factories moved to Florida as a consequence of Cuban political instability and because of high American duties on the finished products. Yet, for years, over 90 per cent of all imported cigars came from Cuba. In 1890 manufacture of cigars in the United States for the first time exceeded four billion per year; 1901, six billion, 1906, seven billion. There was little increase thereafter.

The manufacturers of cigars used both native and imported leaf. The foreign varieties came from Sumatra, Cuba, and Puerto Rico, and in small quantities from the Philippines and Brazil. The East Indian leaf was introduced into the United States in 1876, and within a half-dozen years became of painful importance to domestic growers of wrappers. Aroused by the competition of the Sumatran leaf, the Connecticut Valley farmers in 1882 persuaded Congress to increase the duties on imported wrappers, effective the following year. Special import arrangements following the Spanish-American War stimulated the purchase of cigar leaf from Cuba and Puerto Rico. Leaf shipments from the Philippine Islands to the United States were small, though there was some increase in the number of manufactured cigars coming from that area.

In the era from the Civil War to the First World War the major cigar leaf areas were four. The first three were the familiar ante-bellum centers: the Connecticut Valley (Connecticut and Massachusetts), the Miami Valley (Ohio), and Lancaster County (Pennsylvania). The fourth was made up of sundry districts in Wisconsin, which had grown practically no tobacco before 1860. The cigar leaf produced in New York and Florida was of less commercial importance.

In general, the tobacco grown in the old free states was used in the making of cigars; that grown in the old slave states in the manufacture of chewing tobacco, smoking tobacco, cigarettes, and snuff. Little or none of the Northern tobacco was exported; foreign markets were of cardinal importance to Southern growers. Although Northern tobacco suffered from the importation of rival types, no such threat confronted the Southern leaf. In an average year, for every pound of tobacco grown in the North there were five in the South. The Northern farms were only lightly affected by the Civil War and Reconstruction; not so the Southern plantations.

BRIGHT LEAF AND BURLEY

After Appomattox, there were epic social upheavals in the tobacco-producing areas of the once-Confederate States. Old families declined, new ones emerged. This is the theme of such fictional treatments as Ellen Glasgow's *The Deliverance: A Romance of the Virginia Tobacco Fields*. When evil days descended on the old ruling class and the Emancipation Proclamation became a reality, the tobacco plantations decreased in size. And they had never been as large as the cotton plantations.

On both types of plantations appeared the sharecrop system, in origin a common-sense solution of pressing problems, in development the generator of a dozen problems for every one it solved. Experimental efforts at wage labor failed. The newly-freed Negro, untrained in the ways of capitalism and drawing no distinction between the words emancipation and idleness, was prone to wander off after pay day until his money was spent, leaving the sensitive tobacco crop to languish and perish. And the wages offered by destitute planters were interpreted by the Negro and his Northern sponsors as merely a more economical form of slavery. An occasional ex-slave bought a small farm, but as a class the freedmen remained landless.[7] After a season of confusion and desperate expedi-

---

[7] In his efforts to obtain land, the Negro was sometimes the butt of cruel jokes by those who he thought were his new friends. "As Moses lifted up the serpent in the wilderness, so have I lifted five dollars out of this nigger's pocket," read the deed given to an ignorant Albemarle county (Virginia) Negro by one of these impostors.

ents, during which the planter pined for the good-old-days of settled labor and the ex-slave dreamed of his "forty acres and a mule," two factors became clear: the once slaveholding tobacco planter had his land, which needed tilling, but he had little money for hiring labor; the Negro wanted land for working, but he had little money for paying rent. Therefore the planter furnished the land, the Negro his labor, and they divided the crop. This was the sharecrop system in its elemental form. Perhaps the most popular of the numerous formulas was the fifty-fifty division: the planter (landlord) supplied the land, buildings, tools, work stock, livestock feed, taxes, half the fertilizers and half the marketing cost; the cropper (tenant) furnished labor, half the fertilizers and half the marketing cost. In general, the planter gave close supervision to the cropper's labor.[8]

But bread and meat for the cropper were necessary. Local merchants who had found enough credit to operate were willing to advance the rations (pronounced rătions in both tobacco and cotton areas) at a suitable mark-up over cash prices, provided payment was insured by a crop lien. Sometimes the landlord owned a plantation store ("commissary" was often the term applied) or a crossroads grocery, and he himself advanced the supplies throughout the year. Or the landlord might guarantee the sharecropper's credit with the merchant. The system had grievous defects; there were chances for deceit and corruption by all parties. Whites as well as blacks became sharecroppers and the system fixed itself on large sections of the country. Yet at no time did it embrace more than a fraction of the farms, perhaps not more than a third, and always held the upper South less tightly than the lower South. Landlord and merchant considered tobacco

[8] By way of distinction from the sharecropper, the share tenant had more control of his operations, usually supplying a larger fraction of the costs of production, obtaining a larger fraction of the yield, and arranging for his own credit.

a good credit crop: it was not easily destroyed, stolen, or hidden.

The two main types of tobacco used in the modern cigarette, Bright (or flue-cured) and Burley, were both in a sense "discovered" in the middle third of the last century. However, neither was originally developed for the cigarette. Bright Tobacco was essentially the result of (1), a shift in culture from the heavy loams of middle Virginia to the relatively infertile light grayish soils of the North Carolina piedmont border counties, plus (2), a new curing technique. The lemon-yellow tobacco was clearly recognized before the Civil War, especially in Caswell County, North Carolina, and Pittsylvania County, Virginia, as a leaf mild in taste, handsome in appearance, and greatly to be desired by manufacturers.[9] But the great boom in Bright Tobacco came in the post-war days, when its expansion, as described by the usually prosaic Census Bureau, was "one of the most abnormal developments in agriculture that the world has ever known." And its culture was indeed paradoxical. The highly-treasured Bright Tobacco grew only on thin soils, once classified as shamefully poor. Presently county argued with county as to which had the more poor land. Immediately after the Civil War there was despondency in most farm areas of the South; not so in those parts of Virginia and North Carolina to which Bright Tobacco was spreading. With

[9] In an excellent piece of historical research, Dr. Nannie M. Tilley has exploded the widely-held myth to the general effect that Bright Tobacco, unannounced, sprang suddenly in 1852 or 1853 from the soils and curing barns of Eli and Elisha Slade of Caswell County. Dr. Tilley not only emphasized the evolutionary nature of Bright Tobacco, but proved that the dramatic curing on the Slade farm with wood and charcoal occurred in 1839, that there were four Slade brothers, that their names were Thomas, Abisha, Elias, and William, that the curing occurred on the Abisha Slade farm while being supervised by a slave, Stephen, and that Abisha Slade was the noted cropmaster for Bright Tobacco in the 1850's. Dr. Tilley's conclusions were presented before the Southern Historical Association in 1937, then incorporated in her monumental volume, *The Bright-Tobacco Industry: 1860–1929* (Chapel Hill, 1948).

reference to the meaning of Bright Tobacco a commentator of the 1880's remarked: "Alongside the decline in wealth in old areas of prosperity there are other instances in the South of the growth of thrift and wealth in communities which were poor before the war, but no other section presents such wonderful changes. Comfortable farm-houses have taken the places of rude log-cabins, excellent and convenient barns and outhouses exhibit the new thrift, and new life has been infused into all classes and into both races."

The culture ballooned out from the Caswell-Pittsyl-vania area, dominating the Old Belt of Virginia and North Carolina, then, with the decline in cotton prices, spread into eastern North Carolina during the 1880's, and down into South Carolina the following decade.[10] The extension of Bright Tobacco into South Carolina was greatly en-couraged by the *News and Courier* of Charleston, which distributed seeds, gave instructions, employed professional demonstrators.

For expansion into new areas expert advice was indeed needed. An offspring of a union between very special soil types and a narrowly controlled culture, Bright Tobacco developed into an exacting and distinctive routine. Before the end of the century the plant beds were covered with cloth instead of branches. This innovation not only pro-tected the seedlings against the weather but, much more important, meant partial victory over the fly or flea beetle. More and more commercial fertilizers were used to hurry the crop along, to increase yield, to decrease loss from worm and frost, and to make feasible growth in soils other-wise unserviceable.[11] New market requirements encour-

10 This was tobacco's second introduction into South Carolina. See above, page 56.

11 The time merchant, who in many instances dictated agricultural pro-cedures, gave little encouragement to long-range programs of soil conser-vation, crop rotations and the like, but he welcomed the application of quick-acting commercial fertilizers to the market crops. Time merchants and warehousemen began selling the fertilizers, and obviously their profit on the sale had something to do with their enthusiasm for the article.

aged the process known as priming; growers stripped the leaves from the stalk as they ripened rather than cut the whole plant as had been the custom in the old days, and as continued to be the routine in other areas.[12] The most radical change occurred in curing, when it was discovered that a system of flues was more economical of wood and more controllable than the charcoal-and-wood process used in the Slade formula for Bright Tobacco. This flue-curing was the re-introduction of a method developed in Virginia as early as the 1820's. Priming meant fewer houses, for the curing barns could be used in effective sequence. After being cured, the tobacco was now bulked (packed) for a period before being stripped (from the sticks to which the leaves had been tied during the curing) and sorted. In the 1870's and 1880's the great authority on the cultivation and curing of Bright Tobacco was Major R. L. Ragland of Hyco, Virginia. Experiment stations, established after the Hatch Act, contributed sound advice to farmers.

The first major use of the new Bright Tobacco was for plug wrappers, but soon this low-nicotine content leaf achieved great popularity as a smoking tobacco. Even more significant was its adaptation to cigarettes. Before long "bright canary yellow" had a world-wide reputation. In 1885, Wm. J. Young, manager of the Cameron plants in Australia, remarked: ". . . we have been put to more bother and expense in satisfying our customers with 'gold leaf' and 'Cigarette' tobacco than the business is worth, but we are forced to supply it or lose trade for other goods." Growers of Bright Tobacco for the plug market, particularly those farmers specializing in fancy wrappers, suffered from the competition of Burley leaf.

White Burley (or simply Burley as it was later called), was a rare biological phenomenon known as a sport, a

[12] The way had been paved for this system of priming the whole crop in the ante-bellum period when in some areas the damaged lower leaves, the lugs, had been harvested before the stalk was cut.

sudden deviation from a standard type. As well as can be determined today, the mutation was first noticed during the year 1864 in Brown County, Ohio, among plants grown from seeds obtained across the river in Bracken County, Kentucky. In 1866 a couple of hogsheads sent to Cincinnati brought a fancy price. The leaf was immediately popular with manufacturers as a plug filler because of its highly absorptive properties, which enabled it to soak up a tremendous quantity of liquid sweetenings and sauces. In 1867 White Burley won prizes at various fairs. With this publicity the new leaf rapidly spread over Brown and Bracken Counties, displacing dark tobaccos along the river, and then in the 1870's moved southward over the Kentucky Blue Grass, where hemp was once the staple. Its production was neither as laborious nor as expensive in equipment as Bright Tobacco. Stalk-cutting was the harvesting method; and air-curing was satisfactory as a preparation for market. Through new plant varieties and changes in cultural techniques both Bright and Burley crops became milder as the years went by.

Of course the earlier types, especially the dark fire-cured shipping leaf, continued to be grown in large quantities, and all over the nation numerous small patches were cultivated for home consumption. The yield of the garden plots was estimated in the millions of pounds. These crops were usually cured by sun and air, and used for pipe-smoking. A minor fraction of the garden tobacco was made into crude chewing twists.

To the south of Maryland, a state which kept its old hogshead system of selling, loose-leaf warehouse auction sales during this period largely supplanted the ante-bellum marketing procedure. By statute in Virginia the traditional inspection went out in 1877; trade associations were given virtual control over the warehouses. The manufacturer's need for more exact grades to carry out his brand requirements, and the fact that farm prizing often damaged the best Bright wrappers encouraged loose-leaf

sales. The auction sales of loose leaf first developed its
modern form in Danville, where the hogshead sales had
been least systematized in the ante-bellum period. The
sales were still called "breaks," though no longer were
there hogsheads to be broken open for inspection. Bells
signalled the breaks at many of the warehouses, but as
late as 1904 buyers in Lynchburg were summoned to
Friend's, Lynch's, and Martin's by the traditional tobacco
horns. The most melodious of the trumpet calls was blown
by an old Negro in a white apron who stood outside
Friend's warehouse at Church Street and Tenth:

Slowly

Markets in south Virginia and in the Carolinas moved
with especial rapidity to the loose-leaf sales system. The
hogshead market was more persistent in the Kentucky,
Tennessee, Missouri, and Ohio district than in the older
area, and the technique of sales more complicated in
evolution. From the late 1880's to about 1905 there was
a tremendous increase in the practice of direct buying;
speculators, agents for domestic or foreign manufacturers
individually bargained with the farmer at his barn or in
his wagon as he came to the market towns. Agents for the
American Tobacco Company negotiated at special, announced stations. Curiously enough the Kentuckians called
the street sale of tobacco, loose in a wagon, "the Virginia
method of sale," though this system of vending the raw
leaf, while used at times in the Dan Valley, certainly had

never been typical of the Old Dominion. There was a special sort of private sale in the central market towns, especially in western Kentucky, called "chute selling." Inside a sheltered driveway, the "chute," the buyers stood on a convenient platform to examine the leaf in the wagons. A peculiar and unclassifiable method was used for awhile in the Green River or Owensboro district, where loose tobacco was sold by sample, only the representative leaves being taken into the warehouse and auctioned to the highest bidder.

The Eastern system of loose-leaf auction warehouse sales moved across the mountains to Kentucky and Tennessee soon after the turn of the century. In the Burley district there was consistent expansion of this method, especially after a couple of years of experimentation, but development of loose-leaf sales was slower in the dark tobacco areas further west.

The advance and decline of the various marketing centers in this period reflected (1) the expansion of the Bright and Burley districts, (2) some shift in the methods of buying, (3) development of new transportation facilities, and (4) the changing location of manufacturing enterprises. For the Maryland and eastern Ohio areas Baltimore continued to be the depot for sale. The dark shipping leaf of Virginia still was marketed in such Virginia centers as Lynchburg and Richmond. But the prestige of the James River markets was sapped by the rise of Bright Tobacco to the south, which was sold principally in Danville, Winston-Salem, Durham, Henderson, Wilson, Rocky Mount, Timmonsville, and Darlington. The most important of these Eastern markets was Danville.

West of the mountains Louisville emerged as the country's greatest leaf market. Cincinnati ran Louisville a close second for a large part of the time. And Lexington, with its emphasis on the auction system, was of importance. The four leading markets in the more westerly area were Paducah, Mayfield, Hopkinsville, Kentucky, and the largest market for dark tobacco, Clarksville, Tennessee. Much of the story of railroad building east and west might be written in terms of the rivalry between tobacco market towns.

As was the situation a half-century earlier, the production of tobacco by 1910 was highly localized. The leading tobacco states were Kentucky, North Carolina, Virginia, Ohio, Tennessee. American production during the five years 1906–1910 averaged about 852,000,000 pounds. The 1886–1890 average had been approximately 546,000,000; 1866–1870, 307,000,000. By the 1880's domestic manufacturers with some consistency began to purchase more of the crop than did the exporters.

*1911 * 1941*

[Chapter 7]

FARMER AND LEAF MARKET

THE WAREHOUSE SCENE

One day during the 1936–1937 leaf-marketing season, when he had been employed by his father's company for less than a year, George Washington Hill, Jr., visited a warehouse auction and heard, for the first time, the rhythmic chant of the auctioneer. Whereupon Hill decided to test the mellow cadences in radio advertisements. On the air in June, 1937, the chant was at first merely the introductory note; later it was dramatized to integrate with a sales message. Thus the auctioneer's chant became that part of the leaf sales institution best known to the American public. But there was much more to the auction system, under which about 90 per cent of the American tobacco was sold, than these tuneful shouts.

When a load of tobacco was ready for market, the farmer piled the cured leaf into his wagon, truck or, as was more typical in the flue-cured areas, in a home-made two-wheeled trailer hitched to his automobile. Then he tucked sacks or quilts around the load to preserve the moisture content and headed for the market town. As he rolled by the warehouses—a market of any size would have several—the farmer was pelted by shouts from the door men urging him to drive in. Great one-story buildings, some of them covering almost a city block, the warehouses were of frame or brick construction. They possessed convenient drive-way entrances, a raised concrete or wooden floor to facilitate loading and unloading, and plenty of skylights. Once upon a time the warehouses were equipped with bunk rooms for the farmers, but such accommodations became obsolete.

In the warehouse, the hands of tobacco were slipped from the tobacco sticks onto the flat warehouse baskets, not more than one grade in each basket. In Georgia the tobacco was not tied, but was brought to market in a burlap sheet. The baskets were put on hand trucks, weighed and ticketed. The hookman, using a hooked metal bar, arranged the baskets in orderly fashion. There was no uniform quantity in each basket, but baskets of Burley characteristically averaged a higher poundage than the flue-cured. In the Burley district, where the entire stalk was cured at the same time, a farmer's crop was arranged on the floor in such a manner that the buying force came first to the flying end of the crop, then proceeded, as it were, up the stalk of the plant, reaching flyings, trash, lugs, bright leaf, red leaf, tips, then damaged. The process of selling was quickly done. One warehouseman shouted, "Bid 'er up boys!" Another threw out a starting bid to the auctioneer. The auctioneer began his chant, caught the gestures of the buyers, slipped his figures higher and higher. "Thirty-five - fi - fi - six - six - seven - seven - seven - eight - eight —t." And the sale was over in about ten seconds. The buyers tossed the sample hands back onto the basket and moved to the next hamper. They zipped along at several hundred baskets per hour. Stories were told of sales as high as 700 baskets per hour, but private rules and public laws curbed such excessive speeds. In most places by the 1930's the average had settled down to 360 sales per hour.

After watching the straggling line on the tobacco rows for awhile, even a stranger could detect the various roles. Out in front was the warehouseman, or, more strictly speaking, the sales manager, who saw to it that the business was started on time and moved along smoothly. He built up goodwill wherever he could.[1] The sales manager was likely to remind the buyers, half-banteringly and half-seriously, that this was a widow-woman's tobacco, or that Bob Jones had lost his barn by fire and badly needed the money. And he often bought the tobacco for the account of the warehouse to bolster the market if the bids were not as high as he thought they should be. The dividing line between purchasing to sustain the market and speculative buying was not always clear. It is certain that the speculative enterprises too often undertaken by the warehouseman ill became his professed role of honest broker.

The starter was an employee of the warehouse, sometimes the floor manager himself. His task was to indicate the price at which the bidding should begin. If efficient he was a good judge of tobacco and of the market possibilities. From his point of view, the ideal starting price was only a little below the previous average bids for that particular quality of tobacco before the buyers. If the starter put his price too low, the buyers would cease bidding before a fair price had been reached; if he began too high, the auctioneer would receive no bid until he dropped way back down the scale, and then he often failed to work the bids back into the fair zone.

The auctioneer's chant was less tiring than a straightforward prosaic handling of the bids, and it was thought to be faster. (One modern investigator has discovered a similarity between the auctioneer's tune and the Gre-

---

[1] One partner, a floor manager, might have the hand shaking assigned as his special job. Witness the frank account of his duties given by one of the owners of a Lexington warehouse: He was "more or less pretty man— walked around and entertained the farmers—different things—and watched the warehouse in general."

gorian chants of the Roman church.) Until he "knocked down" the tobacco, the auctioneer was singing over and over again the last bid, this mixed with meaningless syllables, or rapid-fire comments. The classic old-time tobacco auctioneer was the Virginian, Colonel Chiswell Dabney Langhorne, father of Nancy Witcher, Viscountess Astor. Colonel Langhorne was widely imitated and probably had more to do with fixing pattern and patter of auctioneering than any other one man on the warehouse floors. A satisfactory auctioneer was supremely alert. His eyes played over the buyers, who by dumb show, raised the bids. The bidding units were usually determined by the local trade associations. A typical formula was the raising of bids by 10 cent units to $6; by 25 cents $6 to $15; by 50 cents $15 to $30; by $1 over $30. An average buyer simply lifted a finger; another pointed a thumb to his chest; another winked his eye; still another nodded his head. One capitalized on his ability to wiggle his ears when he wanted to make a bid.

The buyers, who operated in sets composed of some five to fifteen men, often shifted as a group from one market to another, as the sales opened first in the Georgia district, then farther north. Of necessity in small towns they stayed at the same hotel, and fish fry and barbecue threw some of them together. Therefore, if a farmer did not get what he thought he should for his tobacco, he might be heard grumbling that there was more competition among the buyers in their card games of an evening than in the warehouses of a morning. Despite careful training, no buyer could be absolutely consistent in his judgment. And periodically the company buyers were subjected to the blandishments of growers, who tried to entertain them at foxhunts and picnics, and sometimes offered them game and liquor. Thus the larger companies employed special agents, officially called supervisors but known in the tobacco regions as circuit riders, who traveled to the various markets, consulted with the buyers, reviewed their pur-

chases, and gave them advice. On the typical Southern
market, buyers represented such large manufacturers and
dealers as the Imperial Tobacco Company, the Export
Tobacco Company (for British-American), Liggett &
Myers, American Suppliers (for American Tobacco Company), R. J. Reynolds Tobacco Company, Universal Leaf
Tobacco Company, and Dibrell Brothers. In addition to
these and the established local dealers, there were the pinhookers.

The pinhooker was a small speculator, usually with no
place of business other than the warehouse floor. He
moved in, quick as a flash, when a basket was selling well
below the market as a result of misjudgment by the regular buyers or because the farmer had carelessly mixed
his grades in one basket; poorly graded tobacco was un-
acceptable to the big companies. He bought his few baskets, hauled them over to one side of the warehouse,
re-classified the hands, and re-sold in a hurry. In his re-
selling he mixed his baskets in the line with those of the
farmers, hoping the buyers would not discover to whom
the tobacco belonged and thus discriminate against him.
Warehousemen often demanded of this operator a reserve
fund, though undoubtedly in some cases the warehousemen financed the pinhookers, sharing profit or the occasional loss. At times the pinhooker bought the tobacco in
the street or at the warehouse door from an impatient
grower wanting to get his cash and hurry home. The term
pinhooker was loosely used. Some purists in the field of
nomenclature insisted that the genuine pinhooker never
operated at the auction sales, but was a buyer of the farmers' tobacco by private negotiations before the regular sale.
Country speculators or barn buyers roving over the countryside were often called pinhookers.

In the warehouse, the farmer, if he were displeased with
the price, had the privilege of "turning the ticket" either by
literally flipping the records face down to indicate that he
had rejected the sale, or by tearing the coupon half-way

across. Although he could sell his tobacco again without extra cost, there was no guarantee that the later sale would be better than the first.

For his services the warehouseman charged special fees for weighing and auctioneering plus a commission which ran 2½ per cent or more of the gross sales price. In 1937 the United States Supreme Court in the case of *Townsend et al.* v. *Yeomans, Attorney General of Georgia, et al.* clearly affirmed the right of the state to fix warehouse charges. At that time Virginia, North Carolina, South Carolina and Georgia had fees regulated by the state. In Tennessee and Kentucky the rates were non-statutory. Although the overhead was great, with large staffs and the warehouses in active use for only part of the year,[2] most warehousemen made substantial profits and naturally were on the alert for movements which jeopardized their business. They had active trade associations, local, regional, and national, to work out smooth marketing procedures, uniform dates for market openings and the like. The Tobacco Association of the United States, organized in 1904 by warehousemen, dealers, and manufacturers, was designed for the general promotion of the trade.

But the warehousemen had many headaches, and at times they would ruefully have swapped their jobs for the worst task of tobacco worming. The floor manager had to boss the unskilled day labor which moved the tobacco to and fro across the floors. The manager had to train the clerical staff in speed and accuracy. Reports were required by both state and federal governments. Farmers must be treated gingerly to save their custom for the next year, even if this solicitude involved a summer loan or private concessions of other types. Another problem was the congregation of crooks in and around the warehouses, persons seeking to fleece the farmer of his crop proceeds.

[2] In off-seasons the warehouses yielded fractional income through use as general farmers' markets, parking lots, hogshead storage, or, in the Burley area, for the drying of blue grass seed.

Obviously the vast majority of the farmers after receiving their checks, cashed them, paid their debts, and went home to sleep in their own beds, but from the amount of money lost to shysters every year officers of the law were tempted to classify the tobacco farmer as the last hope of the itinerant crook. There were the honest, or nearly so, chapmen who hawked their razor blades, apples, and suit samples in and around the warehouses. There was the "corn doctor," a street medicine man who, alongside his strange chemicals, displayed a platter of amputated corns. And there were the local prostitutes, *prix fixé*. But the main trouble was the roving brotherhood of crooks and sharpsters, who by one device or another, stratagem, black-jack, or knockout drops, separated the farmer from his bills. It was said that some of the thieves, men and women, followed the market from the first openings in Georgia and Florida on north. The farmer wanted "a little fun" after his season of labor. He found new "friends," took a drink, and awakened with a splitting headache and without his purse. For years the most characteristic deception at auction time was the loaded pocketbook, usually operated by a team of two. A farmer who had just cashed his tobacco check was spotted by the crooks, who placed under his nose a wallet. One of the crooks picked up the pocket-book, flashed large bills, then, granting that his associate (who posed as a stranger) and the farmer had equal claim with him, the smart talker offered to share with them if they would put up a roll of money to "show faith" while he went to get the large bills changed. The associate immediately put up his "faith money"; the credulous farmer did likewise. First the one crook, then the other disappeared in the crowd, never to be seen by the farmer again. Despite periodic warnings from the police, tobacco farmers for years were victimized in this manner.

The market opening dates were determined each year on a basis of the maturity of the crops in the various sections. By 1941 the flue-cured market schedule was as fol-

lows: The Georgia Belt (markets in Georgia and Florida)
opened during the first week in August; the South Carolina Belt (markets in South and North Carolina) opened
a week or ten days later; the Eastern North Carolina or
New Bright Belt (markets in North Carolina) opened the
last of August or the first of September; the Middle Belt
(markets in Virginia and North Carolina) opened about
the middle of September; the Old Belt (markets in Virginia and North Carolina) opened a week or two later.
Opening dates for the dark air-cured and fire-cured markets ranged from November in Virginia to January in
Kentucky and Tennessee. By custom the Burley Belt
opened the first Monday in December with sales in Lexington; the other Burley markets opened the next day.
The Baltimore market usually was under way by May.
For most types there was a tendency towards earlier and
shorter sales seasons.

The loose-leaf auction system thoroughly dominated the
Southern markets, flue-cured, fire-cured, dark air-cured,
and Burley. In the Burley district the last of the old-style
hogshead auction sales was held during the 1929–1930
season in Louisville. Until the late 1930's Maryland sales
continued to be of the hogshead type, with a special system of bidding on samples. The farmer sorted his cured
leaf, then packed it in hogsheads and shipped the casks
on consignment to Baltimore.[3] Inspectors took six or eight
samples, a pound and a half or a pound and three-quarters
each, from the hogshead, sealed and tied the bundles, and
delivered them to the consignor. Buyers made sealed bids,
and the tobacco was sold to the highest bidder. The buyers
saw only the samples, not the actual bulk on which the

[3] Much of the tobacco was sent to the Baltimore market by so-called
"transfer buyers," who originally bought from those farmers with less than
a hogshead lot of one grade. The "transfer buyers," who started their business by transferring fractional hogsheads to full ones, soon began purchasing entire crops from the farmers. In some of the Maryland counties more
than half the crops were sold to transfer buyers. After 1915 most of the
Ohio tobacco sold in Baltimore was on a re-sale basis, having been purchased
from the farmer in Ohio.

samples were laid as was the case in the old Louisville and Cincinnati markets. The loose-leaf warehouse auction system was started in Maryland in 1939 by Crosby Wyche, a student from the University of Maryland, who opened a warehouse at Hughesville. About a quarter of the Maryland crop was sold under this plan the first season. By 1941 over half the Maryland crop was auctioned. Most of the cigar leaf and a fraction of the dark fire-cured in Kentucky and Tennessee were sold by private bargaining in the country at the farmers' barns.

This evolutionary institution, the warehouse auction system, was theoretically perfect, actually imperfect. In good times the farmers had little complaint, but when prices were low they accused the buyers of collusion and tried either to reform the warehouse auction system or to create substitute marketing machinery. During and immediately after the First World War prices were high. The farmers could hardly believe their ears as they heard the bids for the crop of 1919. About this time a young graduate student at the University of Kentucky interviewed farmers and warehousemen and, in time-honored graduate-student fashion, distributed questionnaires. He reported that both growers and warehousemen were well satisfied with the warehouse auction system.

TROUBLED WATERS OF THE TOBACCO POOLS

When the 1920 crop was put on the warehouse floor some farmers swore that leaf which a year before had brought from 25 to 35 cents sold at 3 and 5 cents per pound. From Kentucky came news that knives were drawn, and buyers threatened and pushed about. A prominent Fayette County church worker was discovered stamping up and down the warehouse, cursing roundly as she found her landlord-share in a load of tobacco to be $2.75, whereas the year before a similar fraction had yielded $325. On

Virginia markets, the season's average for flue-cured was 22 cents as compared with 51 the previous year; on the Lexington markets for Burley, 13 cents as compared with 35 for the 1919 crop. Countless farmers faced immediate foreclosure.

Post-war deflation came with a crash. The total tobacco crop was large, and much of it indifferent or bad in quality. The world leaf market collapsed with the news of glutted warehouses in the East Indies, South America, and elsewhere. At the same time importing countries lacked dollars for the purchase of luxury articles. Although some farmers acknowledged that the basic evil was overproduction, most were unconvinced and insisted that thimblerigged leaf sales were at the root of the evil. Beyond the question of collusion, the warehouse procedure was a simple farce, half gamble and half guess, contended tobacco growers. To prove his point one farmer shifted about on the warehouse floor a basket of tobacco and, according to report, sold it ten different times, fetching prices all the way from 8 to 28 cents per pound. The buyer paying 28 cents had previously bought the hamper for 11.

Inevitably the cry for cooperative marketing was raised. At that time there was only one tobacco cooperative of any significance, the Maryland Tobacco Growers Association, essentially a farmer-owned brokerage agency. Soon other cooperatives appeared. The three leading groups were: the Burley Tobacco Growers Cooperative Association, with headquarters at Lexington, Kentucky; the Tri-State Association, or, more properly, the Tobacco Growers Cooperative Association of North and South Carolina and Virginia, with headquarters at Raleigh and at Richmond; and the Dark Tobacco Growers Cooperative Association, with headquarters at Hopkinsville. The first of these three was incorporated in 1921, the others in 1922.

The Burley Tobacco Growers Cooperative Association, though sustained by many men, was the creation of three: Robert W. Bingham, Aaron Sapiro, James C. Stone. This, the greatest organization of its kind, grew out of a meeting in April, 1921, called by Judge Bingham of Louisville, publisher of the *Courier-Journal* and of the *Times*, and later ambassador to Great Britain. Conservative banking groups followed his lead. Aaron Sapiro, an able self-made lawyer, brought up in a California orphan asylum, had proved himself a master in the handling of citrus-fruit cooperatives. He was an efficient attorney, often described as the only qualified expert in his field, and a contagious propagandist. But without a practical and outstanding tobacco man there would have been just so much flailing of the air. This key individual was Stone, "Jim" Stone as he was known all over the Burley district, a warehouseman long in the tobacco business, who was made president and general manager of the Association. The leadership of the Burley pool possessed prestige, intelligence, and honesty. By November 15, 1921, 55,716 members, representing well over three-quarters of the 1920 Burley crop, had signed the five-year contract. There was practically no violence, this by way of contrast with the Black Patch days.[4]

Requesting direct business, Jim Stone visited the presidents of the largest manufacturing corporations. C. W. Toms, ex-school superintendent and president of Liggett & Myers, gave him the warmest welcome, promising that his company would buy from the Burley pool that propor-

---

[4] When the enemies of the Burley pool were marshalling all possible evidence to prevent its operation in Tennessee, they were able to discover only a few isolated cases of intimidation.

Dan Bowen stated with reference to an agent of the Association:

"Well," he says, "that is the only way you have got and you will have to sell through the pool or else just be a scab, and we will make you join." And my wife opened up then and says, "Well, if that is the way of it you just as well to sign," and I says, "I will sign for two acres of it."

And W. Mattingly claimed that he was threatened:

They said they were going to see that I didn't dump any more tobacco, and they were going to see that there was no loose leaf market from now on, and they were going to see that I didn't do any more talking about the Association, or they would take my damn scalp; that dead men told no tales.

tion of the company's Burley which the pool's tobacco bore to the entire crop. Sure enough, Liggett & Myers made the first significant purchases; others followed. The largest single sale appears to have been made to Reynolds. The pool obtained a net average of 20 cents per pound for the 1921 crop, selling about 68 per cent of the total. The association received 75 per cent of the 1923 Burley crop. By 1924 membership had passed the 100,000 mark. For six consecutive years the Burley pool sold over 100,000,-000 pounds annually.

Embracing flue-cured, fire-cured, sun-cured, and even Burley crops, the Tobacco Growers Cooperative Association of Virginia, North Carolina and South Carolina—the Tri-State—was incorporated February 9, 1922. Clarence Poe, editor of the *Progressive Farmer*, was the prime mover. Before the year 1922 was out, about 80,000 members had signed; by 1925 about 96,000. The Tri-State Association marketed 35 per cent of the crop in its district the first year of its operation, 28 per cent the next. Enthusiasm for cooperatives swept over other tobacco areas. The Dark Tobacco Growers Cooperative Association eventually counted over 70,000 members from Kentucky, Tennessee, and Indiana. Cigar-leaf growers formed the Connecticut Valley Tobacco Association, the Miami Valley Tobacco Growers Association, and the Northern Wisconsin Cooperative Tobacco Pool. Farmers of Maryland strengthened their society. Perhaps 5,000 farmers representing about one per cent of the crop were selling tobacco cooperatively in 1920. The various associations at the peak of their strength in 1923 enrolled almost 300,000 growers, controlling 46 per cent of the nation's leaf. Then the movement subsided. Especially in the dark and flue-cured areas, there were attempts to wriggle out of contracts.[5] By 1930,

---

[5] Among the suits for contract breaking was one brought by the Dark Tobacco Association against Sap Johnson, Negro, whose testimony was something like this: "Yessuh, dat gentman come round gettin up de pool. I axed my white folks about it, and dey sayd that de pool was good. So I signs de contract. I didn't read it—can't do much reading, but I can write my name.

only two groups, the Maryland Tobacco Growers Association and the Northern Wisconsin Cooperative Tobacco
Pool, were actively operating. They represented a membership of 4,800 and 7,900 respectively and crops equal to
about two per cent of the nation's total. The Burley pool,
the Stone pool as it was often called, retained its legal
existence and properties, but the members had refused to
renew their contracts.

The decline of the cooperative movement in the middle
1920's may be credited to the following factors: (a) *An
improvement in prices for most leaf types.* In farmer logic
this circumstance meant that a continuation of the novel
schemes, which involved delayed payment, was unneces-
sary. (b) *A general lack of understanding the nature of
the cooperative.* Particularly in the areas covered by the
Dark Tobacco pool and the Tri-State, the membership
campaigns, based on hatred of the old marketing machinery, had promised too much. There was a high degree
of illiteracy in the Tri-State region. (c) *Weaknesses in
the organic structure of the cooperatives.* The centralized
type of organization was ill-suited to the various classes
of tobacco handled by the Dark Association and the Tri-
State. Furthermore, the monopoly idea was fallacious. In
sharp contrast to the situation in the California citrus
areas, expansion into regions not dominated by cooperatives readily took place. (d) *Loss of faith in the management.* Despite Bingham's defense, in the Burley area
Sapiro's $48,000 fee as counsel was condemned. A crush-
ing blow to the morale of the Tri-State members came
with the exposure that contracts had been made with re-
drying plants owned by responsible officers of the Association.

(e) *The opposition of those local groups believing that
the pools threatened them with disaster.* This was the

Yessuh, my name is Frank Johnson, but everybody hereinabouts, both white
and black, inginerally calls me Saphead Johnson—so I up and signs the
contract 'Sap.' "

decisive factor in the breaking of some pools. Astute observers as early as 1922 discerned that the real conflict
centered not so much around the manufacturers as about
the time merchant and the auction group. The time merchants were accustomed to doing business on a basis of
cash sale at the auction warehouse. Warehousemen did
not soon forget a speech made by Aaron Sapiro in Wilson,
in which he promised that, if cooperative selling were successful, grass would grow in the streets of that market
town. The high rate of tenancy, 80 per cent in some tobacco counties, left the farmer with something less than
full control over his crop. Creditors, time merchants, landlords and others often were affiliated with the warehouse
groups antagonized during the membership campaign.
There is strong evidence that the injunction which in effect kept the Burley pool out of Tennessee was sponsored
by warehousemen, who stood to lose by the development
of cooperatives.[6] Insofar as the associations in membership
drives emphasized their objective as monopoly control, and
this point was made particularly in the dark and flue-
cured areas, manufacturers were concerned over the innovations. The American Tobacco Company and the Imperial Tobacco Company were accused at the time of
having boycotted the cooperatives, specifically of breaking
the Tri-State Association and of encouraging the growth
of flue-cured in unorganized Georgia, a state which increased its production from about 6,000,000 to 40,000,000
pounds in the four years after 1922. The Federal Trade
Commission exonerated the companies from the charges,

    [6] James E. Lipscomb of American Suppliers, Inc., the leaf-buying divi-
sion of the American Tobacco Company, in 1930 wrote to J. H. Dean of
Knoxville Fertilizer Company, "I appreciate fully your cooperation during
the Pool and believe you have done more to forward the growth of tobacco
in Tennessee than any other interest and I want you to know that I, as well
as the Company, certainly appreciate your efforts." In the 1941 trial at
Lexington, Lipscomb explained that by cooperation he meant "keeping the
loose leaf market open—not going into the Pool." He claimed that he fought
the pool only in the sense that he bought on the loose-leaf market. Though
he had nothing to do with the distribution of seeds, "I was glad to see it
done. I did not encourage it in any way."

and indicated that the boll weevil more than anything else
had caused the substitution of tobacco for sea-island cotton along the coast of Georgia.

TOBACCO AND THE NEW DEAL

At the beginning of the 1931 marketing season, farmers
were chuckling over the story of the foresighted Negro
who, in Blackshear, Georgia, put up for auction a small
hamper of tobacco, which sold for less than the warehouse
fees. He was told that he owed 50 cents on the transaction,
a sum which he did not have. "Well," said the warehouseman, "just bring me a chicken next time you come to
town." The following day the Negro appeared with *two*
chickens. When told he owed just one, he replied, "I know
that, boss, but I done brought another hamper of terbacker
and I brought this extra chicken to pay you for selling it!"
And the townsmen smiled at the brave little farmer who,
after a Nashville sale, found himself with a profit of 20
cents, promptly spent for a plug of "eatin' tobacco."

But as the weeks wore on and the dismal picture never
lightened, the tobacco country had not the heart to laugh.
The 1928 Burley crop had averaged 31 cents per pound;
1929, 22 cents; 1930, 16 cents. The 1931 cutting was to
bring less than 9 cents. At the opening of the market in
Owensboro, December, 1931, three thousand farmers,
angered at the average of $4.61 per hundred for dark leaf,
about half the price of the preceding year, broke up the
sales with their shouts and threats. Note, for example, the
case of Dan Wood, a young farmer of the New Canton
section of Virginia. This sharecropper with a wife and
two children took a load of 414 pounds of dark tobacco,
good but not fancy, 30 miles to market. When the carriage
charges were deducted, the check amounted to $5.19; his
share was $2.60.

There was talk of reviving with full vigor the coopera-

tive associations of the 1920's. Indeed the Federal Farm
Board, Herbert Hoover's contribution to the settlement of
the agrarian problem, professed as a major purpose the
encouragement of these groups. Its chairman was Jim
Stone, once president of the Burley Tobacco Growers Cooperative Association. Several new cooperatives were
formed, but in terms of the national situation this movement sponsored by the Federal Farm Board counted for
little. The cooperatives handled an estimated one-half of
one per cent of the 1932 crop.

In defense of their shaky condition the domestic producers of cigar wrappers waged a campaign against the
importation of Sumatra leaf on the thesis that it was produced by convict labor and therefore ran afoul American
import laws. Connecticut and Florida growers pressed for
total exclusion; the manufacturers took a contrary point
of view. The Treasury Department investigated and in
October, 1931, announced that the Sumatra companies
were abolishing the penal system.

Times were bad in 1931, worse in 1932, and when
Franklin D. Roosevelt spoke of the "forgotten man" the
farmer thought he knew whom Roosevelt meant. The
Burley crop of 1932 could buy only one-fourth the goods
that the average crop, 1919–1928, could have purchased.
In the famous hundred-day session of Congress after
Roosevelt's inauguration, the tobacco grower saw with
satisfaction the Agricultural Adjustment Act of May 12,
1933, which included tobacco among the six basic commodities for crop restriction with benefit payments to the
farmer, the costs to be met by the levying of processing
taxes. The farmer was quite willing to become part of a
planned economy if such meant taking the time merchant
from his heels. The Tobacco Section of the Agricultural
Adjustment Administration, which had as its chief John
B. Hutson, turned its attention to those tobacco-producing
sections seemingly in the worst condition, the cigar leaf
areas. By June there had been worked out a plan for pay-

ments to growers of New England, Pennsylvania, and Ohio for reduction in 1933 filler and binder crops. Governmental preoccupation with northerly areas perturbed the largest single group of tobacco farmers, those in the flue-cured district.

With the support of the Raleigh *News and Observer*, a portentous meeting was called by tobacco growers for August 31, in Raleigh. The assemblage asked for federal supervision of grading and marketing, and requested Governor J. C. B. Ehringhaus to close the North Carolina warehouses under martial law until the price of tobacco went to a 20-cent-per-pound average or better. Secretary of Agriculture Henry Wallace spoke of acreage reduction in Southern tobacco crops for 1934, but the farmers were in no mood to wait another year for something to be done. To expedite federal action, about 95 per cent of the flue-cured tobacco growers of the land agreed to reduce their crops for the next year by 30 per cent. The producers hoped that this promise would enable the Secretary of Agriculture to negotiate an agreement with the major buying companies.

At meetings in Washington, Governor Ehringhaus of North Carolina complimented the manufacturers on their achievements, but added, "You have lived, and lived sumptuously . . . The growers at the other end of the line are not receiving anything but the wages of a peon and a slave. That condition cannot be permitted to go on indefinitely." The eight leading buyers, American, Liggett, Reynolds, Lorillard, Philip Morris, Larus, Continental, and Brown & Williamson consented to purchase flue-cured at an average minimum price of 17 cents. Later a purchasing agreement for Burley was signed, applying to the 1932 crop on a basis of approximately 12 cents per pound. The eight companies plus U. S. Tobacco Company and Axton-Fisher joined in this arrangement. A somewhat similar understanding was worked out for the purchase of dark air-cured and fire-cured types. These one-year arrangements were not renewed. Export buyers continued their purchases despite higher prices, largely because of the favorable foreign exchange at this time. The AAA, a term everyone applied to the Agricultural Adjustment Administration as well as to the statute under which it was established, went ahead with its plans to obtain from farmers contracts specifying a limited production on a basis of benefit payments.

As a new and strong girder under the tobacco provisions of the AAA, there was passed by Congress on June 28, 1934, a bill sometimes called the Kerr Act or the Kerr-Smith Act, levying a special tax of not less than 25 per cent on the sales of leaf tobacco produced above the allotment under AAA or by those not contracting with the AAA. In 1935 the AAA made 369,465 contracts with growers. The farmers seemed happy; their incomes had increased. And the crops had been cut below the level of consumption. Then, in January, 1936, the Supreme Court ruled the 1933 Agricultural Adjustment Act unconstitutional (this was the famous *United States* v. *Butler*, 297 U. S. 1). At Roosevelt's request Congress repealed the Kerr-Smith Act in February, 1936, and settled down to contrive a statute which would survive the Supreme Court. Congress passed the soil conservation and domestic allotment act of February, 1936, to encourage enrichment of the soil, but no direct measure for crop control was included.

Again production turned upwards. A dry summer restricted the 1936 crop, but in 1937 the harvest was large; only two earlier crops, 1930 and 1931, had surpassed it in quantity. Congress in February, 1938, passed a new Agricultural Adjustment Act to maintain what was in effect a ceiling on harvest, a floor under prices for five crops, including tobacco. Marketing quotas, to be declared by the Secretary of Agriculture when the stocks of any particular type of tobacco so warranted, were not to be applied until ratified by two-thirds of the growers. The "commodity loans" in practice established a minimum price based on "parity." [7] Farmers planting no more than their individual quotas ("cooperators" was their legal designation), were granted through the Commodity Credit Corporation non-recourse loans on their leaf, usually 85 or 90 per cent of parity. Tobacco grown in excess of the quota could be marketed only under heavy penalty. The constitutionality of the 1938 AAA was tested on a basis of the tobacco marketing quotas under the new statute. On April 17, 1939, a majority of the Supreme Court in *Mulford et al.* v. *Smith et al.*, speaking through Justice Roberts pronounced the act constitutional. The Court had been won by the New Deal.

Impatient with restraints of any sort, both Burley and flue-cured growers rejected AAA controls for the 1939 crop. The Burley cutting was the third largest in history; the flue-cured larger than any previous crop by about 300,000,000 pounds. The total yield in the United States for all types was a record-breaking 1,880,000,000 pounds, one-third of the world's production. As the markets opened there came news of the beginning of the Second World War. Foreign buyers withdrew and now the farmers wanted the government to *do* something. Under a special arrangement export companies returned to the market using Commodity Credit Corporation funds.

THE MODERN TOBACCO FARMER

Along with its attempts to cure the evil of overproduction, Congress tried to reform leaf sales by means of a general

[7] Congress defined parity as follows: " 'Parity,' as applied to prices for any agricultural commodity, shall be that price for the commodity which will give to the commodity a purchasing power with respect to articles that farmers buy equivalent to the purchasing power of such commodity in the base period . . ." The base period for all kinds of tobacco was August 1919–July 1929 until the year 1940, when Burley and flue-cured were given the base period August 1934–July 1939.

system of federal inspection and leaf classification. Once the procedure of government grading had been introduced, the farmer could scan his ticket marked by the federal grader, review the lists of current prices posted in the warehouse, and see whether the bid on his product was consistent with the sales over the district for that particular quality of tobacco.

Under the general terms of a warehouse act passed by Congress in 1916, federal officials were warranted in preparing a grading system for tobacco as well as for other agricultural products. An important service of the cooperatives which flourished during the 1920's was to educate the farmers in the importance of a proper pattern of grading, but the grades adopted by the associations disappeared as the pools went out of existence. Finally, the Department of Agriculture formulated a schedule of grades, and, despite the opposition of various warehousemen and leaf speculators, by 1929 the farmers at several markets on payment of a special fee could have their leaf graded by a federal officer. There were several statutes providing for the collection and publication of tobacco statistics, but the major importance of all these laws was to clear the way for the *magna carta* of the warehouse, the Tobacco Inspection Act of August 23, 1935. Under this act, the Secretary of Agriculture was authorized to set up an inspection system on any leaf market he designated, contingent on a favorable vote of two-thirds of the growers using that market. The Secretary was also directed to publish and distribute information regarding the supply, demand, and market prices. Warehousemen of Oxford, North Carolina, opposed the statute and sought a declaratory judgment as to its constitutionality. The District Court held with the warehousemen, but in 1939 the decision of *Currin* v. *Wallace*, 306 U. S. 1, showed that the Supreme Court was a different body from that which had destroyed the AAA in 1936. Chief Justice Hughes, speaking for the majority, held that the regulations were within the commerce power granted by the Constitution to the federal government.[8]

The actual grading, an indication of kind and quality, was based on a primary subdivision of leaf into classes and types. The Department of Agriculture recognized seven basic classes of the domestic leaf: the first three were non-cigar leaf classes (tobacco used in the making of cigarettes, smoking tobacco, chewing tobacco, and snuff); the next three were cigar leaf classes; and the seventh was a miscellaneous group. The non-cigar leaf classes were divided on a basis of curing methods: class one, flue-cured; class two, fire-cured; and class three, air-cured. The cigar leaf classes were determined on a basis of the major uses of the product: class four, filler; class five, binder; class six, wrapper. The location and uses of these tobacco classes by the late 1930's were approximately as follows:

Class One—Flue-Cured. Flue-cured (the official name for Bright Tobacco) was produced in Virginia, North Carolina, South Carolina, and Georgia, with scattered acres in Florida and Alabama. Most flue-cured was used in the making of cigarettes; some was taken by manufacturers of smoking and chewing tobacco. By the middle 1930's the flue-cured was more valuable than all other classes combined, dominating both domestic and export leaf trade.

[8] An interesting feature of the case was Hughes's summary of the auction system and an analysis of its weaknesses, which were, in large measure, corrected by the federal inspection procedure. "The auction goes forward with extreme rapidity—about one basket every ten seconds—the auctioneer proceeding along one side of a row and the buyers moving with him. The auction is conducted with a technical vocabulary intelligible only to the initiated, bids being made by well-understood gestures." And he added, "It also appears from the record that because of the speed of the sale few buyers have the opportunity to make a satisfactory examination of the tobacco and consequently many errors are made, although on the average the buyers are not supposed to suffer seriously. The effect of the methods used is to introduce an unusual degree of uncertainty in the prices which a grower may receive for tobacco of any particular grade."

Class Two—Fire-Cured. The fire-cured class was grown in Virginia, Kentucky, and Tennessee. Most of the fire-cured tobacco was used in the manufacture of snuff, though a small part of the crop was devoted to the making of a special cigar, the Toscani, slender, tapering, strong, a favorite with newly-arrived immigrants in the days before the immigrant-quota system. Some of the fire-cured, with a type of air-cured known as "One Sucker," went into the making of black fat, a semi-manufactured article for the foreign trade. In the early days fire-cured was the leaf most in demand for export.

Class Three—Air-Cured. The air-cured class was further divided into light and dark, the light being the Burley and Maryland types. The culture of Burley swept over large areas of eastern Kentucky, down into Tennessee, over into Virginia and into corners of North Carolina, Ohio, Indiana, West Virginia, and Missouri. Most of the Burley crop went into the making of cigarettes; a smaller fraction was used in the manufacture of smoking and chewing tobacco. Maryland was likewise predominantly a cigarette tobacco. The dark air-cured, used largely in chewing tobacco, was grown principally in western Kentucky (the One Sucker and Green River were the major types there) and in central Virginia, where the leaf was known as Virginia sun-cured. ·

Classes Four, Five, and Six. Class four embraced cigar-filler types; the principal ones were Pennsylvania seedleaf, grown in and around Lancaster County, Pennsylvania, and several types in the Miami Valley of southwestern Ohio. Puerto Rican filler was also put under class four. Class five, binder types, was produced mainly in the Connecticut Valley, though substantial amounts came from Wisconsin. Less important quantities were grown in New York, Pennsylvania, Georgia, and Florida. The two types under class six, cigar-wrapper, were Connecticut Valley shade-grown and Georgia and Florida shade-grown. These were the most expensive of all types of tobacco to produce,

TOBACCO-GROWING DISTRICTS

MINN.

WIS.

MICH.

55

VIROQUA 54
EDGERTON STOUGHTON
JANESVILLE

IOWA

ILL.

IND.

OHIO

42,43,44
DAYTON

W.VA.

MO.

WESTON

31

31,35

SHELBYVILLE
OWENSBORO 36
HENDERSON 35
PADUCAH 3
HOPKINSVILLE
MAYFIELD 31
SPRINGFIELD
CLARKSVILLE
23 31
MURRAY 22
ARK.

31

N.Y. VT.

N.H.
51,52,61
SYRACUSE
MASS.
53
ELMIRA
52 HARTFORD R.I.
53
CONN.
PA.
LANCASTER 41
YORK N.J.
BALTIMORE DEL.
VA. MD.

MAYSVILLE
KY.
LEXINGTON 31
HORSE CAVE
ABINGDON
KNOX
LYNCHBURG 32
GREENEVILLE 11b
DANVILLE 21
DURHAM GREENVILLE
W.-SALEM KINSTON

TENN.
MISS. ALA.

N.C.

GA.

S.C.

FAIRMONT
LAKE CITY
13

LA.

DOUGLAS 45
TIFTON BLACKSHEAR
NASHVILLE
VALDOSTA
QUINCY LIVE OAK
45,62

FLA.

ME.

U S DEPARTMENT OF AGRICULTURE

FLUE-CURED TYPES
CLASS 1
TYPE
11a OLD BELT FLUE-CURED
11b MIDDLE BELT FLUE-CURED
12 EASTERN NORTH CAROLINA FLUE-CURED
13 SOUTH CAROLINA FLUE-CURED
14 GEORGIA FLUE-CURED

FIRE-CURED TYPES
CLASS 2
TYPE
21 VIRGINIA FIRE-CURED
22 EASTERN FIRE-CURED (CLARKSVILLE AND HOPKINSVILLE)
23 WESTERN FIRE-CURED (PADUCAH AND MAYFIELD)
24 HENDERSON FIRE-CURED

AIR-CURED TYPES
CLASS 3
TYPE
31 BURLEY
32 SOUTHERN MARYLAND
35 ONE-SUCKER
36 GREEN RIVER
37 VIRGINIA SUN-CURED

CIGAR FILLER TYPES
CLASS 4
TYPE
41 PENNSYLVANIA SEEDLEAF
42 GEBHARDT
43 ZIMMER OR SPANISH
44 DUTCH
45 GEORGIA AND FLORIDA SUN-GROWN

CIGAR BINDER TYPES
CLASS 5
TYPE
51 CONNECTICUT VALLEY BROADLEAF
52 CONNECTICUT HAVANA SEED
53 NEW YORK AND PENNSYLVANIA HAVANA
54 SOUTHERN WISCONSIN
55 NORTHERN WISCONSIN

CIGAR WRAPPER TYPES
CLASS 6
TYPE
61 CONNECTICUT VALLEY SHADE-GROWN
62 GEORGIA AND FLORIDA SHADE-GROWN

principally because of the elaborate use of slats or cloth to cover the fields. By way of contrast with the usual filler and binder tobaccos, which were stalk-cut in harvesting, the wrapper types were primed, from the bottom of the plant up, two or three leaves at a time. All the cigar classes were air-cured, though charcoal fires were used extensively in the curing sheds when the weather so warranted.

Class Seven—Miscellaneous Types. Under this catch-all designation were classified Eastern Ohio export, rustica, and Perique. Eastern Ohio export was a Maryland-marketed hogshead-packed leaf cured in various ways. Rustica *(Nicotiana rustica)*, the original tobacco used by the North American Indian before Columbus, was a strong, coarse leaf with high nicotine content, produced in a limited way for the making of insecticides. The most interesting of the Class Seven types was Perique, grown in St. James Parish, Louisiana, and used in the manufacture of fine smoking tobacco.

There was no such thing as a uniform pattern of tobacco farming in the United States. Among the growers were Kentucky mountaineers with small patches of Burley, Carolina landlords with dozens of acres of flue-cured, Cajun farmers with a few rows of Perique, Connecticut corporations with miles of wrappers under cloth. White and black, landowner and tenant, rich and poor cultivated the leaf. Tobacco was raised under various farming systems; sometimes it was the dominant crop, but often it was grown in conjunction with grain or cotton, or as one phase of mixed farming. Especially in the Bluegrass region of Kentucky and in cigar leaf areas of Pennsylvania, tobacco raising was combined with livestock production.

Yet, out of this welter of unstable factors there emerged certain characteristic feaures of tobacco culture. The machine age had come to America, but it barely touched the tobacco farm. There were threshing machines, milking machines, even a few cotton-picking machines, but only the human hand could pull tobacco plants from the beds, hoe them, top, sucker, prime, and put them on tobacco sticks. Sundry mechanical and chemical aids evolved, but, more than any other major crop, tobacco was the translation of aching backs into marketable produce. This vast labor requirement meant an intensive sort of culture. It is probable that the average tobacco field was under five acres.

The routine of culture by 1940 differed in few respects from the procedure of fifty years earlier. The seeds were sown in plant beds, which had been either burned or steamed to kill the weeds and insects and to retard plant diseases. Tobacco cloth was stretched over the seed bed to protect the young plants from insects and weather. In their labors about the plant beds, workers were warned not to use "long green," home-prepared chewing or smoking tobacco which might spread tobacco mosaic virus. Commercial fertilizers were applied to the tobacco fields in largest amounts in the flue-cured districts, in least quantities in the rich Burley lands of Kentucky and Tennessee. In Wisconsin and Pennsylvania farmers spread on their fields quantities of barnyard fertilizers. In choosing leaf varieties, farmers benefited from the brilliant research of plant breeders, who developed disease-resistant strains and, in the flue-cured areas, plants which could profit by heavy applications of fertilizers.

When the young tobacco plants were large enough for transplanting, the farmer carefully drew them from the beds and took them to the prepared fields. On the larger, flatter farms, especially in the Burley regions, horse-drawn "tobacco setters" were employed with profit. In using this machine two men sat on seats swung close to the ground and inserted the plants after the setter had dug a hole and put in water. On small farms the ancient dibble or peg might be used, but more typical was a simple hand instrument with water reservoir which saved much bending.

Then came the field tasks. The crops were plowed, hoed, wormed, topped, and suckered. As the years went by and labor became more scarce there was a tendency to reduce the amount of hoeing. Furthermore, applications of insecticides helped retard the gluts of worms.[9] A drastic change occurred in the practice of topping. In many areas the desire for thinner leaf meant setting the plants closer together and topping higher and later. In the Burley area plants finally were suckered only once, just before cutting, this in order to minimize labor costs and to reduce the chance of spreading plant disease throughout the field. No fields were more distinctive in appearance than those in the shade-grown cigar regions, where hundreds of acres were covered by cloth or, in some cases, by laths.

Particularly under the system of stalk-cutting it was not easy to tell when a field was ripe for harvesting. There was an old saying in the Burley country that when the farmer thought his tobacco ripe he should go fishing for a week! In stalk-cutting the question was whether to *spear* or to *split*. The older method was to split the stalk to a point near the ground, then to cut the plant, all with a spade-shaped knife. Then the stalk was put astraddle the tobacco stick. Under the more efficient spear plan, the plant was cut near the ground with a vicious-looking tomahawk or machete. (Some of these tools were farm-made of saw-blade and wheel-spoke.) Long-handled shears were used in parts of Pennsylvania. The plant was then speared over a steel-pointed cap and thus slipped onto the tobacco stick. This stalk-cut tobacco was taken from field to barn in low wagons, which, in the filler districts, were fitted with racks called tobacco ladders. In the flue-cured area, where the tobacco was primed, the *pullings* were placed in a home-

[9] Among the offenders was the green hornworm, a large and peculiarly unlovely creature. According to Virgil Steed, "A common local description is 'He's so tough he bites the heads off tobacco worms,' and country boys delight in trying to convince their city playmates that the men kill the worms by doing just that. With much pantomime, they illustrate the gruesome details."

made wooden sled and drawn by mule or horse to the barn, where all helpers, men, women, and children, were called to tie the leaves on tobacco sticks. Wooden laths four and a half 'feet long, they were either milled or rived, and, curiously enough, a thousand sticks which had been used for a season were more highly prized than new ones, for the pesky splinters had been worn off the strong ones and the weak ones had been broken and discarded.

Harvesting, whether carried on under cutting or priming methods, was the peak load on the tobacco farms. Since it involved much bending and lifting, and a certain hazard when sticks were placed high in the barn, day labor often demanded double pay. The housewife was glad when it was all over, and the last of the tobacco gum was washed from the men-folks' clothes.

Some tobacco was put on scaffolds in the open air before being housed for the actual curing; this scaffolding was an atrophied remnant of the once dominant scheme of sun-curing. No matter what the type of curing, even where the so-called sun-cured was grown, a barn was essential. And the barn was an important and distinctive part of the architectural landscape in all tobacco regions. In flue-cured districts the barns were tightly-built small log structures, despite their windowless character rather easily confused with some of the older sharecropper cabins. Many of the newer ones, especially on the coastal plain, were made of milled lumber. Standing on end near the flue-curing barns was the fuel wood, cut in the fall or late winter. Where labor or timber was scarce and capital available, progressive farmers introduced oil burners or coal stokers for the curing barns. The barns for fire-curing were somewhat similar in appearance to the flue-curing barns.

In the air-cured districts, such as the Burley region, the barns were much larger than those in the flue-cured areas, for curing here took weeks instead of days, and a barn could be filled only once each season. These great high structures were painted black with a cheap coal-tar, rot-resistant liquid, which could be applied with a heavy white-wash brush. In the horse-country of Kentucky, planters with an eye for appearances relieved this drab-ness by painting the hinged ventilating planks some con-trasting color, a brown or a dark red. For best results the air-curing barn was built on a hill, where it could receive full benefit of the prevailing winds. In both Burley and dark air-cured barns coke stoves aided nature if the weather continued damp. Attached to the big barns were stripping rooms with north windows and stripping benches. Near the smaller flue-curing barns were pack houses for storage; sometimes underneath them or con-veniently nearby there were ordering pits where tobacco could be placed to absorb enough moisture for ease in handling. After the curing process proper, flue-cured, Bur-ley, and most other tobaccos were packed down, "bulked," before being classified for market. The bulking improved quality and induced uniformity of color.

The curing of Perique was so complicated that its grow-ers were required by the federal government to obtain manufacturers' licenses. The plants were stalk-cut and air-cured, suspended on wires in the barns. In two or three weeks the tobacco was stripped from the stalks, stemmed, then lightly twisted into one-pound hands or "torquettes" and packed into large oaken barrels where it was sub-jected to pressure from powerful screwjacks. Every few weeks the pressure was removed and the torquettes, moist with their own rich, winey juices, were loosened then re-packed. After months of this fermentation under pressure the Perique was ready for market. The older method of packing in little wooden boxes and pressing with lever and fulcrum had about passed away. A few of the farmers, mostly for their own use, prepared carottes, hard-packed four-pound rolls, in the eighteenth-century Natchez manner.

In most tobacco areas the farmer graded his tobacco and

marketed it in loose, unprized fashion. The basic farmer divisions were keyed to the position of the leaves on the plant. The farmer graded his flue-cured crop, beginning with the top and going down, as tips, leaf (probably divided into dark and bright shades), wrappers if any (though this was not a natural group), cutters, lugs, then the ground leaves called primings. The principal difference in the Burley farm classification was that instead of using the term lugs, the farmers said "flyings." And the cutters of the flue-cured area became lugs in the Burley country. In Maryland the farmer's classification, coming down the stalk, was usually tips or dulls, bright, seconds, then ground leaves.

Perhaps the most curious of all twists in farm terminology was the variant use of the term *trash*. In the days before the Burley-blend cigarette, there was little or no demand for those thin lower leaves, the bright flyings; the valuable part of the Burley plant was the heavier leaf higher up on the stalk used by chewing-tobacco manufacturers. So cheap and relatively useless were the lower leaves that they were called trash and sometimes the farmer simply gave them to the dealer. But with the great popularity of the cigarette the once "trash" developed into the most valuable part of the plant. Yet the term trash continued to be used! Further west of the Burley district, in the Green-River and One-Sucker sections, the very bottom leaves and the worst of the lot were still called trash.

In the tobacco areas, shifting consumer demand created changes more significant than new definitions of old words. A review of the leaf types used in the manufacture of the various tobacco products is helpful for an understanding of conditions in the different tobacco districts. Cigars were, of course, made of the basic domestic cigar leaf types, classes four, five, and six, and of various imported leaf. Snuff was manufactured of the dark fire-cured. Going into chewing tobacco were, arranged in order of their importance, Burley, dark air-cured, and flue-cured.

The smoking mixtures were, in the main, composed of Burley, with a lesser amount of flue-cured and sometimes a seasoning of Perique or Turkish. Well over half of the tobacco going into the cigarette was the flue-cured; subsidiary types, in descending order of importance, were Burley, imported Turkish, and Maryland. In this period both foreign and domestic markets reflected a radical increase in demand for the most important cigarette tobaccos and a decline in the demand for other types. Once the dark-fired types were the principal export leaf items, but by the late 1930's over three-fourths of the leaf exports consisted of flue-cured.[10]

The new era meant great changes in the acreage devoted to the various types. A comparison of the years 1909–13 with the years 1935–40 shows that the cigarette types (flue-cured, Burley, and Maryland) increased in acreage 128 per cent; fire-cured and dark air-cured types suffered a reduction of 50 per cent; and the cigar types experienced a decline of 48 per cent. There was much painful readjustment in the contracting areas, especially in western Kentucky, in the adjacent Tennessee counties, and in central Virginia, those sections where the fire-cured and dark air-cured types were grown.

In terms of millions of pounds, total domestic production moved upwards from an annual average of 1,181 in the 1910's to 1,331 in the 1920's, and 1,395 in the 1930's. The bumper crop of 1939 was 1,881 millions, distributed among the major categories as follows: 1,171 flue-cured,

[10] The increased exports of flue-cured and Burley did not fully compensate for the decline in other types. Export markets were threatened by competition from other lands. And foreign governments subsidized domestic production, developed systems of exchange controls and barter agreements, and worked out preferential tariffs. The best customers for leaf tobacco by far in the average years of the 1920's and 1930's were Great Britain and China, the British taking from a third to a half of the American exports. Ten of the 20 trade agreements made in the years 1934–1939 included provisions of benefit to growers and manufacturers. Eight countries made concessions on leaf tobacco imports, five on manufactured tobacco. Most characteristic were promises that there would be no increase in tariff rates already in effect.

TOBACCO (UNSTEMMED EQUIVALENT) USED IN MANUFACTURE OF TOBACCO PRODUCTS, UNITED STATES, 1900-1946

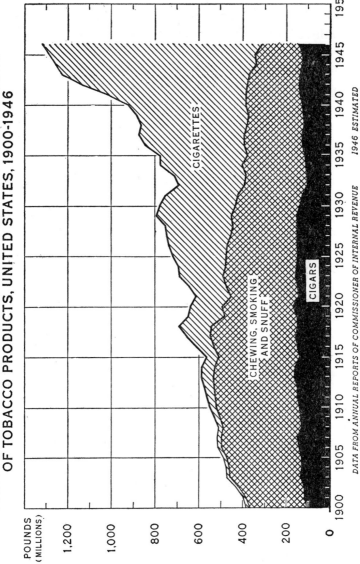

POUNDS (MILLIONS)

CIGARETTES

CHEWING, SMOKING AND SNUFF

CIGARS

DATA FROM ANNUAL REPORTS OF COMMISSIONER OF INTERNAL REVENUE

1946 ESTIMATED

U. S. DEPARTMENT OF AGRICULTURE

BUREAU OF AGRICULTURAL ECONOMICS

396 Burley, 138 cigar leaf, 99 fire-cured, 33 Maryland, 44 all others. According to the census of 1940, tobacco, the seventh most important crop in the United States, represented 5.5 per cent of the value of all crops, but occupied only 0.6 per cent of the cultivated acreage.

MARSHALL'S "REALLY GOOD FIVE-CENT CIGAR"

Domestic consumption of tobacco products showed a moderate per capita increase—6.39 pounds in 1911 and 8.10 pounds in 1941—but, as already suggested, the significant development was the shift in the forms in which the leaf was passed on to the consumer. The fictional every-man-woman-and-child during the year 1911 smoked 78 cigars, chewed 2.50 pounds of tobacco used 1.70 pounds of smoking tobacco, dipped .31 pounds of snuff, and smoked 108 cigarettes; by 1941 this imaginary creature annually smoked only 45 cigars, chewed only .78 pounds of tobacco, used 1.46 pounds of smoking tobacco, dipped .30 pounds of snuff, but smoked 1,551 cigarettes.[11]

The most dramatic changes, of course, were the rise of the cigarette, and the decline of the quid and the cigar. A few old-time professional men unashamedly chewed their tobacco, but, by and large, plug and twist were now restricted to the agricultural and industrial laborers.[12] Sales of plug and twist tobogganed unwept, unsung. The fraternity around the hot stove chewing its cud was inarticulate, and braved neither verse nor imagery. Not so the

[11] Obviously the per-capita-consumption basis is a helpful but an imperfect device for indicating changes in tobacco habits. The ratio of adults (potential tobacco-users) to total population was much higher in 1941 than in 1911.

[12] Chewing became less popular with professional athletes. Spit-ball pitchers, who had depended on a tobacco-licorice combination for lubrication, were confronted by a prohibitory rule in 1920 barring that particular type of curve ball in the professional leagues. Tolerant officials permitted the old pitchers, who depended on the spit ball, to continue its use, but the practice was forbidden newcomers.

TOBACCO PRODUCTS: CONSUMPTION PER CAPITA
IN THE UNITED STATES, 1900-1946

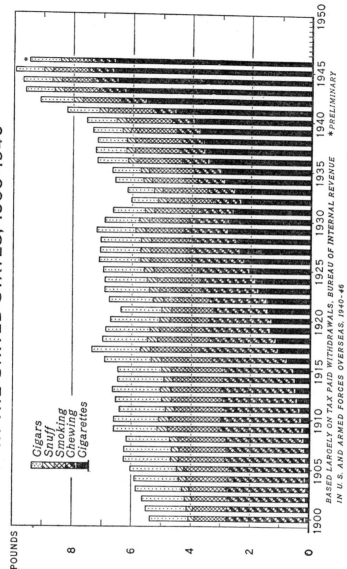

POUNDS

Cigars
Snuff
Smoking
Chewing
Cigarettes

*PRELIMINARY

BASED LARGELY ON TAX PAID WITHDRAWALS, BUREAU OF INTERNAL REVENUE

IN U. S. AND ARMED FORCES OVERSEAS, 1940-46

U S DEPARTMENT OF AGRICULTURE

BUREAU OF AGRICULTURAL ECONOMICS

smokers of the cigar. To them their tobacco was more than just a habit; it was a religion to be vested with appropriate ritual.

In an inspired scrambling of James Barrie and Jeremy Bentham, one devotee of the cigar celebrated the year 1938 by informing the *New York Times* that, "A cigar, rightly made, is esthetically as important as a piece of sculpture or a poem; and, measured in terms of the greatest good to the greatest number, it ranks high in the list of man's inventions." By silent election the high priest of the cigar cult was Thomas Riley Marshall, Hoosier humorist and statesman, and vice-president of the United States during the First World War. Until Winston Churchill's visage became a household picture in America, Marshall was the most famous cigar smoker of the twentieth century. And, at least in substance, he *did* make the remark about the five-cent cigar.

It was during Wilson's first term and Marshall, of course, presided over the Senate. The Republican, Joseph Little Bristow of Kansas, was making an emphatic speech, listing the *needs* of the country. In the pause after Bristow's sweeping peroration, Marshall whispered loudly to one of the Senate secretaries, "What this country needs is a really good five cent cigar!" Later his friends regretted that Marshall was remembered only for this sally, his constructive statesmanship forgotten.[13]

The declining per capita consumption of cigars was in evidence some four or five years before Marshall's election to the vice-presidency, but the increase in population caused a rising total consumption until after the First World War. Organizations of cigar men determined to check the downward sales then in evidence, but they struggled against an overwhelming current. Nostalgic clerks

[13] After Marshall's death in 1925, a large tobacco company unsuccessfully tried to buy from Mrs. Marshall exclusive rights to the good-five-cent-cigar yarn. Yet, the General Cigar Company claimed that Marshall said, "By golly, it is a good cigar," when first he smoked their Wm. Penn. Accordingly the company embossed this exclamation on the Wm. Penn boxes.

claimed that the true cigar connoisseurs were disappearing. In this generation the cigar box and band became less ornate. Once appearance of box and band was a decisive factor in the cigar purchase, and the cigar, often sold in saloons, caught the spirit of the brass rail and of the lush paintings that inflamed Carry Nation. The lithographing in the old days might include seductive nudes, the Great Sandow, or college athletes, all surrounded by gold medals of which the product was supposedly worthy. With the adoption of the Eighteenth Amendment and with more extensive national advertising, this type of art declined. Also completely passed was the noble gesture of manufacturing on special order wedding cigar bands, showing the picture of bride and groom.

The cigar was the last of the tobacco products to remain a hand-fashioned article. Now there was a complete machine, one which could turn out good long-filler cigars. Partly successful devices were made by Hammerstein, and by the Universal Tobacco Machine Company, but perhaps to Rufus Lenoir Patterson more than to any other single man should go the credit for producing the intricate mechanism which removed the cigar-making machine from its old classification with the impossibles and made it a thing to be bolted to the factory floor and belted to factory power. The cigar-making machine, usually given the birth-date of 1917, turned out some 4,000 finished cigars per day. The machines were quietly used for awhile in the 1920's by manufacturers who feared to disturb those consumers believing that they were getting a genuine handmade article. By 1929, when probably half the cigars were machine made, George Washington Hill decided to spread abroad the virtues of the machine product and to war against the hand-wrought article. Thus was launched the notorious spit campaign, the low point in the merchandising of tobacco products in the three hundred years and more which had elapsed since John Rolfe and his fellow settlers pondered ways to compete in the home market with the West Indian leaf. The public, though toughened over the years, found repulsive such legends as, "Spit is a horrid word . . . Why run the risk of cigars made by dirty, yellowed fingers and tipped in spit?"

As experts had predicted, the effect of the machines was a rapid concentration of the trade into fewer hands. In round figures there were 22,000 cigar factories in 1910, about 6,000 by 1929. By 1940 the number was 3,800, of which 30 were in the 40,000,000 and more class. The large factories became even larger, and the industry gave more attention to less expensive cigars, which were widely advertised. By the 1930's the General Cigar Company, featuring its White Owl, and Bayuk Cigars, Inc., concentrating on Phillies, apparently led the field. Yet all the brands of these two companies presumably made up less than one-fourth of the national production of cigars.

Considerable hand industry continued, especially for the fancy, exclusive types. And with the hand worker there survived, in some factories, the reader. In 1931 readers were directly involved in the great Tampa strike, during which citizens got out injunctions, and policemen carried riot guns. Apparently the gentlemen on the elevated chairs, reading alternately in English and Spanish, included in their repertoire not only the daily newspapers and the Spanish classics but also a seasoning of communistic propaganda, by way of supporting the Tampa Tobacco Workers Industrial Union, affiliated with the Red International. At least such was charged by the operators of the factories, who dismissed the readers, an act bringing on the strike of 7,000 cigar makers. When the factories reopened, the reading stands had been dismantled.

A year after the Tampa upheaval there occurred a strike among the cigar workers of Havana with far-reaching effects on the manufacture of fine cigars for the American market. The cigar rollers of Havana struck and most of the independent manufacturers left Havana. Among those departing was the establishment producing La Corona and related brands. This factory, controlled by the American Tobacco Company, was moved from Havana to Trenton, New Jersey, where American girls were trained to roll cigars in a plant air-conditioned to duplicate Cuban atmosphere. American girls were satisfied with piano playing instead of hearing possibly troublesome literature. And further, they did not smoke the Corona Coronas which Havana rollers had consumed at the rate of a dozen or so per day per worker.

During the calendar year 1941 the American public spent $2,139,953,000 for all tobacco products. Of this sum, $281,429,000 went for cigars; $1,527,686,000 for cigarettes. It was clearly the age of the cigarette.

[Chapter 8]

THE CIGARETTE AGE

CAMELS LEAD THE WAY

When placed on the market in 1913, Camels, the first modern cigarette, created something akin to panic in the cigarette divisions of companies producing older brands. No less an authority than the Supreme Court of the United States, 328 U. S. 791, has affirmed that the R. J. Reynolds Tobacco Company with its Camels "revolutionized the cigarette industry."

These cigarettes descended on a scene relatively peaceful, though characterized by stepped-up advertising since the dissolution. Companies spread their sales efforts over several brands. They revived the plan of giving premiums, and a man bought not so much a box of cigarettes as a Yale pennant, a miniature oriental rug, a silk flag, a map of Portugal, or a picture of Lillian Russell. In some measure the cigarette was still in the Crack-R-Jacks stage; the product was purchased partly for the prize anticipated. And it was somewhat like opera; it must smell of foreign lands before it commanded respect. Once the market had been dominated by the straight domestic cigarette, made of the bright flue-cured. Since about 1895 public favor had

been turning to straight Turkish and to Turkish blend cigarettes. Despite the usual formula of about 60 per cent
domestic (flue-cured) and 40 per cent Turkish, the Turkish blend had a pronounced Turkish flavor.[1]

After the anti-trust decision of 1911, the cigarette business of the old American Tobacco Company had been distributed among three of the four great successor companies: the new American Tobacco Company, Liggett &
Myers, and P. Lorillard. The R. J. Reynolds Tobacco Company had never entered the cigarette business in the days
of the combination and the new era found it with none
at all.

The favorite of the moment was Fatima, a Liggett &
Myers product in the Turkish blend classification, selling
15 cents for 20 cigarettes. (Fatima was the first popular
cigarette to be sold in the modern cup package of 20's.) In
their attempts to compete with Fatima, American introduced Omar, and Lorillard developed Zubelda, both
Turkish blends. The Reynolds Company rather gingerly
edged over into the 10-for-5-cent Virginia (flue-cured)
class with Reyno, but achieved no particular success.

Then, in the year 1913, members of the R. J. Reynolds
establishment created a new blend, largely bright flue-
cured, a seasoning of Turkish, and, most distinctive of all,
cased or sweetened Burley. The Burley was treated somewhat as though it was being prepared for plug tobacco.
Burley had been earlier used in cigarettes, but, so far as
can be determined, never in exactly this way. Later, probably about 1916, Maryland leaf was added to the blend
for its burning qualities. By way of doing courtesy to the
prevailing bent for the oriental, Reynolds christened his

[1] Although the evidence is vague, almost certainly several of the brands
in the straight-domestic classification were seasoned with a sprinkling of
Turkish. Marcus Feder, sometimes called the "father of the American cigarette," added a little Turkish tobacco to native leaf and produced the well-
known Sweet Caporals, originally manufactured by F. S. Kinney and later
by the American Tobacco Company. In promoting this brand Harvey Con-
over created the famous slogan, "Ask Dad, He Knows."

new product Camel, a short, easily-remembered name. Not quite realizing the epochal importance of the occasion, he launched his first real sales campaign in Cleveland, Ohio. Refusing to pin all his hopes on Camels, for safety's sake Reynolds pushed Reyno, his flue-cured cigarette, and Osman, a new blend of flue-cured and Turkish, at the same time. A stroke of genius was to present Camels as a high-grade brand, to boast of the elimination of blankets, pictures, and coupons, and to give this economy as an excuse for the initial price of only 10 cents for 20 cigarettes. The first trials were successful; Camels were well liked.

Next, Reynolds determined to concentrate on one brand, and to support that brand with forceful advertising. It was easier for him to adopt this system than it would have been for American, Liggett, or Lorillard, each of which owned several brands representing a considerable investment in advertising. As selling was then understood, it would have appeared foolish to discard goodwill built up through the years. But all of Reynolds' brands were new, and he had little to lose by dropping one or by minimizing another. The Winston-Salem group in its national campaign of 1914 adopted a program known in the trade as the "teaser" type. There were curiosity-provoking advertisements such as, "Camels! Tomorrow there will be more Camels in this town than in all Asia and Africa Combined!" At last came the picture of the package. During the spring-board year, 1914, though less than a half billion Camels were sold, nearly $1,500,000 were spent in advertising the brand.

At first the older, more experienced cigarette manufacturers merely shrugged their shoulders. George Washington Hill, of American Tobacco Company, later admitted, "I thought it was a joke: I thought they were wasting their money." But the new brand simply swept others aside and sales experts of rival firms frantically pleaded with their production men for competing articles. Chemists and laboratory men discovered that the most novel feature of the

Camel blend was the cased and dipped Burley. Even non-specialists could see that concentrated, one-brand advertising was of equal or greater importance.

In the American Tobacco Company the great salesman, Vincent Riggio, demanded something really modern to sell. Accordingly, the Hills developed a good Burley blend. So cased and sweetened was the Burley that after it was dipped it was run through a wringer. In his search for a name, George Washington Hill thumbed through the properties of the company and came upon the brand Lucky Strike, coined years before by Dr. R. A. Patterson. Next, Hill supervised the artists as they designed the package with its bull's-eye circle, but he delayed the sales campaign until he could find an effective slogan. When C. A. Penn, vice-president in charge of manufacturing plug tobacco, remarked that the amount of heat used in making the cigarette was equivalent to a cooking process, the senior Hill hit upon the phrase, "Lucky Strike, It's Toasted." The first advertising campaign showed a piece of toast with a fork through it. Before the end of the year 1916 the cigarette was sold in Buffalo; in 1917 it was successfully distributed in other sections. This was the beginning of what was to become the most expensive sales campaign in the entire history of merchandising.

In evolutionary rather than revolutionary manner Liggett & Myers developed its product, Chesterfields. Actually the brand was inconspicuously launched in the year 1912 while the various successor companies were expanding their lists under the prevailing conception that eggs should not all be put in one basket. It appears that the original Chesterfield cigarette was an undistinguished blend of domestic tobaccos, but revisions soon took place in factory ingredients and in advertising policy.[2] The

[2] In lieu of formal birth announcements, the following record is informing. Circular No. C-51, April 30, 1912, from W. Duke, Sons & Co. Branch of Liggett & Myers Tobacco Company, Durham, N. C. offered Chesterfield cigarettes "IN SLIDE BOXES of 10s" at $3.75 per thousand, less 2 per cent for cash. The firm would appreciate the stocking of Chesterfield cig-

character of the cigarette eventually fitted into the formula trend established by Camels, though by reputation Chesterfields had less extraneous flavoring matter than either Camels or Lucky Strikes. This quality may have represented an unwillingness on the part of Liggett & Myers to depart too far from the original recipe. By 1915 the Chesterfield cigarette was promoted energetically in the modern package of 20's rather than in the earlier slide-and-shell package of 10's. Thus there were three "standard brands" by 1917: Camels, Lucky Strikes, and Chesterfields.

The upward spiral of cigarette sales began in the competitive situation created by the introduction of Camel cigarettes, the per capita consumption increasing from 108 in 1911, to 166 in 1914, to 248 in 1916. The next conspicuous stimulus was offered by the First World War. In 1917 the per capita consumption was 337; by 1919, 426. With men in camps and overseas, use of both the roll-your-own and factory-made varieties sharply increased. The government in April, 1918, took over the entire output of the Bull Durham factory; the famous product was now used largely as the "makin's" for hand-rolled cigarettes. In Europe the Young Men's Christian Association assumed the thankless task of setting up the post exchanges, successors to the old time sutlers, who had operated on the all-the-traffic-will-bear idea. The Y.M.C.A. sold $12,546,661 worth of tobacco products, a large part at very reasonable rates. By October 1, 1918, Camels (then costing 15 cents in the United States) were sold for 7 cents; Fatimas (bringing 20 cents in the United States) for 8 cents. Of course much tobacco was given away to the soldiers.

---

arettes as "we feel sure that in 'CHESTERFIELD' Cigarettes we have a blend that will fill a long-felt want on the part of the consumer . . ." Further, " 'CHESTERFIELD' Cigarettes are made of the very best domestic tobacco that can be secured, and we guarantee the quality of same. Each package of 'CHESTERFIELD' Cigarettes contains a painted bower satin insert for the consumer, and this insert is unquestionably the most attractive satin insert ever used."

The cheaper varieties of Turkish cigarettes were less in evidence, partly because of the popularity of the new blends and particularly because of the wartime transportation difficulties, factors especially embarrassing to the Lorillard concern, owner of the major brands in the Turkish category. The Reynolds company, on the other hand, was in a peculiarly advantageous position. During the war, government contracts among the cigarette manufacturers were allotted on a basis of domestic sales, and as Camel sales were ranging from 30 to 40 per cent of the total American consumption at the outbreak of the war, the Reynolds company benefited greatly by this arrangement. At the low sales price in France, Camels became exceedingly popular with the armed forces. This momentum helped the Reynolds company to maintain its lead for a dozen years after the war.

"Watch me and see if I don't give Buck Duke hell," remarked the energetic R. J. Reynolds to his friend Josephus Daniels soon after the Supreme Court decision of 1911. But in no direct way did Reynolds have a chance to challenge Duke, for the founder of the American Tobacco Company assumed the chairmanship of the British-American Tobacco Company, which did not sell in the United States domestic market. In 1923 Duke resigned his executive position with British-American. By this time his interests had largely turned to textile, aluminum, and hydro-electric power projects.

It was natural that James B. Duke should have concentrated his principal legacy on Trinity College, less than an hour's walk from the old Duke homestead, near Durham. For more than a quarter of a century his family had given generously to the little institution. These contributions to Trinity had reached the millions when, in 1924, a year before his death, James B. Duke created the Duke Endowment, originally valued at some $40,000,000. Provisions were made for organizing around Trinity College a new university, for aiding other colleges, for erecting and supporting hospitals and churches, and for the care of aged ministers and orphans in the Carolinas. The Endowment with Duke's later legacies classified James B. Duke as a philanthropist exceeded in the amount of his gifts only by Rockefeller and Carnegie.

During the early 1920's the three major Burley-blend cigarettes, Camels, Chesterfields, and Lucky Strikes, products of Reynolds, Liggett & Myers, and American, dominated the American market. The Camel brand was clearly in the lead, by 1925 accounting for some 45 per cent of the sales. Belatedly Lorillard determined to move into the "standard brand" field, and in 1926 placed on the market Old Gold.[3] With high advertising expenditures, supported by a bond issue of some $15,000,000 in 1927, Lorillard achieved a segment of the market, though sales were well below the point maintained by each of the so-called Big Three.

In the year 1925 Percival S. Hill died, and his son, George Washington Hill, became president of the American Tobacco Company. More than any other person, George Washington Hill was captured by the tobacco industry. His was a peculiar single-mindedness. James B. Duke in his later years turned his interests to other fields. Not so George Washington Hill. In his youth he trained strenuously in market and factory. In 1904 he left Williams College and went to the leaf market at Wilson, North Carolina, where he hustled tobacco from the warehouse floor after it had been purchased. He followed the leaf market over the flue-cured belt. Then in Durham, where he enjoyed an occasional penny-ante game, he managed the top floor of the stemmery. After being tried out at

[3] Although Benjamin Belt, president of Lorillard, probably never heard of it, about the year 1880 one of the tobacco brands of Beard & Roberts of Kernersville, N. C., was Old Gold, presumably a plug. Certainly as early as 1885 the Kimball Tobacco Company was marketing a cigarette under the trade name Old Gold.

various jobs, he was sent to Wilson to be saddled with the
Wells-Whitehead Tobacco Company, making Carolina
Bright cigarettes. After this he took to the road, selling
Carolina Brights and later Wilson Straight Cuts. It was
the modern version of the wagon-trade school for future
tobacco executives.

Next came the first major test. In 1907 he was charged
with the management of Butler-Butler, Inc., a subsidiary
manufacturing various tobacco products and spreading its
advertising over many brands. Looking back on his experiences, Hill recalled that he then and there made up
his mind "that the future of the tobacco busines in this
country, at least, seemed to be along the lines of cigarettes." Accordingly he persuaded his father to let him
concentrate on this one product. Furthermore he decided
to center on one brand, Pall Mall, which was a Turkish
article, not to be confused with the domestic-blend cigarette made under that name in 1937 and thereafter. He
made the most of the red package ("gorgeous" was Hill's
word), developed dealer displays, and introduced what
has become standardized cigarette practice, the use of
magazine back-covers for advertising. Pall Mall emerged
as the largest selling cigarette in the high-grade classification. Hill then pushed a cigarette for the mass market,
Egyptian Straights. His device here—and it was the
method of others too—was the gift-in-every-package. The
prize, obviously an outgrowth of the nineteenth century
cigarette cards, was a little silk flag. The ladies collected
them from their gentlemen friends and with the bits of
silk pieced out pillows for their horsehair sofas of the
time.

George Washington Hill played a key role in creating
the Lucky Strike cigarette, and, when he took his father's
place as president of the American Tobacco Company, he
was already a master-hand at selling tobacco products.
Concentrating on his principal brand, Hill began planning promotion schemes with his advertising agency, Lord

& Thomas, of which Albert Davis Lasker, once gatherer of testimonials for Peruna, was president. The sensational feature of the Lucky Strike campaign of 1927 was the bold use of testimonials from women, not only the opera stars of foreign birth but native American women. Next came the campaign which ranged the whole candy industry against the American Tobacco Company, "Reach for a Lucky instead of a Sweet." "The way I got that campaign," recounted Hill, "I was riding out to my home. I got to 110th Street and Fifth Avenue; I was sitting in the car and I looked at the corner, and there was a great big stout negro lady chewing on gum. And, there was a taxicab—it was in the summertime,—coming the other way. I thought I was human and I looked, and there was a young lady sitting in the taxicab with a long cigarette holder in her month, and her skirts were pretty high, and she had a very good figure. I didn't know what she was smoking; maybe she was smoking a Camel.

"But, right then and there it hit me; there was the colored lady that was stout and chewing, and there was the young girl that was slim and smoking a cigarette,—'Reach for a Lucky instead of a Sweet.'

"There it was, right in front of you. That campaign really went to town, as everybody knows."

Actually the battle cry may have been in imitation of a Lydia E. Pinkham slogan of 1891, "Reach for a Vegetable Instead of a Sweet." The candy manufacturers were driven to distraction, and the Federal Trade Commission warned Hill that cigarettes should not be sold as reducing devices. He seemed satisfied to abbreviate his slogan to "Reach for a Lucky Instead," and to run the future-shadow series, double-chinned and heavy-belted silhouettes behind normal figures. Technical honors of war in this jousting probably went to an interested bystander, Lorillard, a firm which diplomatically advertised, "Eat a Chocolate. Light an Old Gold. And enjoy both! Two fine and healthful treats!"

In his advertising Hill outwitted wiser men because he himself had much of the average man's taste. And he was dispensing a mass product. Like "Private" Allen, the ex-Confederate soldier running for office in Mississippi, he was perfectly willing to let the generals vote for his opponents, if the privates would only vote for him. Hill's advertisements were characteristically aggressive, sometimes in poor taste. Occasionally they were simply impish, as in the "HER HERO" edition of the old Bull Durham advertisement, showing the traditional Bull Durham sign, with benefit of a decently-placed fence paling, being subjected to warm glances by a lonesome cow, bovine tongue hanging out. Hill's competitors often felt that he struck unfairly, as when he wrote of the *sheep dip* in those cigarettes not possessing the virtues of the Lucky Strike toasting process.[4] R. J. Reynolds Tobacco Company vented its anger by spending $300,000 in March, 1930, on a full-page advertisement, "Turning the light of Truth on false and misleading statements in recent cigarette advertising."

To meet the new type of competition, the Reynolds firm changed its advertising agency and employed William Cole Esty, who had earned distinction among his confrères through his creative talents in coining such phrases as "Undie Odor," when shepherding the Lux account. Early interested in stage magic, Esty moved into Reynolds via a program, "It's Fun to be Fooled," indirectly ridiculing the Lucky Strike toasting process. In this tournament between American and Reynolds at the end of the decade, American for the moment came out ahead, in 1930 displacing the primacy enjoyed by Camels. Though less sensational in its sales policy than either Reynolds or American, Lig-

---

[4] Loyal inhabitants of Winston-Salem in the old days were convinced that Lucky Strike salesmen had initiated whispering campaigns against Camels. At any rate, there was no commodity about which rumors could be more readily spread than cigarettes, whether it was the time-worn story that lepers were found in such and such a factory, or that a certain combination of control numbers on a cigarette package would win from the manufacturing company a new car.

gett & Myers held Chesterfields well within the orbit of the Big Three.

The decade of the 1920's marked the real beginning of monumental advertising on the part of the tobacco companies. Annual budgets of $10,000,000 for a company were not at all uncommon; in 1926 the Reynolds firm spent about $19,000,000. Advertisements were now directed at women as well as men, and per capita consumption of cigarettes doubled during the decade. The figure for 1920 was 419; for 1925, 690; for 1930, 972. And the American cigarette was becoming more popular in foreign lands. In 1931, when on their British-goods-are-the-best tour of South America, the Prince of Wales and Prince George smoked cigarettes made in the United States. Although the rest of their party used the British article, one of the 96 pieces of baggage assigned the princes was a satchel filled with their favorite American brand.

THE ALL-AMERICAN CIGARETTE

The exact processes employed by the major manufacturers were closely guarded trade secrets, but basic formulas were common knowledge in the tobacco trade. About 1940 the leaf tobacco going into a typical cigarette was probably from 50 to 65 per cent flue-cured; from 20 to 35 per cent Burley; from 8 to 15 per cent Turkish; from 2 to 5 per cent Maryland. Whatever ratio the manufacturers considered ideal, undoubtedly they made adjustments on a basis of availability of the various crops. The character of the cigarette was, by gradual stages, greatly changed in the 1920's and 1930's as larger and larger crops of flue-cured were grown in the new areas of Georgia and Florida. In these southernmost regions the average leaf was lighter and probably milder than in the older belts, though by itself it would not have made a satisfactory smoke.

The leaf purchased loose on the auction warehouse floor

was subjected to a re-drying process, for "farmer's order" was a semi-perishable condition. Companies might carry flue-cured up to three weeks, Burley up to two months without spoiling, but these were the safety limits. After redrying, the tobacco was packed in large hogsheads, about the same size and shape as used in colonial times, approximately a thousand pounds to the cask. These were stored for aging in large, well-ventilated warehouses. Some of these storage warehouses were of almost unbelievable dimensions. A single structure in Lexington, Kentucky, owned by the American Tobacco Company held 40,000,000 pounds of tobacco. Inventories were built up by the best managers when prices were low or when crops were especially good, but the cardinal reason for the large supply on hand year after year was the necessity for aging the leaf before it could be used. The changes which took place, essentially chemical in their nature, left the tobacco milder. The length of the storage period varied; much of the tobacco aged for a couple of years or more.

When ready for manufacture, the tobacco was hauled from the warehouses, stripped of the hogshead staves, and, for proper handling, given a moisture content by ordering machines. Then the domestic leaves were stemmed, an operation once carried on by hand, but now performed largely by machines. ("Green stemmeries," where tobacco was stemmed before aging, were introduced by several companies in the 1930's.) The strips, that part of the tobacco remaining after the stems had been removed, were again given the proper moisture content, then blended and flavored.

For convenience the non-tobacco ingredients in the cigarette may be separated into two divisions. First, there was the hygroscopic agent, designed to preserve the moisture in the tobacco. Nearly all manufacturers used glycerin; at least one employed diethylene glycol. Second, there were what the layman would call the flavorings proper: honey or sugar-syrup, rum, licorice, chocolate, essences of prune or peach, coumarin, and other redolent substances. The possibilities of combining natural and artificial flavors to point up the natural tobacco aroma were almost infinite. For a long time the fragrant tonka bean was used, but synthetic coumarin, more subject to laboratory control, in considerable measure replaced nature's article. The tonka bean, with its vanilla-like aroma, was the seed of a tropical tree found in the jungles of South America. The ground-up tonka beans were given a three months' soaking in rum, and the resultant liquid, rich in natural coumarin, was sprayed over the tobacco. From the southeastern part of the United States came deer's tongue, sometimes called dog's tongue, hound's tongue, Carolina vanilla, vanilla leaf, or vanilla plant. Because it contained coumarin it was sometimes used as a substitute for vanilla and other flavors. Families living near the swamps of South Carolina and Florida profited by the demand for deer's tongue, collecting the plant, selling the leaves to merchants, who dried, baled and shipped them.

A typical manufacturing process began with the blending of Burley and Maryland strips, which were then dipped in a cooked solution made of sugar, licorice, and other flavors. The sweetened Burley-Maryland strips were next mixed with the flue-cured strips and aromatic leaf, two types which earlier had been blended together and given an appropriate amount of moisture. The tobacco was then sprayed with glycerin and "bulked" (left piled up) for one or more days. After this, the blended tobacco was put on the cutter-line, where it was shredded. Next the tobacco was dried, sprayed with coumarin-flavored rum, stored and cooled, ready for the cigarette machines. As the procedures were simplified, some manufacturers apparently eliminated the dipping and applied all flavoring materials in one spraying. The makers of the Lucky Strike brand in their earliest advertising emphasized the various drying-out and heat treatments interspersed in their processes.

The cigarette-making machines were almost unbeliev-
ably intricate and efficient contrivances, which had grown
out of the earlier inventions of Bonsack and others. Great
spools of cigarette paper unreeled. Tobacco was spread
along the belt of paper, which was turned up and about
the shredded leaf, and sealed with casein or some other
tasteless adhesive. Self-sharpening knives clipped this almost endless tube of tobacco into cigarettes at a high rate
of speed. The basic machines dating from before the First
World War maintained a standard output of some 600
cigarettes per minute, more than triple the rate of the
Bonsack contrivance of 1884. About 1931 there were installed new devices made possible by improved types of
ball bearings, which allowed still greater speed. Belt con-
veyors took trays of cigarettes to packing machines, which
manufactured the cups around the cigarettes, complete
with foil, label, and revenue stamp. The most important
general changes in factory management consisted of the
expanding use of labor-saving machinery and the continual adoption of simplified processes. These developments reduced manufacturing costs per unit of output,
and enabled the industry with a minimum of difficulty to
grant the wage demands of the 1940's.

The manufacturer of the 1920's and 1930's was dependent on foreign sources not only for his aromatic tobacco, as the Turkish began to be called, but also for his
cigarette paper, supplied mainly by the Société Anonyme
des Papeteries de Mauduit and the Société Nouvelle des
Papeteries de Champagne of France. Although there were
earlier developments of interest to the antiquarian, the
revolutionary fact in the history of cigarette paper in the
United States was the shipping of the first carload from
the Ecusta Paper Company, Pisgah Forest, North Carolina,
on September 2, 1939. It was just in time. The Second
World War had broken out the previous day with Germany's attack on Poland.

In the background was the person of Harry H. Straus,

an energetic six-feet-one-inch man, who had arrived in this country from Germany at the age of eighteen, and finally become a salesman of cigarette paper, French made. He prospered, controlled a French establishment, then determined to make cigarette paper in America and from the fiber of the flax plant itself, not the linen rags such as were supplied the French manufacturers by the rag pickers of Poland, Russia, and the Balkans. American manufacturers were interested in his plans. They were receiving good spools from France, but they were troubled by the knowledge that the industry was keyed to raw materials from unstable eastern Europe. After basic research had been carried on in the laboratories of Duke University and elsewhere, Straus eventually created a process whereby the straw from linseed-oil type flax could be used in the making of paper equal or superior to the best of that from the French mills. His decisive experiments were completed about the time of Munich, and American cigarette manufacturers, now thoroughly frightened, scurried to lend him money for the construction of a plant.

In the mountains of western North Carolina, Straus's engineers and chemists found the Davidson River, silt-free, pouring from Pisgah National Forest. Around about were mountain men and marginal farmers, ignorant of factory ways but teachable. In May of 1939, when seventeen buildings had been completed, French artisans, skilled paper-workers from the French mills, arrived and with four interpreters assisting they taught the Carolinians the art of papermaking. The plant expanded until it could supply the demands of all domestic manufacturers, had they thought it wise to concentrate their purchases in this one firm. A new era dawned around Pisgah Forest, for the Ecusta Paper Company spent millions of dollars in meeting its payrolls. Once the seed-flax farmers of California, Minnesota, Oregon, and the Dakotas paid a dollar and a half an acre to have the straw removed after the seed had been gathered. Now they received a dollar or two per acre for that straw.

By 1939 the 100-per-cent American cigarette was almost a reality. There was freedom from the rag pickers of eastern Europe, but the manufacturers still depended on the farmers of Turkey, Greece, and Bulgaria for the "salt-and-pepper-leaf," the aromatic Turkish type. The annual importation was about 50,000,000 pounds. During the next decade a significant beginning was made in the production of this leaf within the boundaries of the United States.

AND STILL THE COFFIN NAIL

Out in Kansas a traveling Chautauqua company staging scenes from *Carmen* presented its cast against a backdrop showing a dairy rather than a cigarette factory. Carmen herself entered carrying a pail of milk. Doubtless such editing was good policy in rural areas before the First World War. The anti-tobacco movement, principally anti-cigarette, was far from dead.

In the heart of the tobacco country, within the religious denomination that had profited most from the tobacco industry, a crushing motion of condemnation was sustained. The anti-tobacco forces obtained a rule from the 1914 General Conference of the Methodist Episcopal Church, South, that the Committee on Admissions should require all preachers-on-trial "to agree to abstain from the use of tobacco." It appears that the decisive memorial was presented by the Northwest Texas Conference, which requested that the Discipline be changed from *advising* abstention to *requiring* it of candidates for the ministry. Mr. M. T. Haw urged acceptance of the proposed rule, topping off his speech with a lachrymose story of his own conversion to the antitobacco cause through the efforts of his mother, who carried home her point by requiring him to clean out his father's cuspidor! The presiding officer at the Conference was none other than Bishop Kilgo, ex-president of Trinity College and an old friend of the Dukes. Although the Bishop reputedly wore a battery of cigars in his waistcoat at the time, after a heated debate he put the question. Observers both within and without the denomination condemned the hypocrisy of allowing the elder clergy to keep their pipes, cigars, cigarettes, and quids while refusing this solace to the younger men.

About this time several of the nation's most popular figures, among them Elbert Hubbard, John Burroughs, Thomas A. Edison, and Henry Ford, condemned the cigarette. And who were more fitted to speak for America than the author of *A Message to Garcia*, "The Sage of Slabsides," "The Wizard of Menlo Park," and the creator of the Model T? [5] In reply Percival S. Hill of the American Tobacco Company cited the bill of health given the cigarette by the *Lancet* of England, and, going even further, Hill countered with the positive-benefit theory. "Millions of American men have convinced themselves that cigarettes are good for them." But something should be done by way of concerted defense, thought leading manufacturers. The answer was the formation of the Tobacco Merchants Association in 1915 under the inspiration and encouragement of Charles Dushkind, first secretary of the organization.[6] The major task of the trade organization was to curb, if possible, hostile legislation.

During the First World War it appeared as though the enemies of nicotine were crushed in the mad dash to prepare cigarettes for shipment overseas, the nation mean-

[5] It must be remembered that Edison was attacking the cigarette, not other forms of tobacco. When his quartered-oak desk was opened in 1947 on the hundredth anniversary of his birth, from the upper right-hand drawer spilled forth cigars and an old-fashioned twist, Murray's Special Chewing Roll.

[6] Contributions to T.M.A., as the Tobacco Merchants Association was called, became sizable. While the payments by the American Tobacco Company and the American Cigarette and Cigar Company totaled only $1,000 in 1916, they exceeded $131,000 in 1931, $202,000 in 1933.

while singing, "While you've a lucifer to light your fag, smile, boys, that's the style!" But not all were silenced. Dr. Clarence True Wilson, head of the Methodist Temperance and Moral Board, charged that the "tobacco trust" had taken advantage of American patriotism and supplied cigarettes so full of "dope" that the soldiers were becoming drug addicts! But much intolerance was also on the other side; one champion of the cigarette wondered if the espionage act were not broad enough to cover reformers and ministers who hinted that cigarettes were bad for young soldiers.

The nominal victory of the prohibitionists in the passage of the Eighteenth Amendment revitalized the anti-tobacco movement. The lead in the new attack on tobacco was taken by the Women's Christian Temperance Union, which, at its Victory Convention in St. Louis in November, 1919, voted to fight against tobacco by general educational program, but refused a resolution favoring prohibitory legislation. About this time special plans for expounding the evils of tobacco were announced by several church organizations; most of the efforts were directed toward the youth of the land. And Billy Sunday, impassioned revivalist, said, "Prohibition is won; now for tobacco." Then, in January, 1920, Miss Gaston announced her candidacy for the presidency of the United States on an anti-tobacco platform. She actually filed platform and declaration in South Dakota, though later she attempted to organize a movement to elect Bryan.

Lovers of individual liberty, of tobacco, and of the profits derived therefrom viewed all these developments with misgivings. *Tobacco*, the organ of the tobacco trade, thought the new anti-tobacco movement quite serious, and blamed "heedless smokers and careless spitters" for strengthening the cause of the reformers. Weary of prohibitions, liberal men mixed sadness and sarcasm in their comments on the new American be-it-enacted complex. The Association Opposed to National Prohibitions, seeing

the W.C.T.U. in every woodpile, sponsored the organization in Cincinnati on October 9, 1919, of the Allied Tobacco League of America. The United States Tobacco
Association, claiming to represent 90 per cent of the growers of the leaf, named a committee to raise a "war chest"
for use in fighting the enemies of tobacco. In Albany, New
York, the Smokers' League Against Tobacco Prohibition,
formed "to establish and conserve the rights of the citizens of the United States to the use of tobacco," was
granted a charter by the Secretary of State, August 8,
1921. The officials of the Tobacco Merchants Association
discussed the problem with various members. Counsel was
appointed for almost every state to report unfavorable
legislation. As a pressure group, the T.M.A. had already
made an enviable record.[7]

For awhile it appeared as though the cigarette prohibition states, which had dropped in number to nine at the
beginning of 1915 and to five by 1920, would be increased.
An Indiana legislator meant business and advocated, as
punishment for smoking in public, imprisonment at hard
labor. Kansas decided to take seriously its prohibitory act,

[7] The following items are extracted from President Werthiem's report
made at the office of the association to the annual meeting of the board of
directors, Tuesday, February 19, 1918:

"It has successfully opposed and frustrated all efforts to enact hostile
legislation, both federal as well as local. . . ."

"The adoption of the tax rates advocated by the T.M.A. instead of the
flat increase of 100 per cent, as recommended by the Treasury Department
in connection with the War Revenue Bill, the difference being about
$40,000,000 per annum."

"The elimination from the Chamberlain Bill of the provision prohibiting
the sale of tobacco products at military camps, etc. The serious consequences
of such law need hardly be dwelt upon. The prohibition clause found its
way into the Military Bill and was passed by the Senate almost on the
last day of the Session. But our opposition to that measure was so strenuous
and our arguments so convincing that Senator Chamberlain withdrew that
clause at the following session of the Congress."

"The defeat of anti-tobacco legislation in a number of States.

"To counteract anti-tobacco propaganda.

"(a) It made an extensive investigation and campaign to remove the fake
tobacco cure menace.

"(b) It distributed thousands of pamphlets that it has had printed demonstrating the harmlessness of the use of tobacco products."

and before the end of the year 1920 the state supreme court affirmed the constitutionality of the statute. Miss Gaston received the good news from Kansas with great joy, packed her bags, went to campaign for effective enforcement, and advised the Kansans to adopt Carry Nation tactics. While in Topeka, she made public a letter which she had sent to President-elect Harding, urging him to give up his cigarettes. "The United States has had no smoking President since McKinley. Roosevelt and Taft and Wilson all have clear records. Is not this a question of grave importance?" she asked. Whereupon a group of Atchison men, seeking to salvage the honor of Kansas, purchased (of course illegally) a carton of cigarettes and sent them to Harding with a letter proclaiming their resentment of the "pernicious audacity on the part of a female who writes you such an insulting letter under a Kansas date line." Schooled in the fence-jumping exercises of the 1920 campaign, Harding had no difficulty in side-stepping the issue presented by Miss Gaston. "I think it is fine to save the youth of America from the tobacco habit," wrote Mr. Harding. "I think, however, the movement ought to be carried on in perfect good faith and should be free from any kind of hypocrisy or deceit on the part of those who are giving it their earnest attention." [8]

In 1921 Utah gave legal force to the official Mormon attitude, and forbade the sale of cigarettes. Then the agitation in the state capitals and elsewhere began to subside. As early as February, 1921, experienced observers saw signs of relief from the anti-tobacco pressure. Before the year was out, Iowa, Arkansas, and Tennessee repealed their ineffective statutes. In 1923 even the Utah legislature allowed cigarette sales under certain restrictions, though the public use of tobacco was still under such severe regulations that one member of the state legislature

[8] The next few years were to show that Miss Gaston had made strong allies in Kansas. In 1925 the Lyon County Chapter of the W.C.T.U. advocated a revision of the song about Old King Cole who called for his pipe.

threatened to introduce a law prohibiting the public sale of corned beef and cabbage, inasmuch as the fumes from the dish were quite as obnoxious to some individuals as was tobacco smoke to others. Only North Dakota and Kansas now had general anti-cigarette-sales laws on their books. Actual enforcement of anti-tobacco rules in North Dakota seemed to be limited to a prohibition of public smoking on the part of minors. It was well-known that the law officials of Kansas had given up attempts to put into effect the anti-cigarette statute of that state, a fact thrown in William Allen White's face when the Sage of Emporia in 1923 came to New York and criticized the lax enforcement of the Eighteenth Amendment there. North Dakota allowed its statutes to catch up with custom in 1924. Three years later, 1927, Kansas repealed her restrictions as a result of a campaign led by ex-servicemen. After that, Utah was the only state in which even a partial effort was made to prohibit the sale of the fags to adults. The State of Utah sustained before the United States Supreme Court the validity of its law prohibiting tobacco advertisements on billboards, placards, and street cars.

After Miss Gaston's death in 1924, the most prominent leader in the anti-tobacco cause was Dr. Charles G. Pease, president of the Non-Smokers' Protective League. This vegetarian and teetotaler personally arrested astonished smokers, including gentlemen in evening clothes, if they were violating ordinances. There are many tales of this David who faced before the courts the Goliaths of the tobacco industry. It is said that his life was threatened more than once, and that he was twice visited by undertakers who offered to show him their wares. "Tobacco is many times more poisonous than opium," proclaimed Dr. Pease. Dr. Daniel H. Kress, chairman, and Dr. Harvey W. Wiley, vice-chairman of the National Anti-Tobacco Convention Promotion Committee were other notable figures. Dr. Wiley, it will be recalled, was father of the Pure Food and Drugs Act of 1906 and later affiliated with *Good*

Housekeeping's laboratory. Numbered among the strange allies accumulated by these leaders was the Honorable Cole Blease, who condemned Coca-Cola and also recommended an act preventing the sale of cigarettes and cigarette paper within the boundaries of his state of South Carolina.

In the medical pronouncements of the 1920's the doctors often marked off the extreme claims of the anti-tobacconists as *not proven* or else presented a mild defense of the weed. Dr. O. Victor Limerick, director of the Department of Pharmacology of the Brooklyn, New York, Diagnostic Institute, wrote an essay, "The Psychology of the Tobaccophobe," for the *Therapeutic Gazette* of Detroit, in which he concluded that tobacco helped in the incessant problem of adaptation. "The history of human experience, as well as the results of exhaustive investigations conducted by men highly trained in scientific research, point to the fact that the moderate use of smoking tobacco is not harmful to either the body or mind." In the light of the urbanization and industrialization of modern life, one of the more significant estimates was made by W. E. Dixon, in the English periodical, *Nineteenth Century*. He judged that, "for ordinary man, under the strained conditions imposed by residence in cities, the use of tobacco fulfils a necessary, beneficial, and harmless function." In *Scribner's Magazine* Dr. James A. Tobey presented a conservative summary by admitting various opinions among medical men, noting the enigma of mouth cancer, and the dangers of tobacco to some persons especially when used in excess. In his judgment, "When used in reasonable moderation, tobacco does not exert a harmful effect on the average person. No one would claim that it is highly beneficial, though there are unquestionably occasions when tobacco may exert a soothing or sedative effect which may be psychologically helpful."

The tobacco industry, as such, from time to time attempted quiet "educational" campaigns, such as National

Tobacco Week, with exhibitions showing processes, and charts indicating the place of tobacco in the national economic life. Quite different was much of the cigarette advertising undertaken by the individual companies in the late 1920's. Dr. Tobey, while decrying the extreme zealots of the anti-cigarette group, declared them "no more unreasonable and bigoted than are some of the predatory, mercenary, and rapacious commercial tobacco interests, whose sales methods and advertising ethics, or lack of them, are, to put it mildly, definitely malodorous." Senator Smoot, of anti-tobacco Utah, condemned the "orgy of buncombe, quackery and downright falsehood and fraud." Church and other reform groups followed this theme, criticizing specifically what they called the appeal being made to convert the youth and the women of the land to the tobacco habit. William K. Anderson, in an article entitled "Will They Force Us to It?" in *The Christian Century* (December 18, 1929), commented on "the blatant and disgraceful advertising methods of cigarette companies in recent months," and then turned to the subject of women in the cigarette advertisements. "First the woman appears in the advertisement—merely a pretty girl who becomes part of the picture; then she is offering the man a fag; next she asks him to blow the smoke her way; finally she lights hers by his. The one encouraging thing about this development is that the grade of women pictured in the posters has distinctly deteriorated in the process, until now we see at the turn of the road the most voluptuous, greasy-haired Medusa that was ever used to advertise anything."

About the time William Howard Taft was President of the United States, a visiting Englishwoman while dining in a fashionable restaurant flourished a cigarette and asked a headwaiter, "May ladies smoke here?" With emphasis that dignitary replied, "Ladies may, madam, but ladies never do." The cigarette made its first noticeable impression on the woman of the international circles. Then, about the end of the First World War, many women accepted the cigarette as though it were the major symbol of their emancipation. By the early 1920's in the urban centers of the northeast women smokers were plainly in evidence; by the middle 1920's they could be seen in small town and village. This was the era of the "flapper," with her bare knees, bobbed hair, rouged cheeks, and frank language. And the cigarette was part of her costume, limited as it was.

To fight against the use of cigarettes by women, all the old arguments in opposition to tobacco were advanced, plus some new ones. Dr. Kellogg and others said that smoking would cause women to have moustaches. Certainly it would jeopardize their ability to bear children, and the health of any children who might be born to them. Women were discharged from their jobs, dismissed from college, for the crime of smoking. In 1921 Congressman Paul B. Johnson of the Sixth Mississippi District offered a bill to prevent women from publicly smoking in the District of Columbia. President Harding's sister, Mrs. Carolyn Votaw, was quoted as saying, "I despair of working any permanent regeneration in the character of a girl who refuses to sign and abide by the anti-cigarette pledge." Families were split on the question. Fortunately not many men went as far as a husband in San Francisco, who, according to newspaper report, was so furious with his wife when he caught her smoking that he put her on the floor, sat on her, and made her eat a pack of cigarettes. The famous woman preacher from England, Miss Maude Roydon, in 1928 found her invitation to speak, once extended by the Women's Home Missionary Society of the Methodist Episcopal Church of Oak Park, Illinois, withdrawn when it was learned that she smoked. The explanation that smoking "is done not at all by the women of our churches" was hooted at by most metropolitan dailies.

Miss Roydon herself remarked, "I feel that until the Church bans smoking entirely among its male members it is not in a very strong position in dictating what its women members should do about it." [9]

By the depression year 1929, much of the opposition to smoking by women had disappeared. They were being given special smoking rooms by theaters, railroads, and steamship lines. Bryn Mawr had lifted the ban in 1925; many other colleges followed. The Student Government at Smith College voted to permit smoking, and President William Allan Neilson sustained their verdict, while disagreeing with its wisdom. He delighted the students by commenting, "It is a dirty, expensive, and unhygienic habit—to which I am devoted." If they were going to smoke, smoke like gentlemen, he said. But the amiable Neilson was forced by dormitory fires to restrict the students' smoking to two fireproof rooms. "The trouble is, my dear young ladies," he remarked when closing his address, "you do not smoke like gentlemen." Miss Frances Perkins in an article in the *New Republic* (May 7, 1930), scolded American women for their bad manners with their new plaything. Her title, "Can They Smoke Like Gentlemen?" was answered in the well-they-haven't-as-yet vein.

The 1930's provided a decade of relative quiescence on the anti-tobacco front. There were, to be sure, fugitive sheets and strange-looking brochures that showed up in odd places.[10] It was symbolic of the decade that North Dakota

[9] The women took to the cigarette much more readily in England than in America. When, in 1930, word was spread about that women of the royal family smoked, an English newspaper commented: "The news is not at all startling. Long before smoking had ceased to be thought freakish or fast for the average English woman, royal ladies having cosmopolitan ways smoked, as did their French and Russian cousins." It was remarked that Princess Louise, Victoria's daughter and King George's aunt, was especially fond of "gaspers," the strong, cheap cigarettes.

[10] Among the various anti-tobacco pamphlets was an essay written by Roland M. Harper, University, Alabama, entitled, "Some Social and Moral Effects of Tobacco," and dated March, 1938. Mr. Harper made a point for couples to keep in mind when doing their family planning. "There seems to be a tendency for smokers, especially of cigarettes, if they have any

in 1937 repealed its unenforced law, dating from 1921, which had made smoking in public carriers or public eating places a misdemeanor. In their Five-Year Meetings the Friends were less concerned about tobacco than formerly. As the Methodists North and South closed the schism of almost a hundred years' standing, they retained on their books the earlier anti-tobacco rules, as well as a denunciation of slaveholding, but the nicotine regulation remained practically a dead letter.

Not from the ranks of the Gastons and the Peases, but from the biologists came the most damning accusations leveled against tobacco. In March, 1938, Dr. Raymond Pearl, eminent scientist and Professor of Biology, Medical School, Johns Hopkins University, reported to the New York Academy of Medicine on "The Search for Longevity." In the course of his paper, based on what he felt were the first life tables showing the relationship between tobacco smoking and longevity, he stated, "Smoking is associated with a definite impairment of longevity. This impairment is proportional to the habitual amount of tobacco usage by smoking, being great for heavy smokers and less for moderate smokers." At the same time, Dr. Pearl reported an inability to demonstrate any relationship between moderate drinking and the life span. Though *Time* magazine suggested that Dr. Pearl's findings would frighten the manufacturers and "make tobacco users' flesh creep," the average American, when he read of the scientist's report, appeared to be happier over the drinking item than downhearted over the smoking report. But, according to George Seldes, ex-newspaper man and author of *Lords of the Press* and other exposure documents, the newspapers, fattening on tobacco advertising, ignored or buried with inconspicuous position the Pearl report. Ickes

children at all, to have more daughters than sons. . . . It is not intended to imply here that girls are in any way less desirable than boys, but merely to record an observation, for the benefit of those who may prefer one or the other."

spoke of the refusal of the papers to publish the findings. Dr. Pearl ruefully observed that he had paid for many items from a clipping bureau, but Seldes insisted that these accounts were mostly from small-town papers, not great metropolitan dailies.[11]

The average American preferred to turn from scientific treatises to the famous words of G. L. Hemminger, first published in the *Penn State Froth*, November, 1915:

> Tobacco is a dirty weed. I like it.
> It satisfies no normal need. I like it.
> It makes you thin, it makes you lean,
> It takes the hair right off your bean.
> It's the worst darn stuff I've ever seen.
>   I like it.

THE BATTLE OF LEXINGTON, KENTUCKY

Partly as a sop thrown to the anti-tobacco groups defeated on the cigarette prohibition programs, but principally as an expedient for the remedying of treasury deficits, states began to levy special taxes on tobacco products. Iowa led the way in 1921 by taxing cigarettes. In 1930 the number of states taxing tobacco products had grown to 12; by 1941 to 27, and the amount collected exceeded $100,000 annually. On cigarettes, the most popular item of taxation, the levy was usually set at two or three cents per pack of twenty, this in addition to the federal tax, which, from 1919 to 1940 was six cents. Internal revenue receipts from tobacco yielded to the federal government about $80,000,-

---

[11] In September, 1935, two and a half years before the Pearl report, *Fortune* magazine attempted a summary of the medical aspects of tobacco and came to these conclusions: "Tobacco like alcohol is a substance to which some people are allergic. And if you are allergic to tobacco, you simply can't smoke. But that is not tobacco's fault." However, "This much can be said: that the *possible* benefit to be derived from tobacco is always less than the *possible* harm."

000 in 1915, $450,000,000 in 1930, and $698,000,000 in 1941.

In the early 1930's Congress, in planning new taxes, considered proposals to increase internal revenue duties. Protesting against further taxation, manufacturers claimed that the tobacco industry, contrary to popular opinion, was not absolutely "depression proof," that sales of cigarettes had now turned downwards. In 1930 production was 124,-000,000,000 cigarettes; in 1931, only 117,000,000,000; in 1932, 107,000,000,000. Not until 1934 were the 1930 sales exceeded.

Confronted by reduced personal incomes and rising state taxes, many cigarette smokers curtailed their purchases of the standard packages; others turned to less expensive smoking, to the hand-rolled varieties, or to the ten-cent brands. Dealers obligingly broke open a package for the indigent customer; ordinarily the loose cigarettes then sold for one cent each. During those hard days of 1932 a customer in McClellanville, South Carolina, asked for a single cigarette. The merchant handed one to the man who carefully put an egg on the counter and departed! Granulated tobacco and cigarette paper were in demand. Men were re-learning the art of rolling-your-own. And some cleaned up their old pipes. As a compromise with the machine age there appeared small hand-operated cigarette-making devices which could be purchased for less than a dollar. For use in hand-rolled cigarettes and pipes, Liggett & Myers pushed Velvet and Duke's Mixture; Reynolds initiated a Prince Albert campaign; American announced a million-dollar drive for the distribution of Bull Durham.

The most serious threat to the primary brands of the Big Three came from the "ten-centers," which were of inconsequential importance in the market until the year 1931, when the major companies tried to cure the depression by raising their prices. Old ten-cent trademarks were renovated, new ones created. Notable in the market during 1931 and 1932 were the following brands listed at ten cents for the package of twenty: White Rolls, put out by the old smoking-tobacco manufacturers, Larus & Brother Company of Richmond; Paul Jones by Continental Tobacco Company; Twenty Grand by Axton-Fisher. Brown & Williamson Tobacco Corporation, also making Raleighs, reduced Wings from fifteen to ten cents. In the group was the brand, Marvels, manufactured by Stephano Brothers. For awhile in 1932 the ten-cent cigarettes represented about one-fifth of the total domestic consumption, but their sales were reduced the next year when the large companies cut the prices of the "standard brands." In 1934 and 1935, when the Big Three again raised their prices, the ten-cent brands made a fractional recovery, accounting for some 10 or 12 per cent of the total cigarette sales. Then, bolstered by judicious advertising, the sales of the ten-cent group rose to about 17 per cent of the total by 1939. It was during this same depression period that the mentholated cigarettes made their most important advance in sales, though they had been developed several years earlier.

Also born in the depression was the Philip Morris English Blend, introduced in January, 1933.[12] This cigarette was distributed for sale on a 15-cent basis at a time when Camels, Lucky Strikes, Chesterfields, and Old Golds were on the retail market at a slightly lower figure. With the Big Three brands and Old Gold being sold to dealers at $6.00 then $5.50 per thousand, less 10 and 2 per cent discounts, Philip Morris put its price at $6.85 per thousand, less the usual discounts, and urged that the package price be kept at 15 cents per package of 20 to afford the retailer a satisfactory margin of profit. Because of this factor, retailers gave the Philip Morris cigarettes favored displays and personal endorsements which assisted in making a suc-

---

[12] Soon after the First World War one of the brands distributed by the English Philip Morris Company had been usually termed simply "Philip Morris," but it was an expensive Turkish blend article.

cess of the initial campaign. A research project proved to the satisfaction of the makers of Philip Morris that, if diethylene glycol were used as a hygroscopic agent, cigarettes were less irritating than with the glycerin product. Therefore diethylene glycol was adopted, a fact presented to the medical men in their journals. In 1933 the advertising agents for Philip Morris discovered a dwarf, John Roventini, whose resplendent uniform created effective counter displays, and whose penetrating and metallic voice became a lively trademark on the radio.

In the 1930's it was apparent that the "lesser brands," meaning Old Gold, Philip Morris, Raleighs, and a host of others, were becoming more and more important as a group. The brands outside the Big Three leaders probably accounted for only a tenth of the cigarette sales in 1930, a fourth in 1940. Yet not a one of these lesser brands was a close rival of Camels, Lucky Strikes, or Chesterfields. The Lorillard Company, makers of Old Gold, conducted an impressive prize contest in 1937, the awards totaling $200,000. Some 2,000,000 people submitted answers to the rebus puzzles. Libraries found their dictionaries torn to pieces by frantic contestants; many public reading rooms temporarily withdrew from circulation their reference works. Despite this boost, sales experts estimated that in the late 1930's Old Golds were pushed out of fourth place by Philip Morris, and that by 1940 they had been passed by Raleighs.

The Big Three possessed compact organizations with old and shrewd heads. The directors were almost invariably officers or department managers. Manufacturing operations were concentrated in a few plants: the American Tobacco Company made its cigarettes in Durham, Reidsville, and Richmond; Liggett & Myers, in Richmond, Durham, and San Francisco; R. J. Reynolds, in Winston-Salem. Every now and then a company had trouble with minority stockholders (there was friction in the American Tobacco Company over the officers' bonus plan in the early

1930's), but usually the corporations ran smoothly enough. As the years went by, the center of power in a cigarette-manufacturing company characteristically shifted from the production branches to financing and selling. By the 1930's even the most conservative executive recognized that advertising meant success or failure for his firm, though the exact ratio of sales to display inches was too elusive for computation.

During the year 1931, a banner season, the tobacco companies spent an estimated $75,000,000 on advertising cigarettes, cigars, and smoking tobacco. This was the year that the R. J. Reynolds Tobacco Company launched a bombshell campaign to exploit its newly-adopted cellophane wrapping, spending a million dollars in one week of promotion. (The firm offered a $50,000 prize for the best statement of the advantages of the new covering, a reward won by a driver of a milk truck in Boston.) In the depth of the depression, advertising expenditures were reduced, though an upswing was noticeable in 1937. The most distinctive feature of cigarette advertising in the 1930's was the increasing use of the radio. By 1940 the leading companies were spending over half of their advertising budget on this, the newest publicity medium.

But there were skeptics over the land who claimed that this clamor was so much stage effect, that the major companies were actually in combination when purchasing leaf tobacco and selling the finished products. They were critical of the income earned by the great companies despite the general depression. Farmers were incensed at the statistics recited by Hugh S. Johnson before the Senate in 1935, "The total amount paid to producers in the nine principal tobacco States didn't equal the net profits of the big four cigarette manufacturers in '32." Was there such a thing as a "duopoly," or a "triopoly," even though the monopoly no longer existed? Was there some combination contrary to the Sherman Act? In no sense were these new questions. Ever since the day of the 1911 decision some men had denied that free competition had been restored, and company executives had been assailed for robbing farmer and customer.

There were fruitless governmental inquiries in the 1920's, but with the New Deal came a quickened interest in business control. Accordingly a two-year investigation was undertaken by the Department of Justice under the supervision of Thurman Arnold, Assistant Attorney General, and, on July 24, 1940, an Information was filed accusing the principal tobacco companies, their subsidiaries and affiliates, and the individuals engaged in managing the corporate defendants, of violating the Sherman Anti-Trust Act. Chief of the government prosecutors was a special assistant to the Attorney General, Edward H. Miller, thirty-four years of age, a Harvard graduate, tall, and blond. Just as Patrick Henry was lucky in arguing his jury case in the friendly climate of Hanover County, Virginia, equally fortunate almost two centuries later was Miller in localizing the case in the Eastern District of Kentucky, the heart of the Burley tobacco district, unhappy for years over leaf tobacco prices.

The major corporate defendants were eight in number: the American Tobacco Company, Liggett & Myers Tobacco Company, R. J. Reynolds Tobacco Company, P. Lorillard Company, the Imperial Tobacco Company, British-American Tobacco Company, Ltd., Philip Morris & Co., Ltd., Inc., and Universal Leaf Tobacco Company, Inc. Their subsidiary or affiliate corporations numbered twenty-six; individual defendants, thirty-three. It was agreed that only the Big Three, American, Liggett, and Reynolds, their subsidiary and affiliate corporations, and their managing officers would stand trial, and that the rest would abide the decision. Furthermore, at the request of the court, the three major defendant companies combined their defense as much as possible.

The case, which came on for trial June 2, 1941, was heard in the court room on the second floor of the new post office building in Lexington, Kentucky. Judge H. Church Ford had particular difficulty in supervising the selection of a jury. Those citizens actively engaged in raising tobacco were excused by the court. Finally chosen were the usual dozen plus two alternates, both of whom finally served. In the fourteen there were eight merchants, two insurance salesmen, an oil agent, an operator of a tourist camp, a high school principal, and a clerk in a bus company. Although four of these jurors stated that members of their immediate families (fathers or brothers) were tobacco farmers, and another testified that he owned a farm on which tobacco was raised, they all promised that they would be unbiased in rendering a verdict.

Conspicuous among the individual defendants was George Washington Hill, president of American. From Reynolds came S. Clay Williams, chairman of the board of directors since 1935. A large, forceful man, he had started with his company as assistant-counsel in 1917. Also representing Reynolds was James A. Gray, president since 1934. He somehow evoked a sense of stability with his words, "I live in the same house I was born in, in Winston-Salem." As chief executive of Liggett & Myers there appeared James W. Andrews, who, on September 1, 1936, had succeeded C. W. Toms as president of the company. William W. Flowers, chairman of the board, died just one week before the opening of the trial. Judge, jury, defendants, counsel, witnesses, and spectators suffered through sweltering weather. The box was removed from around the jury in an effort to reduce the temperature. On through the hot days and into the autumn the case ran, twenty weeks. There were over two million words of testimony and written exhibits.

The prosecution insisted that the defendants were guilty of combination to dictate harsh and oppressive terms in both the purchase of leaf from the farmers and in the sale of the finished products to the dealers. By way of indicating possible motive, the court allowed the question of individual incomes to be reviewed, despite strenuous objections from the defending counsel. An interested jury heard a staggering calendar of corporate and personal profit. Perhaps most impressive was the announcement of compensation received by George Washington Hill. Other than salary or dividends, his special payments or bonuses from his company were $842,000 in 1930, $891,000 in 1931, $705,000 in 1932.

In presenting its case, the Department of Justice did not undertake to prove specific agreement among the defendants, but maintained that the decisive question was the existence of conditions such as would naturally follow collusion. Prosecuting attorneys pointed out certain irregularities that had developed in the warehouses from time to time, such as the buying of a basket before the starter had quoted an opening bid, this in an effort to be first in reaching the "top" price. The prosecution insisted that there were "top" prices on some markets beyond which the buyers refused to go. The government did not assert that the auction system itself was illegal, but insisted that the defendants shaped it to their own purposes, and were domineering and arbitrary in the establishing of new markets. The companies maintained large inventories in order to be more independent of the growers, so said the prosecution. The manufacturers were also accused of policing retail prices, of a despotic use of the "direct" list, a list of customers who could buy directly from the company without having their goods routed through the jobbers. The prosecution emphasized the identity of prices asked by the companies for their finished products.

The defendants objected to much of the evidence as irrelevant to a charge of conspiracy, and disavowed company or executive responsibility for disconnected incidents involving their buyers at the warehouses or salesmen on the road. For the manufacturers Dr. Theodore Otte Yntema, economist, testified that "price uniformity is not inconsistent with competitive rivalry among business men, even though there is complete independence of action." The defendants insisted that some cooperation in working out leaf market arrangements was necessary to prevent chaos and to insure that enough buyers would be present to guarantee competition for the farmers' tobacco. Manufacturers were proud of their expansion of business, their contribution to the government by way of taxes, and the enlargement of opportunities for the farmer. In proof of competition in the industry, they pointed out the decline in the proportion of business controlled by the Big Three.

For the spectators the high point of the trial came Tuesday and Wednesday, September 2nd and 3rd, when George Washington Hill testified. In his usual black suit, black bow tie, white shirt, white handkerchief (definitely with hat *off* in Judge Ford's court room), the heavy-browed executive entertained jury and audience, giving the impression of Olympian self assurance. One question by Miller brought from Hill the blunt reply, "I don't choose to answer." His horrified attorney leaped into the confusion to explain to the court that the witness meant he did not understand the question! The witness agreed that the question was confusing and affairs settled down. He intrigued his hearers by a bit of showmanship based on his book, "The Selling Principle of Demonstration," and his contraption to illustrate sales force, a machine consisting of two cogs, the smaller one, "demonstration through salesmanship," the larger, "the synchronization of the advertising therewith," all presented with the utmost seriousness.

As economists, government officials, warehousemen, merchants, auctioneers, leaf dealers, jobbers, government inspectors, statisticians, consumer-union experts, and all the rest were examined and cross-examined, the more thoughtful spectators recalled a statement made by one of the jurymen to the court before the case started, "I don't know whether I am capable of sitting on the jury like this." He was not certain that he could understand such a case.

On October 27, 1941, the jury brought in a verdict of guilty for the three major companies and one subsidiary, American Suppliers (American Tobacco Company's leaf-buying company), and thirteen executives. There had been a directed verdict of acquittal in the case of three of the subsidiaries. The trial was a personal triumph for Miller, his first major case. The general public, apprehensive over the tension between the United States and Japan, paid little attention to the verdict. On appeal, the Circuit Court sustained the decision of the District Court. The Supreme Court consented to a review on specified and limited grounds, heard the case argued November 7 and 8, 1945, and gave the verdict June 10, 1946 (328 U.S. 781), affirming the judgment of the lower courts. The major point of the decision was the technical question of whether actual exclusion of competition was necessary for conviction. The Supreme Court decided that actual exclusion of competition was not necessary for conviction; the *power* to exclude competition was the essential question. Judge Burton delivered the opinion of the Supreme Court, which refused to review the question of fact. "The present opinion is not a finding by this Court one way or the other on the many closely contested issues of fact." The question was simply the application of the law to the facts as they were found by the jury and which the Circuit Court had held should be affirmed. Judge Frankfurter agreed with the general verdict but wished there had been a chance to consider the alleged errors in the selection of the jury.

*1941 * 1948*

[Chapter 9]

THE END OF TOBACCO ROAD

High national income, "war nerves," and aggressive advertising drove upwards the curve of cigarette consumption during the Second World War. Per capita use moved from 1,551 in 1941 to 2,027 in 1945.[1] Yet, such was the demand, people spoke gravely of the cigarette shortage. Among those pondering the scarcity of cigarettes and the defensive retreat to the pipe was Dr. Earnest Albert Hooton, Rhodes Scholar, Harvard anthropologist, and author of *Why Men Behave Like Apes and Vice Versa,* who, according to report, gave the following verdict: "The boys in the fox-holes, with their lives endangered, are nervous and miserable and want girls. Since they can't have them, they smoke cigarettes. The girls at home, with their virtue not endangered, are nervous and miserable and want boys. Since they can't have them, they too smoke cigarettes. So, what happens? The briar pipe resumes its rightful place as the companion of the philosophic male whose gonadal

[1] If tax-free cigarettes shipped to the armed forces are included, the figures become 1,580 for 1941 and 2,334 for 1945. In the year 1941 production was 217,934,925,000; in 1945, 332,164,670,000.

preoccupations have vanished with the years." Less whimsical and more ignorant of Freud was the man on the street, who, minimizing the phenomenal increase in consumption, ascribed the scarcity of cigarettes to hoarding and to the black market.

Of particular comment was the unsatisfied demand for cigarettes during the winter of 1944–45. There was some private and informal apportioning by dealers, but cigarettes were never officially rationed as were foodstuffs and gasoline. When American society was called on to face the gasoline and tobacco shortage, the ill tempers in evidence proved that ours was indeed an automobile and cigarette civilization. There was a plethora of fly-by-night brands, and a revival of the roll-your-own movement. Women, about a third of whom were now smoking, insisted on having some sort of tobacco, and many of them, unable to buy their accustomed cigarettes, turned to the pipe. A representative of the tobacconists estimated that 200,000 pipes were sold to women during the three months of October, November, and December, 1944.

Because of transportation difficulties, at times cigarettes were scarce on the battle fronts. According to one analysis of morale, the favorite "gripe" of the average soldier was his inability to get as many cigarettes as he wanted. The Camp Lee (Virginia) *Traveler* found a vicious circle: the soldiers in worrying about a possible shortage were smoking more than usual and thus helping to create the very situation they were fearing! Though no form of tobacco followed the steep curve of cigarette use, soldiers, sailors, and marines used all types of tobacco. Traditional geographical patterns held true. When regiments from the Wisconsin-Minnesota area were stationed at Camp Lee, the post exchange was compelled to stock a large supply of snuff. And in war factories where smoking was forbidden both snuff and chewing tobacco were adopted by nicotine-hungry workers.

The only bland faces in the cigarette picture belonged

to the members of the Anti-Cigarette Alliance, who pronounced the so-called shortage a wholesome thing for
America. Manufacturers, though pleased with the long-
time prospect, were driven to distraction by the clamor
from dealers, the lack of manpower, and the diminishing
stocks of key raw materials such as Turkish leaf, hygroscopic agents, and sugar. A common plan was to modify
the blend by reducing the Turkish and increasing the
other leaf ingredients. Hygroscopic materials became particularly scarce because they were needed in the manufacture of explosives. In its search for substitutes one
company turned to the ginseng root, an herb found growing wild in the mountainous sections of eastern North
America as far south as Georgia. Later another firm reportedly developed a type of hygroscopic material from
apple juice. Corn syrup sometimes took the place of sugar
solutions.

Two Britishers, Winston Churchill and W. Somerset
Maugham, provided the cigar industry with notable war-
time advertising, Churchill's cigar was quite as characteristic as Franklin D. Roosevelt's cigarette or Stalin's
pipe. In 1942 the Cigar Institute of America was represented at the world premier of the film version of "The
Moon and Sixpence" by Maugham, who freely used the
cigar in his novels and short stories.[2] Higher national income, more consistent advertising—the typical display
showed a pretty girl admiring a steady-looking man smoking a Corona—meant a stronger market. Demand soon
exceeded supply, partly because of the difficulties in pro-
curing factory laborers and in obtaining satisfactory raw
material, especially Sumatra wrappers. Although there
was an actual decline in factory production, dollar volume
of retail sales went up because of the emphasis on higher

[2] Both on- and off-stage the use of tobacco became a vehicle of social expression. With the dominance of the cigarette, the spirit of the eighteenth-
century snuff ritual partly returned. Exaggerated tobacco mannerisms on
screen and stage are satirized by Giles Playfair in an essay, "Smoke Without Fire," *Atlantic Monthly*, April, 1948.

priced brands. Per capita consumption dropped from 45 in 1941 to 38 in 1945 (39 if tax-free shipments to the armed forces are included in the statistics), despite the tremendous increase of imports from Cuba during the war years. Machines continued to crowd out the hand-made article; in 1944 cigar-making machines were reported as producing 85 per cent of all American cigars.

At the end of the war, American cigarettes became the standard of value in the European black market, a tragic parody on the economy of the colonial South, when the leaf was the medium of exchange.[3] Many Americans in Europe during the years 1946 and 1947 made fabulous profits. Early in 1947 most of the 3,000,000 pounds of parcel post going monthly from the United States to Germany consisted of cigarettes. A carton purchased tax-free by the American manipulator for about a dollar could be converted into reichmarks equivalent to approximately $100. It was, to quote an editorial writer in the *New York Times*, "a kind of tobacco road to wild inflation." Even the Berlin Barter Mart, established to eliminate the black markets, discovered that its "barter unit" was adjusted to the cigarette standard. By May, 1947, the United States government set up postal regulations for the suppression of the demoralizing traffic in cigarettes. Leaf shipments to Europe in 1948 were, in part, aimed at the same goal.

The post-war period saw no change in the basic trends

[3] To the British House of Commons Mr. Harold Davies, M. P. for Leek, on February 20, 1946, complained: "You have a 'cigarette economy' from Paris to Peking, and nobody seems to do anything about it."

In the European prisoner of war camps the cigarette was found to possess most of the features of metallic currency. One captured British economist, R. A. Radford, later reported: "Although cigarettes as currency exhibited certain peculiarities, they performed all the functions of a metallic currency as a unit of account, as a measure of value and as a store of value, and shared most of its characteristics. They were homogeneous, reasonably durable, and of convenient size for the smallest or, in packets, for the largest transactions. Incidentally, they could be clipped or sweated by rolling them between the fingers so that tobacco fell out." Their principal disadvantage was the fact that they were in great demand for non-monetary uses.

of consumption. Cigarette production for 1948, estimated at 387,000,000,000 (about 350,000,000,000 of which went into the domestic market), exceeded all records. The movement upward was accelerated by powerful advertising campaigns; some of the claims made for particular brands were extravagant enough to be denounced by the Federal Trade Commission. A great figure in the advertising world passed away with the death of George Washington Hill on September 13, 1946.[4] According to statisticians, Hill had spent in the promotion of Lucky Strike cigarettes over a quarter of a billion dollars, the greatest sum ever devoted to advertising a single product. The policies of his successor, energetic Vincent Riggio, apparently displeased George Washington Hill, Jr., who resigned as an officer in 1948 after making doleful predictions for the future of the company. In January, 1949, however, Harry M. Wootten's authoritative estimate of cigarette production for the previous year placed Lucky Strikes in the lead, followed by Camels and Chesterfields. (With these and subsidiary brands, the Big Three—American, Reynolds, and Liggett & Meyers—controlled approximately 84 per cent of the American market.) Fourth and fifth places were assigned the Philip Morris and the Old Gold brands.

To keep up with the increasing demand, leading tobacco companies expanded their facilities. American Tobacco Company established a Lucky Strike factory in Louisville. Liggett & Myers broke ground for a new plant in Durham. In their operations, the management now had to recognize organized labor; the most important group was the Tobacco Workers International Union, which, while originating in 1895, experienced its greatest growth in the late 1930's and the early 1940's. By 1948 this organization, affiliated with the American Federation of Labor, consisted of about 38,000 members.

By way of contrast with the cigarette, other tobacco

---

[4] This colorful individual is thought to have been the inspiration for one of the characters in Frederic Wakeman's novel, *The Hucksters* (1946).

products considered as a whole suffered from declining sales. Cigar manufacturers had hopes of reversing the pre-war downward movement, and the 1946 production figures were a respectable 5,617,000,000. Then sales fell off. Particularly conspicuous was the contracting market for smoking tobacco; many pipe-smokers were turning to the cigarette. Snuff sales held up surprisingly well, exceeding the average of the late 1930's. This phenomenon probably reflected the strengthened purchasing power of Negro women in the South Atlantic and Gulf states. The war sustained the market for chewing tobacco, but soon thereafter the downward trend was resumed. More eloquently than in bare statistics, the fate of tobacco chewing can be registered in the disappearance of the cuspidor. With the rubber-salvage campaign of 1942, Secretary Ickes unceremoniously yanked the mats from beneath the Congressional cuspidors. By 1945 the United States District Court in Washington, D. C., authorized the elimination of the cuspidor from federal buildings over the nation. A body blow was struck at the spittoons in the great metropolitan center of New York when the Board of Health in 1946 ruled that no longer were they obligatory in gathering places. Then, in the following year, the charwomen of New York through their union announced that they refused to clean spittoons any more. Yet in 1947 about 100,000,000 pounds of chewing tobacco were manufactured for the stout-hearted citizens who stubbornly persisted in masticating the weed.[5] In the calendar year 1941 Americans spent $2,139,953,000 for tobacco products; in 1947, $3,779,659,-

[5] The following news item concerning extracurricular activities in the realm of higher education in North Carolina appeared in *Tobacco: A Weekly Trade Review,* 1946:

"Raleigh, N. C. Nov. 7—Although he was not present to defend his title, S. Ray Thompson, of Charlotte, retained his North Carolina tobacco-spitting crown at the State College Forestry Club's annual Rolleo in Hill forest near Durham.

"The longest 'juice fling' was made by Henry H. George of Cherryville, who spat 15 feet, 3½ inches. But that hardly was within spattering distance of the champ's record of 21 feet, 2 inches established in 1945."

ooo. The per capita consumption of all tobacco products increased from 8.10 pounds in 1941 to 9.32 in 1947.[6]

The upward swing in tobacco consumption troubled several groups in America. Careless smokers caused fire losses totaling hundreds of thousands of dollars annually. Medical research confirmed earlier conclusions that tobacco was definitely bad for some people. Three investigators at the Mayo Clinic cautioned against the use of cigarettes by patients who suffered from peripheral vascular disease or arterial injury. A serious charge was made by Dr. Alton Ochsner of New Orleans, regional medical director of the American Cancer Society. Speaking at Duke University, October 23, 1945, he announced that "there is a distinct parallelism between the incidence of cancer of the lung and the sale of cigarettes, and it is our belief that the increase is due to the increased incidence of smoking and that smoking is a factor because of the chronic irritation that it produces." Among those reminding the nation of Dr. Raymond Pearl's statistics was Gene Tunney, Lieutenant Commander, U.S.N.R., in charge of navy physical training. The former heavyweight champion, in an article "Nicotine Knockout, or the Slow Count," published in December, 1941, remarked: "You do get a 'lift' when you light a cigarette. But it's exactly like the lift you get from cocaine, heroin, marijuana." Tunney's vehicle, the *Reader's Digest*, was a consistent thorn in the flesh of cigarette manufacturers.

In 1946, when the North Carolina Baptist Convention was debating the offer to Wake Forest College of the millions from the Smith Reynolds Foundation, contingent on removal of the institution to Winston-Salem, there was a moment of embarrassment when a young clergyman chose to dramatize the issue by holding a Bible in one

[6] Preliminary estimates indicated the following per capita consumption for 1947. The figures in parenthesis represent adjustments made by the inclusion of tax-free products shipped to forces overseas. Cigars 39; cigarettes 2,343(2,415); chewing tobacco .67 pounds; smoking tobacco .72 pounds; snuff .27 pounds; total 9.32(9.53) pounds.

hand and a package of Camel cigarettes in the other. He proclaimed that the people had to make their choice. Fortunately for Wake Forest, the presiding officer at the moment was the ripe parliamentarian, former Governor J. Melville Broughton, who tolerantly but effectively squelched this outburst. Though scotched, the general anti-cigarette movement was not dead. Rumors of impending campaigns came out of Chicago, the field which Miss Gaston had so assiduously cultivated. The New York chapter of the Religious Society of Friends partially returned to its old enthusiasm, citing the excessive use of tobacco as one factor in the moral collapse of the world. In June, 1948, Representative Walter K. Granger of Utah introduced in the national House of Representatives a bill proposing a committee to investigate the tobacco and cigarette problem. During the last hours of the year 1948 the House Small Business Committee issued a report critical of the Big Three.

Federal income from tobacco taxes soared to new heights because of increased cigarette consumption and advanced rates. In 1940 the cigarette schedule was changed from $3.00 to $3.25 per thousand; in 1942 to $3.50 per thousand. This last rate meant, of course, seven cents for the usual package of 20 cigarettes. The yield from federal excise taxes for the fiscal year 1948 was $1,300,280,000. And the states, following a trend set in the days before the Second World War, moved farther into the field of tobacco taxation. During the fiscal year 1948 the 38 states levying cigarette and tobacco taxes collected an estimated $339,321,000, and approximately two-score municipalities levied an extra tax on cigarettes. By that time federal excise taxes, federal import duties, and state taxes totaled well over $1,650,000,000 per annum. The sum promised to increase, as legislators in the ten non-taxing states pondered ways of increasing their revenues. New Jersey, which had hitherto avoided special cigarette taxes, posted a schedule of three cents a pack on July 1, 1948.

As for crop methods, the farmer adopted whatever techniques offered a saving in labor and an increase in poundage. Man-power scarcity was such that men and women from Jamaica were imported during the crop seasons; sometimes college and high school students helped with the harvesting, especially in the shade-grown wrapper areas of Connecticut. Commercial fertilizers and barnyard manures were applied more heavily, even in the Burley area beginning in 1942. In some belts, the plants were crowded more closely together. Poundage per acre went up sharply; the national figures moved from 966 in 1941 to 1,182 by 1946. In the flue-cured areas perhaps a fourth or more of all the barns were equipped with oil burners, saving both the labor of gathering wood and the scarce timber supply. So great was the demand for leaf during the war that all qualities, mediocre as well as good, approached the ceiling price. Accordingly the average farmer concentrated on quantity rather than quality, a lesson difficult to unlearn with the elimination of ceiling prices in the post-war period and a return to buying on a strict basis of grades. Growers profited by continued research and experimentation in crop rotation, the application of commercial fertilizers, and plant breeding. By the 1940's perhaps the most significant results were the good-yielding disease-resistant varieties such as: Kentucky-16, a Burley type credited to W. D. Valleau and E. M. Johnson; and Oxford-26, the 400-strains, and other flue-cured types developed by E. G. Moss, T. E. Smith, James Bullock, and E. E. Clayton. In the Southern areas tenantry and sharecropping declined in the face of good prices and the easier credit facilities offered by the Farm Security Administration and its successor, the Farmers Home Administration. By way of contrast, in the shade-grown districts there evolved a sort of vertical combination in the industry: an increasing percentage of the crop (types 61 and 62) was raised by the large cigar-manufacturing concerns. By 1948 the manufacturers directly or indirectly produced approximately a half of the expensive shade-grown tobacco. Because of the shortage of fine wrappers from the East Indies, the domestic shade-grown expanded in the 1940's. The acres for this crop in the Connecticut Valley, which had dropped to 6,100 in 1942, moved to over 10,000 by 1948. To obtain a domestic supply of another tobacco ordinarily imported, Turkish, was a more difficult task.

In this period private and public institutions undertook an experimental program for the American production of Turkish tobacco, or aromatic as it was now called, and, in effect, placed the crop on a commercial basis. The General Education Board, tobacco companies, agricultural experiment stations of North Carolina, South Carolina, and Virginia, and Duke University supported the research efforts. The project was directed by Drs. F. R. Darkis, F. A. Wolf, and Paul Gross of Duke University.[7] Much hand labor was required in the cultivation of the small plants, crowded some 50,000 to 70,000 per acre (ten times the usual number of domestic plants per acre), harvested by the leaf priming method, and cured by a sun and air process. The relatively poor and rocky soils of the eastern slope of the Blue Ridge proved particularly suited for this type of tobacco, and it was an area badly needing a new cash crop. Aromatic tobacco invited the use of barnyard rather than chemical fertilizers; this feature encouraged livestock in a section never strong in that field of husbandry. The planting for 1948 was estimated at about

[7] For a score of years Duke University, beneficiary of a central figure in the tobacco industry, had been a center of tobacco research, a large part of it under the general supervision of Dr. Paul Gross. The most creative efforts were in the following areas (the name in parenthesis indicates the scientist taking immediate charge of the project): (1) an investigation of the nature of the aging process (Dr. F. R. Darkis); (2) experiments in the control of blue mold, a tobacco disease (Dr. F. A. Wolf); (3) the creation of cigarette paper from domestic raw materials (Dr. Gross); (4) the development of processes for evaluating the quality of tobacco by chemical means (Dr. Darkis); and (5) the growing of aromatic tobacco (Dr. Darkis). Dr. Wolf, author of *Tobacco Diseases and Decays*, directed fundamental investigations as to the nature of the aroma in aromatic tobacco. This quality appeared traceable primarily to the resinous exudate from glandular hairs.

100,000 pounds, a figure insignificant beside the normal import totals of more than 50,000,000 pounds, but important as indicating what could be done. Another approach to the problem was attempted in Kentucky, where Burley was crossed with aromatic. The resultant leaf, air-cured in regular Burley fashion, was of undetermined commercial importance.

In the years during and immediately after the war, most of the leaf was grown and marketed under the provisions of the 1938 Agricultural Adjustment Act and its amendments. By 1948 tobacco was the only one of the basic commodities specified under the act remaining under crop control, though the plan of allotments had not been consistently applied to all types during the years.[8] On a basis of the non-recourse loans, the Commodity Credit Corporation by 1948 had taken over more than 2,000,000,-000 pounds of tobacco which had failed to bring parity-basis prices on the open market. No wonder that a farm leader in the tobacco country pronounced the parity-price statute the greatest law for the good of the farmer since formation of the Constitution! Farmer-cooperatives were eventually used in the physical and financial management of the tobacco coming under the government stabilization plan. In the Burley area the Burley Tobacco Growers Co-operative Association, chartered in 1921, was reactivated and in 1941 operated under an agreement with the Commodity Credit Corporation; in the flue-cured area a new corporation, the Flue-Cured Tobacco Cooperative Stabili-

[8] From 1938 to 1948 marketing quotas were in effect on flue-cured and Burley, save for the year 1939 when they were rejected by the growers in the referendums. Marketing quotas were applied to fire-cured and to two types of the dark air-cured (type 35, One Sucker; and type 36, Green River) in 1938, disapproved by growers in 1939, not proclaimed for the years 1940, 1944, and 1945 (the supply on hand being less than the statutory reserve-supply level), in effect 1941 and 1942, proclaimed then withdrawn for 1943, in effect for 1946, 1947, and 1948. Quotas were never proclaimed for Maryland tobacco, Virginia sun-cured, or any of the several types of cigar leaf, though parity-based loans were applicable to these as well as other kinds of tobacco.

zation Corporation, was formed in 1945. Despite criticism, the warehouse auction system appeared to be more firmly entrenched than ever, clearly winning out over the hogshead sales in the Baltimore market, and, in 1945, even invading the cigar district under the sponsorship of the Lancaster County Tobacco Growers Cooperative Association. Manufacturers, remembering the broad charges made against them in the anti-trust trial of 1941, took little or no part in determining the details of leaf marketing. In 1948 the special flue-cured marketing committee, representing buyers, growers, and warehousemen, set the speed of sales at 400 per hour. In that same year the Burley Auction Warehouse Association announced that sales would begin on November 15th, about a fortnight earlier than usual.

Within the framework of crop control measures, total poundage went up. In the year 1946 a record-breaking 2,322,000,000 pounds were harvested. The 1947 yield was 2,108,000,000; the 1948 crop somewhat less. North Carolina, far ahead of its nearest rival, Kentucky, was accepted as the leading state in tobacco production. Once the apologetic appendage of the so-called Virginia District, North Carolina now grew about 40 per cent of the nation's leaf, and manufactured some 50 per cent of the cigarettes produced in America.

The wisest heads in the tobacco country knew that government support of leaf prices was no permanent solution of the sales problem. During the year 1947 farm and market leaders formed in the flue-cured area Tobacco Associates, Inc., farther west The Burley and Dark Leaf Tobacco Export Association, both organizations designed to expand foreign consumption. The flue-cured producers gave especial attention to events in Great Britain, the principal outlet for their exported tobacco, where for three centuries smokers had become accustomed to what they called "Virginia" leaf. In 1940 American farmers heard that the British, for political reasons, were requiring their manufacturers to mix quantities of Turkish with the American tobacco. This threat to the flue-cured growers appeared to subside after the United States went to war and much leaf was purchased for lend-lease shipment to Great Britain. But there were agricultural and fiscal developments within the British Empire which jeopardized the flue-cured exports. In New Zealand, Northern and Southern Rhodesia, and Canada flue-cured crops greatly increased, and this leaf, because of the system of imperial preference, promised eventually to displace much of the American-grown tobacco in the British market. Particularly menacing was the Canadian crop, established partly through the help of American citizens, many of whom annually left the southeastern states to teach the Canadians to prime and cure. And by 1945 rival flue-cured crops from Brazil disturbed American exporters.

As a matter of fact, however, it was neither the Canadian leaf nor flue-cured from any other part of the world which gave most serious injury to those Americans supplying the British market; it was the post-war economic crisis in Great Britain. On the tobacco front the situation became acute during the year 1947, when the British determined to save their dollars, about an eighth of which were normally accounted for by purchases of American leaf tobacco. As early as February, 1947, Americans were warned of a possible reduction in British imports. (Churchill, a notorious tobacco-user and leader of the Opposition, took Dalton's reference to the large British tobacco imports as something of a personal taunt.) Then the British government increased taxation in an effort to cut the consumption of tobacco by one-fourth and thus save about $30,000,000 in tobacco purchases in the United States. The British domestic situation did not improve and, in October, 1947, the government absolutely banned importation of American tobacco. Export grades of flue-cured went tumbling in prices as Imperial Tobacco Company recalled its buyers from the warehouse markets. Farm leaders fruitlessly sought an arrangement whereby the American government would purchase leaf, eventually to be sold to the British. And plans were made for a 27 per cent reduction in the flue-cured crop acreage for the year 1948. In 1948 British restrictions were eased, but the leaf export market appeared tied to the European Recovery Program, the "Marshall Plan."

The growers of tobacco rejoiced as they were assured that some of the billions of dollars appropriated for carrying out the European Recovery Program would be spent for tobacco shipments. In June, 1948, Paul G. Hoffman, administrator of the Economic Cooperation Administration, announced an allotment of $7,427,000 for tobacco. Before the end of the year, the agency had authorized over $100,000,000 for the procurement of American leaf. Among the ineffectual opposers of the plan to permit tobacco purchases under the European Recovery Program were Northern dairy interests, infuriated at Southern attempts to remove taxes on oleomargarine. This same dairy group also tried to repeal the 1940 act which, purposing to restrain foreign competition in American types of tobacco, levied an embargo on tobacco seeds and plants.

According to some analysts, there was danger that the declining markets abroad in a circuitous way might lower the quality of the manufactured product offered the domestic consumer. Once much of the low-grade tobacco was exported. With acreage controlled and tobacco consumption rising, the manufacturer might of necessity turn to leaf once classified as unfit for the American market.

Out in the tobacco belts, the farmer enjoyed unusual prosperity. Increasing demand, crop controls, and stabilization corporations had enlarged the profits of tobacco culture. It was often remarked that Jeeter Lester would hardly know the old place along Tobacco Road. Croppers had become owners; there were washing machines, refrigerators, radios, and often two-car garages. The gap was closing between urban and rural standards of living.

[Chapter 10]

BIBLIOGRAPHICAL NOTES

The following bibliographical notes are presented as a brief guide for further reading, and as an acknowledgment of at least the principal secondary sources used in the preparation of this book. Because of limited space, the lists are highly selective.

For an orientation in the basic materials there is nothing better than Jerome E. Brooks, ed., *Tobacco: Its History Illustrated by the Books, Manuscripts and Engravings in the Library of George Arents, Jr.* (4 vols., N. Y., 1937–1943). All serious research in the history of tobacco must either begin or end with the Arents Collection, now administered by the New York Public Library. Helpful introductions to the general literature have been prepared by Everett E. Edwards, author of *Bibliography of the History of Agriculture in the United States* (U. S. Dept of Agric., *Misc. Pub.*, no. 84, Washington, 1930) and of many other bibliographical aids. Encyclopedic in scope and meticulous in character is L. C. Gray, *History of Agriculture in the Southern United States to 1860* (2 vols., Washington, 1933). There has been exhaustive treatment of the origin and development of only one type of American leaf, Bright Tobacco, covered in the authoritative researches of Nannie May Tilley. Her manuscript, originally prepared as a Ph.D. thesis at Duke University, 1939, was published under the title, *The Bright-Tobacco Industry, 1860–1929* (Chapel Hill, 1948). The story of manufacturing for the score of years after the dissolution of the trust is adequately treated by Reavis Cox, *Competition in the American Tobacco Industry, 1911–1932: A Study of the Effects of the Partition of the American Tobacco Company by the United States*

Supreme Court (Columbia Univ., *Studies,* no. 381, N. Y., 1933). Virgil S. Steed, in his *Kentucky Tobacco Patch* (Indianapolis, 1947), sensitively presents the reactions of a modern tobacco farmer to the day-by-day problems of culture. The sole attempt of its kind is J. J. Gottsegen, *Tobacco: A Study of Its Consumption in the United States* (N. Y., 1940). Out of date, but still helpful when used in conjunction with modern research work, is Meyer Jacobstein, *The Tobacco Industry in the United States* (Columbia Univ., *Studies,* XXVI, no. 3, N. Y., 1907). The best volume on the cigar industry is W. N. Baer, *The Economic Development of the Cigar Industry in the United States* (Lancaster, Pa., 1933). Probably the most usable brief introduction to the history of tobacco production in America is the essay by W. W. Garner and others, "History and Status of Tobacco Culture," U. S. Dept. of Agric., *Yearbook,* 1922, 395 ff. (also published as *Separate,* no. 885). A worthy companion-piece, broader in scope, is J. P. Troxell, "Tobacco," *Encyclopaedia of the Social Sciences,* XIV (N. Y., 1934). There is much merit in a general survey by G. K. Holmes, "Some Features of Tobacco History," *Agricultural History Society Papers,* II, Am. Hist. Assn., *Report,* 1919 (Washington, 1923), 387 ff. The most comprehensive recent survey of the leaf tobacco situation is C. E. Gage, *American Tobacco Types, Uses, and Markets* (U.S. Dept. of Agric., *Circular,* no. 249, Washington, 1942). An essential reference work is, of course, Allen Johnson and Dumas Malone, eds., *Dictionary of American Biography* (21 vols., N. Y., 1928–1937).

CHAPTER 1

●THE DISCOVERY OF "THAT BEWITCHING VEGETABLE"

On the early phases of the story there is no substitute for the scholarly "Introduction" to Brooks, *Tobacco,* I. For the European background see the attractive summary, George Arents, Jr., "Early Literature of Tobacco," *South Atlantic Quarterly,* XXXVII, 97 ff. In addition to Gray's volume, the student should examine the all-important works of G. L. Beer: *The Commercial Policy of England Toward the American Colonies* (Columbia Univ., *Studies,* III, no. 2., N. Y., 1893); *The Origins of the British Colonial System, 1578–1660* (N. Y., 1908); *The Old Colonial System, 1660–1754* (N. Y., 1912). There is much significant material in P. A. Bruce, *The Economic History of Virginia in the Seventeenth Century* (2 vols., N. Y., 1895). An old but good survey is R. A. Brock, "A Succinct Account of Tobacco in Virginia, Historical, Agricultural, and Statistical, 1607–1790, with Some Mention Incidentally of Its History in Maryland," *Tenth Census* [1880], (1883), III, 806 ff. For the story of the leaf across the bay also see N. D. Mereness, *Maryland as a Proprietary Province* (N. Y., 1901); and M. S. Morris, *Colonial Trade of Maryland, 1689–1715* (Johns Hopkins Univ., *Studies,* XXXII, no. 3, Baltimore, 1914). Various phases of the developments in North Carolina are covered in R. D. W. Connor, *Rebuilding an Ancient Commonwealth* (4 vols., Chicago & N. Y., 1928–1929), I; and in J. C. Robert, "The Tobacco Industry in Ante-Bellum North Carolina," *N. C. Hist. Rev.,* XV, 119 ff. In several volumes T. J. Wertenbaker, authoritative interpreter of seventeenth and eighteenth century movements, emphasizes the rigor of British policy immediately after the Restoration. Especially see his *Virginia Under the Stuarts* (Princeton, 1914).

CHAPTER 2

FIRST AMERICAN ARISTOCRATS

Sweet Scented and Oronoko: To supplement Gray, reference should be made to A. O. Craven, *Soil Exhaustion as a Factor in the Agricultural History of Virginia and Maryland, 1606–1860* (Univ. of Ill., *Studies,* XI, no. 1, Urbana, 1926). A classic account of early tobacco culture is William Tatham, *An Historical and Practical Essay on the Culture and Commerce of Tobacco* (London, 1800). Bruce in his *Economic History,* II, 566 ff. presents a notable evaluation of the colonial tobacco industry.

Great Planters of the Tidewater: The basic theme is well covered in L. B. Wright, *The First Gentlemen of Virginia: Intellectual Qualities of the Early Colonial Ruling Class* (San Marino, Calif., 1940), a major source of information in the preparation of this section. In addition, for William Byrd of Westover see particularly J. S. Bassett, ed., *The Writings of "Colonel William Byrd of Westover in Virginia Esqr."* (N. Y., 1901); and Maude H. Woodfin, ed., *Another Secret Diary of William Byrd of Westover, 1739–1741: With Letters & Literary Exercises, 1696–1726* (Richmond 1942). The Fitzhugh story is illuminated by letters published in the *Virginia Magazine of History and Biography,* I, and by Gilbert Chinard, ed., *A Huguenot Exile in Virginia* (N. Y., 1934). On Carter the authoritative work is by Louis Morton, *Robert Carter of Nomini Hall, A Virginia Tobacco Planter of the Eighteenth Century* (Williamsburg, Va., 1941). For the Maryland story see C. A. Barker, *The Background of the Revolution in Maryland* (New Haven, 1940). Stimulating interpretations are contained in T. J. Wertenbaker, *The Golden Age of Colonial Culture* (N. Y., 1942); in John Fiske, *Old Virginia and Her Neighbours* (2 vols., Boston & N. Y., 1898); and in W. E. Dodd, "The Emergence of the First Social Order in the United States," *Am. Hist. Rev.*, XL, 217 ff. For exaggerated emphasis on the larger implications of tobacco culture see the chapter, "Tobacconalia," in M. D. Conway, *Barons of the Potomack and the Rappahannock* (N. Y., 1892). In the text, Quary's remark is taken from T. J. Wertenbaker, *The First Americans, 1607–1690* (*A History of American Life*, II, N. Y., 1938).

Tobacco Merchants of Britain: In addition to the works by Gray, Beer, and Mereness, see particularly J. S. Bassett, "The Relation Between the Virginia Planter and the London Merchant," Am. Hist. Assn., *Report*, 1901 (Washington, 1902), 551 ff.; and St. G. L. Sioussat, "Virginia and the English Commercial System, 1730–1733," Am. Hist. Assn., *Report*, 1905 (Washington, 1906), 71 ff. Sioussat's essay; William Coxe, *Memoirs of the Life and Administration of Sir Robert Walpole, Earl of Orford* (3 vols., London, 1798); and A. J. Henderson, *London and the National Government, 1721–1742: A Study of City Politics and the Walpole Administration* (Durham, 1945) are best for Walpole's excise plan and its background. Inspection statutes are described in Gray, in Mereness, and in V. J. Wyckoff, *Tobacco Regulation in Colonial Maryland* (Johns Hopkins Univ., *Studies*, extra vol., n.s., no. 22, Baltimore, 1936). A careful analysis of the "Sotweed Factor" is discovered in L. C. Wroth, "The Maryland Muse . . . ," Am. Antiquarian Soc., *Proceedings*, n.s. XLIV, 267 ff. Regarding Jefferson's letter to Mrs. Paradise see the distinctive study by A. B. Shepperson, *John Paradise and Lucy Ludwell of London and Williamsburg* (Richmond, 1942).

The Parson's Cause: For tobacco as currency see Beer, *The Origins of the British Colonial System, 1578–1660;* C. P. Gould, *Money and Transportation in Maryland, 1720–1765* (Johns Hopkins Univ., *Studies*, XXXIII, Baltimore, 1915); and W. Z. Ripley, *The Financial History of Virginia, 1609–1776* (Columbia Univ., *Studies*, IV, no. 1, N. Y., 1893). The case itself is covered with more enthusiasm than accuracy by William Wirt in his *Sketches of the Life and Character of Patrick Henry* (Philadelphia, 1818). A more substantial narrative is in W. W. Henry, *Patrick Henry: Life, Correspondence and Speeches* (3 vols., N. Y., 1891), the source of the quotation from Henry's speech. To correct the legendary account of the Parson's Cause reference should be made to Ann Maury, ed., *Memoirs of a Huguenot Family* (N. Y., 1853). For an evaluation of the case see C. H. Van Tyne, *The Causes of the War of Independence* (Boston and N. Y., 1922). The quotation from the "unhappy gentleman in a Maryland parish" is taken directly from Gould's volume.

CHAPTER 3

NEW FIELDS AND CHANGING MARKETS

In surveying the industry east of the mountains from the Revolution to the Civil War the present author's earlier work, J. C. Robert, *The Tobacco Kingdom: Plantation, Market, and Factory in Virginia and North Carolina, 1800–1860* (Durham, 1938), has been extensively paraphrased.

The Revolution and Diplomacy: Major reliance for this section is placed on I. S. Harrell, *Loyalism in Virginia: Chapters in the Economic History of the Revolution* (Durham, 1926). Of special importance is F. L. Nussbaum, "American Tobacco and French Politics, 1783–1789," *Political Science Quarterly*, XL, 497 ff. Useful materials also may be found in Gray; Allan Nevins, *The American States During and After the Revolution, 1775–1789* (N. Y., 1924); S. F. Bemis, *Jay's Treaty: A Study in Commerce and Diplomacy* (N. Y., 1923); and C. A. Beard, *Economic Origins of Jeffersonian Democracy* (N. Y., 1915). St. George Tucker's letter is taken from M. D. Conway, *Omitted Chapters of History Disclosed in the Life and Papers of Edmund Randolph* (N. Y. and London, 1888); Wolcott's derogatory comment from the appendix to Beard; Mason's comment from Henry, *Henry*.

Frontier Planters and the "Spanish Intrigue": The great authority is A. P. Whitaker, whose relevant works are: *The Spanish-American Frontier* (Boston and N. Y., 1927); *The Mississippi Question, 1795–1803* (N. Y., 1934); ed., "Documents: James Wilkinson's First Descent to New Orleans in 1787," *Hispanic American Hist. Rev.*, VIII, 82 ff. See also the interpretation given in L. D. Baldwin, *The Keelboat Age on Western Waters* (Pittsburgh, Pa., 1941). Best on the early tobacco industry in Mississippi is B. L. C. Wailes, *Report on the Agriculture and Geology of Mississippi* (State Printer, 1854). Latrobe's tobacco capitals and their origin are discussed in Glenn Brown, *History of the United States Capitol* (2 vols., Washington, 1900–1903); C. E. Fairman, *Art and Artists of the Capitol of the United States of America* (Washington, 1927); and in similar works. There is no single volume covering the story of tobacco in the Middle West in the pre-Civil War period. Gray is helpful; and some aid may be obtained from J. B. Killebrew, "Report on the Culture and Curing of Tobacco in the United States," U. S. *Census*, 1880, III, 583 ff. Many items are available in Mary Verhoeff, *The Kentucky River Navigation* (Filson Club, *Publications*, no. 28, Louisville, 1917). P. W. Bidwell and J. I. Falconer, in their *History of Agriculture in the Northern United States, 1620–1860* (Washington, 1925) give suggestions concerning the culture of tobacco in Ohio and Connecticut.

of manufacturing centers during the Civil War in Clark, *History of Manufactures in the United States, 1607–1928*.

The Birth of the Golden Calf: Invaluable for a general survey of the post-Civil War period are the following essays in the *Tenth Census* [1880] (1883), vol. III: J. B. Killebrew, "Report on the Culture and Curing of Tobacco in the United States," 583 ff.; and J. R. Dodge, "Statistics of Manufactures of Tobacco . . . ," 881 ff. Incorporated in Killebrew's work is Brock's essay on the colonial industry already mentioned. The history of Durham and of the development of the Blackwell factory is told in: W. K. Boyd, *The Story of Durham, City of the New South* (Durham, 1927); H. V. Paul, *History of the Town of Durham, N. C.* (Raleigh, 1884); J. W. Jenkins, *James B. Duke: Master Builder* (N. Y., 1927); J. K. Winkler, *Tobacco Tycoon: The Story of James Buchanan Duke* (N. Y., 1942); William A. Guthrie, "Durham County," *Western North Carolina: Historical and Biographical* (Charlotte, 1890), ch. xvi; and Tilley, *Bright-Tobacco Industry*. For the Winston-Salem narrative see: D. P. Robbins, *Descriptive Sketch of Winston-Salem* (Winston, 1888); and Mrs. A. V. Winkler, *Souvenir of the Twin Cities of North Carolina, Winston-Salem, Forsyth County. Descriptive and Historical* (Salem, N. C., 1890). Sketches in S. A. Ashe, ed., *Biographical History of North Carolina* (8 vols., Greensboro, 1905–17), covering the Dukes, Reynolds, and Hanes are helpful. General developments may be traced in Connor, *North Carolina*.

The Old Guard and Newcomers: There is a summary of the Virginia manufacture in the post-bellum years in B. W. Arnold, Jr., *History of the Tobacco Industry in Virginia from 1860 to 1894* (Johns Hopkins Univ., *Studies*, XV, nos. 1–2, Baltimore, 1897); and suggestions in an essay by John Q. James, "When Richmond's Leaf Industry Was Saved by Men of Stout Heart," *Richmond Times-Dispatch*, March 18, 1945. The Richmond industry is treated in Andrew Morrison, ed., *The City on the James* (Richmond, 1893); and on the same subject there are helpful notes in Paul, *History of the Town of Durham, N. C.* For developments in St. Louis see the volume by Stevens. Jacobstein is of some aid here. For details of the manufacturing processes see Tilley's volume.

W. Duke & Sons: See Boyd, Jenkins, Winkler, and Paul, already cited, and the sketches in Ashe, *Biographical History of North Carolina*. The story of the machines, as well as of almost everything else connected with the development of Bright Tobacco, is best covered in the writings of Tilley. Duke's comment with reference to the cigarette is taken from Boyd.

The Tobacco Empire: The history of the "tobacco trust" has been told many times. The basic events are thoroughly treated in *Report of the Commissioner of Corporations on the Tobacco Industry* (3 parts, Washington, 1909, 1911, 1915). Good summary accounts may be found in Eliot Jones, *The Trust Problem in the United States* (N. Y., 1921); and Henry Seager and C. A. Gulick, Jr., *Trust and*

Corporation Problems (N. Y., 1929). Contrasting narratives are presented by Jenkins, favorable, and by Winkler, more critical. James A. Thomas recalls his adventures in two books: *A Pioneer Tobacco Merchant in the Orient* (Durham, 1928); and *Trailing Trade a Million Miles* (Durham, 1931). The memoirs of Josephus Daniels are invaluable as the reminiscences of a critical contemporary: *Tar Heel Editor* (Chapel Hill, 1939); and *Editor in Politics* (Chapel Hill, 1941). The Reynolds quotation is drawn from the latter volume.

CHAPTER 6

THE AGE OF CONFLICT

Night Riders versus *Hill Billies:* The two best accounts of the night riders are: J. O. Nall, *The Tobacco Night Riders of Kentucky and Tennessee, 1905–1909* (Louisville, Ky., 1939); and J. G. Miller, *The Black Patch War* (Chapel Hill, 1936). A colorful contemporary sketch is Martha McCulloch-Williams, "The Tobacco War in Kentucky," *Review of Reviews*, XXXVII, 168 ff. See also Marie Taylor, "Night Riders in the Black Patch" (M. A. Thesis, U. of Ky., 1944); Theodore Saloutos, "The American Society of Equity in Kentucky: A Recent Attempt in Agrarian Reform," *Jour. Sou. Hist.*, V, 347 ff.; O. B. Jesness, *The Cooperative Marketing of Tobacco* (Ky. Agric. Exp. Station, *Bul.*, no. 288, Lexington, 1928); W. H. McCord, "The Development of the Tobacco Markets in Kentucky With a Preliminary Sketch of the Earliest History of Tobacco" (M. A. Thesis, U. of Ky., 1920); and W. E. Connelley and E. M. Coulter, *History of Kentucky* (Charles Kerr, ed., 5 vols., Chicago and N. Y., 1922). Conflict in the eastern district is treated in Nannie May Tilley, "Agitation Against the American Tobacco Company in North Carolina, 1890–1911," *N. C. Hist. Rev.*, XXIV, 207 ff.

"Blood Money" and the Trust-Busters: Tilley's article, just mentioned, provides an intelligent account. The autobiographical works of Josephus Daniels offer good background material by an opponent of the Dukes. P. N. Garber, *John Carlisle Kilgo: President of Trinity College, 1894–1910* (Durham, 1937), suggests the effect of the anti-trust agitation on Trinity College. Running narratives are available in the works of Jenkins and Winkler. Beveridge's role is explained in C. G. Bowers, *Beveridge and the Progressive Era* (Boston, 1932). Quotations from the newspapers of North Carolina are taken directly from the works of Garber and Daniels. Daniels' account of his talk with Washington Duke may be found in *Tar Heel Editor*. The Page quotation is taken from Garber, *Kilgo*. Cox's book begins to be of value at this point.

325 ff.; and in H. B. Rowe, *Tobacco Under the AAA* (The Institute of Economics of the Brookings Institution, *Pub.*, no. 62, Washington, 1935). A review of the volume by Woofter is of aid in interpreting the background of New Deal legislation. Accounts in the *New York Times* and in *Business Week* fill out the story. The Ehringhaus quotation is taken from the essay by Knapp and Paramore.

The Modern Tobacco Farmer: Of especial importance is the bulletin Gage, *American Tobacco Types, Uses, and Markets.* There are available many government publications, state and federal, giving the details of crop management. A little-known phase of the industry is described in "Perique Harvest," *The St. Jamesian* (I, no. 2, 19 ff.). An intelligent report is offered by J. B. Hutson in his work entitled *Consumption and Production of Tobacco in Europe* (U. S. Dept. of Agric., *Tech. Bul.*, no. 587, 1937). Superb analyses of demand movements are W. H. Fisher, *Economics of Flue-Cured Tobacco* (Richmond, 1945); and B. W. White, Jr., *Trends in Demand for Tobaccos of the Southern States* (Ky. Agric. Exp. Station, *Bul.*, no. 431, Lexington, 1942). Many farmer-problems are suggested in the articles in *Law and Contemporary Problems*, I, no. 3. Descriptions of the lives of tenants may be found in Federal Writers' Project, *These Are Our Lives* (Chapel Hill, 1939). The landlord point of view is expressed in Steed's volume. Helpful details are available in the brochures by Weeks and Floyd, and Lancaster et al.

Marshall's "Really Good Five-Cent Cigar": The authoritative life is C. M. Thomas, *Thomas Riley Marshall: Hoosier Statesman* (Oxford, O., 1939). See the works of Baer, White, and Gage. A good summary essay is C. A. Werner, "The American Cigar," *American Mercury*, II, 27 ff. Beautifully illustrated and well prepared articles are in *Fortune.* See especially "Rufus Lenoir Patterson's Cigar Machine," *Fortune*, I, no. 5, 56 ff.; "Cigar Bands," *Fortune*, I, no. 5, 77 ff.; and "La Corona," *Fortune*, VII, no. 2, 74 ff.

CHAPTER 8

THE CIGARETTE AGE

Camels Lead the Way: Excellent material is available in the testimony and exhibits of the anti-trust suit of 1941. Cox provides a critical survey of the industry to the year 1932. See these essays: "Good Taste in Advertising [Lucky Strikes]," *Fortune*, I, no. 2, 60 ff.; "Camels of Winston-Salem," *Fortune*, III, no. 1, 45 ff.; "The American Tobacco Co.," *Fortune*, XIV, no. 6, 96 ff.; B. D. McNeill, "The Town of a Hundred Millionaires [Winston-Salem]," *North American Review*, CCXXXII, 101 ff.; and C. A. Werner, "The Triumph of the Cigarette," *American Mercury*, VI, 415 ff. An analysis of the early stages of the Reach-for-a-Lucky campaign is provided by Philip Wagner, "Cigarettes vs. Candy: War Correspondence from a New Battle Front," *New Republic*, LVII, 343 ff. from which the Lorillard advertisement, mentioned in the text, is quoted. Major developments are sketched in the *Literary Digest*, the *New York Times*, and *Business Week*. In the last-named periodical, Feb. 26, 1930, there is a colorful essay entitled, "George Washington Hill, Advertiser." An authoritative treatment of cigarette advertising may be found in H. H. Borden, *The Economic Effects of Advertising* (Chicago, 1942). The last years of James B. Duke and the first years of the Duke Endowment are covered by Jenkins, Winkler, Cox, and Daniels. The Reynolds quotation in the text is taken from Daniels, *Tar Heel Editor;* Hill's testimony as to the Reach-for-a-Lucky slogan, from testimony in the trial of 1941.

The All-American Cigarette: For ingredients and processes of manufacture there are suggestions in the works of Gage and White. Note also B. F. Lemert, *Tobacco Manufacturing Industry in North Carolina* (mimeographed, National Youth Administration of N. C., Raleigh, 1939), especially ch. v. If used with care, advertising brochures distributed by leading companies clarify some points. For materials other than tobacco going into the manufactured product, see Evelyn M. Schwartztrauber, "It Isn't Just Tobacco," *Foreign Commerce Weekly*, VII, no. 9, 6 ff. The creation of the American cigarette paper industry has been well covered by the periodicals; for example note Don Wharton, "America's White Paper," *Forbes: The Complete Business Magazine*, XLVI, no. 10, 16 ff.

And Still the Coffin Nail: The de-nicotinized version of Carmen is recounted by Gay MacLaren, "Morally We Roll Along," *Atlantic Monthly*, CLXI, no. 4, 441 ff. Particularly significant is the anti-tobacco protest by W. K. Anderson, "Will They Force Us to It?" *Christian Century*, XLVI, 1576 ff. A sound survey of the tobacco controversy is offered by Dr. James A. Tobey in *Scribner's Magazine*, LXXXVIII, 420 ff. The *Literary Digest* provides invaluable summaries of newspaper opinion. In several instances newspaper and magazine quotations as given in the *Literary Digest* have been used in the text when the original journals were not available. Mrs. Dwight Whitney Morrow tells of "President Neilson of Smith" in the *Atlantic Monthly*, CLXXVIII, 43 ff. The story of the Tobacco Merchants Association is clarified during the 1941 anti-trust trial. Wertheim's report is Government Exhibit no. 714, *Record on Appeal*. Hemminger's verse may be found in Christopher Morley, ed., *Familiar Quotations . . . by John Bartlett* (11th edn., N. Y., 1937).

The Battle of Lexington, Kentucky: The history of cigarettes during the 1930's is well presented in a series of articles in *Fortune:* "One Out of Every Five Cigarettes [Ten-Cent Cigarettes]," *Fortune*, VI, no. 5, 44 ff.; "Spuds," *Fortune*, VI, no. 5, 50 ff.; "Philip

Morris & Co.," *Fortune*, XIII, no. 3, 106 ff.; "The Old Gold Contest," *Fortune*, XVI, no. 1, 49 ff. Also see Borden. The record of the trial is entitled, *In the United States Circuit Court of Appeals for the Sixth Circuit: The American Tobacco Company, American Suppliers, Inc., George Washington Hill, James E. Lipscomb, Jr., Paul M. Hahn, and Vincent Riggio, Appellants vs. United States of America, Appellee . . . Record on Appeal* (Record, 8 vols., Exhibits, 6 vols.).

CHAPTER 9

THE END OF TOBACCO ROAD

The *New York Times* and its *Index* are invaluable for tracing recent developments. Such newspapers as the *Durham Morning Herald* and the *Lexington Herald* provide local news of the tobacco industry. The trade magazines *Tobacco* and *Business Week* furnish information of a national character. Among current publications the *Annual Report on Tobacco Statistics* (U. S. Dept. of Agric., Production and Marketing Adm.) is essential. Also helpful is *The Tobacco Situation* (U. S. Dept. of Agric., Bureau of Agricultural Economics). A one-volume analysis of scientific production is offered by W. W. Garner in a work entitled, *The Production of Tobacco* (Philadelphia, 1946). American culture of Turkish is described in F. R. Darkis and Robert Mattison, *Aromatic Tobacco: Instruction for its Production in the Southeastern United States* (Duke Univ., *Tobacco Bul.*, no. 1, Durham, 1947). An exceedingly suggestive editorial, entitled "Change on Tobacco Road," appeared in the *New York Times*, Nov. 19, 1947. An interesting survey of cigarette currency is available in R. A. Radford, "The Economic Organization of a P.o.W. Camp," *Economica*, n.s., XII, 189 ff. The recognized expert in preparing current estimates of the production of cigarettes is Harry M. Wootten, whose conclusions appear in *Printer's Ink*.

INDEX

Crumpton, William M., manufacturer, 92
Cuba, 3, 4, 96, 150, 179–180, 228, 272
"Cuban blade," a tool, 178
Culpeper, John, 13
Culpeper's Rebellion, 12–14
Curing tobacco, methods of, 18, 60–61, 185–186, 219–221, 277–278
Currin v. Wallace, 212
Cuspidor, 104, 274. See also Chewing tobacco, use of

Dairy interests, oppose tobacco purchases under European Recovery Program, 282
Dale, Sir Thomas, 7, 8
Dalton, Sir Hugh, 281
Daniels, Josephus, 160, 167, 235
Danville, Va., as leaf market, 67, 163, 187–188; as manufacturing center, 79, 94, 129–130
Darkis, F. R., Dr., research work of, 278
Dark Tobacco District Planters' Protective Association, 154–156, 158–159
Dark Tobacco Growers Cooperative Association, 202, 204–205
Darlington, S. C., as leaf market, 188
Dausman, Henry, manufacturer, 80
Davies, Harold, member of Parliament, 272
Davies, Samuel, clergyman, 37
Davis, Jefferson, bail bond signed, 130
Dean, J. H., of Knoxville, Tenn., 206
Debts, owed by colonial planters to British merchants, 25–32, 44–48. See also Credit system
Deer's tongue, used in manufacture of cigarettes, 242
Delaware, Lord, 7
Deliverance, a pinnace, 7
Deliverance, The, by Ellen Glasgow, 181
de' Medici, Catherine, 4
Denmark, 108, 175
Department of Justice, 167, 261, 263
Dibrell Brothers, leaf dealers, 197
Dickens, Charles, visits tobacco factory, 86–87; criticizes American tobacco habits, 103–104

Diethylene glycol, as a hygroscopic agent, 241, 259
Digges, Edward, planter, 17
Digges family, 24
Digges Neck, a plantation, 17
Dill, Adolph, manufacturer, 131
Dill, J. G., manufacturer, 131
Dill's Best, trade name, 131
Dime Durham, trade name, 144
Dingley Act, tariff measure, 165
Dipping, practice described, 102, 173. See also Snuff, use of
"Direct" list, 263
Dixon, W. E., defends use of tobacco, 251
Dolan, Thomas, financier, 147
Dow, Neal, opposes use of tobacco, 111
Drake, Sir Francis, 5
Drummers, cigar, 173–174
Drummond, James T., manufacturer, 133
Drummond, John Newton, manufacturer, 133
Drummond Tobacco Co., 146–147
Duke, Benjamin Newton, on farm, 139; in factory, 140; as philanthropist, 161; as trustee of Trinity College, 162–163. See also Duke family; W. Duke & Sons; W. Duke Sons & Co.
Duke, Brodie, 139–140. See also Duke family
Duke Endowment, 235
Duke family, 141–143, 160, 163, 246
Duke, James Buchanan, on farm, 139; as manufacturer, 138–140, 143–152, 166, 169; as philanthropist, 161, 235–236; mentioned, 128, 235. See also American Tobacco Co., of 1890, of 1904; Duke family; W. Duke & Sons; W. Duke Sons & Co.
Duke of Durham, trade name, 126
Duke's Mixture, brand of tobacco, 257
Duke University, 235–236, 244, 278. See also Trinity College
Duke, Washington, on farm, 138; as manufacturer, 94–95, 138–140, 143, 160–161; as philanthropist, 161. See also Duke family; W.

A NOTE ON THE TYPE IN WHICH
THIS BOOK IS SET

Waverley, the type used in this book, is a new design produced by the Intertype Corporation. Named for Captain Edward Waverley, the hero of Sir Walter Scott's first novel, it is inspired by the spirit of Scott's literary creation rather than actually derived from the typography of that period. Indeed, Waverley is a wholly modern typeface, if not by definition, certainly by association with the designs of our best contemporary typographers.

The book was composed, printed, and bound by H. Wolff, New York.